Tim Price

Plays: 1

For Once: 'A gentle yet forensic examination of family crisis in a rural town. As the pain, anger, love and anxiety of mother, father and son bleed out in interweaving monologues, the cords that connect them are at once strangulating, sustaining and strained to snapping point . . . This is sharp-eyed writing, full of humanity and compassion.'   *The Times*

Salt, Root and Roe: 'Its mixture of the whimsical and the shocking, windy Welsh garrulousness and sudden moments of intense feeling, is undoubtedly distinctive. There may be more than a touch of Dylan Thomas's *Under Milk Wood* in the play's more poetic passages, with stories of mermen and villages under the sea, but it is also a piercing account of sisterly love and the agonies of Alzheimer's . . . It captures both the horrors of old age and the ties of family love with unmistakable compassion.'   *Daily Telegraph*

The Radicalisation of Bradley Manning: 'Get bullied, resist. Get bullied, resist. Get bullied, leak 250,000 classified US diplomatic cables along with half a million army reports about the wars in Iraq and Afghanistan. That's the basic pattern Tim Price picks out in his impressionistic, semi-fictionalised account of the life and now very troubled times of Bradley Manning, twenty-four, the world's most infamous rogue US soldier . . . At heart, though, this is a sympathetic portrait of a vulnerable, bright kid who hit one too many brick walls of rejection and flipped in a way that combined his socio-political preoccupations with his inner demons.'   *Daily Telegraph*

I'm With the Band: '[Price's] central thesis is that the debate should not be myopically focused on whether Scotland would be better off alone. With centuries of shared history, emotion, psychology and kinship there will be unexamined impacts on Wales, Ulster and England too . . . A compelling allegory on the issue of Scots independence . . . A play for all nations, on these isles at least.'   *Independent*

Protest Song: 'In Tim Price's urgent, heartfelt monologue, Danny is [a] rough sleeper, a man who likes order, but whose life has become chaotic through addiction, marriage breakdown, and the loss of a child . . . The cry of protest it invokes is a strong one against the inequalities we all condone by our continued failure to do anything about them . . . But the piece does suggest, through the metaphor of a piano with damaged keys, that when something is broken you have to find a way to work around it. It's the only way the music will be heard.'

Guardian

Tim Price is a Welsh playwright and screenwriter. His plays include *For Once*, *Salt, Root and Roe* (winner of Best English Language playwright at the Theatre Critics of Wales Award), *Demos*, *The Radicalisation of Bradley Manning* (winner of the James Tait Black Prize for Drama), *I'm With the Band*, *Protest Song* and *Teh Internet is Serious Business*. He is associate playwright at the Traverse Theatre and co-founder of Welsh new writing company Dirty Protest.

TIM PRICE

Plays: 1

For Once
Salt, Root and Roe
The Radicalisation of Bradley Manning
I'm With the Band
Protest Song
Under the Sofa

with an introduction by the author

B L O O M S B U R Y
LONDON • NEW DELHI • NEW YORK • SYDNEY

Bloomsbury Methuen Drama

An imprint of Bloomsbury Publishing Plc

50 Bedford Square, London WC1B 3DP, UK
1385 Broadway, New York, NY 10018. USA

www.bloomsbury.com

**BLOOMSBURY and the Diana logo are registered trademarks
of Bloomsbury Publishing Plc**

This collection first published in the Contemporary Dramatists series
in Great Britain in 2014. Plays that were published in previous editions
may contain script changes in this publication.

For Once first published by Bloomsbury Methuen Drama 2011
Copyright © 2011, 2014 Tim Price

Salt, Root and Roe first published by Bloomsbury Methuen Drama 2011
Copyright © 2011, 2014 Tim Price

The Radicalisation of Bradley Manning first published
by Bloomsbury Methuen Drama 2012 and reprinted in 2013
Copyright © 2012, 2013, 2014 Tim Price

I'm With the Band first published by Bloomsbury Methuen Drama 2013
Copyright © 2013, 2014 Tim Price

Protest Song first published by Bloomsbury Methuen Drama 2014
Copyright © 2014 Tim Price

Under the Sofa first published by Bloomsbury Methuen Drama 2014
Copyright © 2014 Tim Price

Introduction copyright © Tim Price 2014

Tim Price has asserted his right under the Copyright, Designs and Patents Act
1988 to be identified as the author of this work.

British Library Cataloguing-in-Publication Data
A catalogue record for this book is available from the British Library

ISBN: PB: 978-1-4742-2196-2
ePub: 978-1-4742-2198-6
ePDF: 978-1-4742-2197-9

Library of Congress Cataloging-in-Publication Data
A catalog record for this book is available from the Library of Congress

Typeset by Country Setting, Kingsdown, Kent CT14 8ES

Contents

Tim Price
Chronology

2011	*For Once* (Hampstead Theatre, London)
	Salt, Root and Roe (Donmar Warehouse at Trafalgar Studios, London, which won Tim Price the Best English Language Playwright prize at the Theatre Critics of Wales Award)
2012	*The Radicalisation of Bradley Manning* (National Theatre Wales: winner of the James Tait Black Prize for Drama 2013
2013	*Praxis Makes Perfect* (National Theatre Wales)
	I'm With the Band (Traverse Theatre, Edinburgh)
	Protest Song (National Theatre, London)
2014	*Teh Internet is Serious Business* (Royal Court Theatre, London)

Introduction

I have discovered it is impossible to introduce a collection of your own plays without sounding pompous. I have tried and failed, so I'll dispense with the thousand words I have written trying to navigate my embarrassment and just ask you to forgive the self-regarding nature of these reflections.

On a wall in my office, I have a piece of paper pinned that says 'Make story your God'. A diktat from Anthony Nielson, a man who understands that a talking polar bear needs to move the story along. Deifying story is something I try when I find myself enjoying writing too much. It is an easy trap to fall into, with a witty put-down, dazzling simile or over-articulated emotion. The problem is, all of those things say more about the writer than the story.

If story is my God, then I cannot also serve my ego. I take a perverse pride in my ability to 'kill babies'. Babies are the pieces of your writing you are proud of because you recognise yourself in them, rather than their service of your story. No matter how pink, gorgeous and fat the baby is, your faith as storyteller compels you to place your hand over its perfectly formed nose and mouth and squeeze until the arms no longer flail, the legs cease to kick and the only sound left is you praying to your God for forgiveness.

Looking over these plays is much like looking over a killing field. I don't really read these plays and feel a warm glow, I feel relief that I kept temptation at bay and I didn't ruin a great story. I am the vehicle for story, not the other way round. I take pride in my discipline and little else. So with this in mind, I have been unnerved to discover that despite my best efforts, there are some things that recur in these plays.

Resistance appears to be what I explore in every story. It is not a conscious choice but it seems these are the stories I am drawn to. In *Under the Sofa* Julie goes on a journey where she discovers

the courage to audit her guilt following a family tragedy. Sid in
For Once finds the courage to shine a light on his community's
complicity in his friends' deaths. Anest and Iola in *Salt, Root
and Roe* follow the laws of a more ancient code than those set
down by society. Bradley (now Chelsea) Manning is the cog
that jams in the American military industrial complex. Barry
in *I'm With the Band* refuses to accept Damo's austerity, and
Danny in *Protest Song* resists both the flowering of hope from
Occupy, and later, that hope's desiccation.

Under the Sofa is the oldest play in this collection. It is significant
as it is the first play I ever wrote that, I was sure, deserved to
be heard. Everything before would need coercion and
determination to see the light of day, but on finishing *Under the
Sofa* I knew it would have a life without me. I had moved to
London, with no plans, no work, but with the clear feeling that
if I were to grow as a writer I needed to leave Wales. After six
months of going to every scratch night and watching as much
theatre as I could, I facebooked Duncan Macmillan, who was
curating Paines Plough's 'Later' season and asked if I could
take part. I wrote *Under the Sofa* and it was performed by Raquel
Cassidy at Trafalgar Studios. During the performance a
middle-aged audience member sat next to me, and she
groaned in recognition when Julie describes the feeling of being
pregnant. It was the first time I'd witnessed my imagination and
a stranger shaking hands in agreement, and in the darkness I felt
credibility creeping towards me.

In 2010 I wrote my first full-length play, *For Once*, for Orla
O'Loughlin when she was artistic director of Pentabus.
Pentabus would host writers' weeks where the company would
bring writers to its rural base in Ludlow and stage 'interventions'
where writers were confronted with rural issues, such as fox-
hunting, racism or food inequality. The Sherman Cymru in
Cardiff had responded to Orla's call out for writers and sent
them *Under the Sofa* and Orla invited me to take part.

Still deeply inexperienced in creating plays, I wrote a monologue
using what I'd learned with *Under the Sofa* (using an animal to

project frustrated emotions on to, etc.) which would later become a large part of Sid's monologue. I asked Orla if she'd be interested in a play where we meet Sid's parents and she commissioned the play in a posh café in King's Cross station. I wrote two more monologues, but struggled to know how to end it. It was Orla's idea for characters to speak their own lines in others' stories, and also her idea to dramatise the final moments of Sid's monologue. With those two decisions *For Once* discovered its own theatrical idiom, and I learnt the incalculable value of working with brilliant directors.

My second play followed four months later, produced by the Donmar Warehouse as part of their Trafalgar Season directed by Hamish Pirie. Hamish and Orla couldn't be more different in their natures, but couldn't be more similar in their loyalty and faith in writers. When they joined forces at the Traverse Theatre years later, they created an extraordinary environment for writers. I had read a news story about two identical twins walking into the sea together and could not get the image out of my head. In the Marathon kebab house in Chalk Farm at around three o'clock one night, Hamish told me that he wanted to do a play 'about suicide'; I modestly explained that I had the best play about suicide ever, and despite being a freelancer, and subsidising his career with bar work, Hamish commissioned me to write the play, I suspect by selling the power generator on his canal boat. It has been a mark of my career that I have continually fallen at the feet of directors I do not deserve.

Salt, Root and Roe is certainly my Welshest play. I wanted to write a Welsh story and tackle the poetry that blights our dramatic writing head on. We had two fantastic twins, in Anna Carteret and Annie Calder-Marshall. Following the play Annie adopted two cats and called one 'Ti'n' and the other 'Gwybod'. It was this play that also started my professional romance with designer Chloe Lamford, who created a stunning design with a wave breaking through the floorboards and engulfing the set with light. Hamish's production was rightly nominated for an Olivier for outstanding achievement in an affiliated theatre.

With each play I write I try to discover a bespoke theatrical form for its story. This comes from both wanting to innovate, and understanding that the fear of the unknown is more manageable than the fear of the known. I would rather agonise over discovering a new form than agonise over whether the play is not as good as the last one. If it feels distinctly different, comparison is impossible. Also I feel a duty to not only tell a story but also, as National Theatre Wales Artistic Director John McGrath puts it, 'to ask questions about what theatre is and what it can be'.

Work that challenges my preconceptions about form, and narrative, by the likes of Marius Von Mayenburg, Lucy Prebble, Simon Stephens and nearly the entire output of National Theatre Wales has left me with an ever-shifting idea of what theatre can be.

My third full-length play, *The Radicalisation of Bradley Manning*, very nearly didn't happen. National Theatre Wales was launched in 2009 and I had been floating around the company for a while. I had a meeting with Artistic Director John McGrath with a stack of ideas ready to pitch, when he asked me what I thought was missing from his first-year programme. 'A political play,' I said. 'Then write me one,' he said, and like all the best directors, he got what he wanted by making me think it was my idea. And so I went off and created a play which imagined the global geopolitical scene if Wales was the size of Russia and NTW agreed to programme it in 2011. In the meantime I had been following WikiLeaks for years. I remember watching *Collateral Murder* in my room on Brick Lane, in a shared house with Joel Horwood. It was an extraordinary document of war. We are a generation that understands visual grammar far better than text. A written account of the attack by an American Apache helicopter on civilians in the street would have a negligible impact compared to the power of watching a man crawling for safety with his legs blown off, targeted once again mercilessly by an American 30mm cannon. Having spent the years trying to make sense of the documents WikiLeaks were releasing from Africa, with this video I now understood what they were trying to do. They were speaking truth to power. So when Chelsea Manning was arrested, I followed her case intently. One week before National Theatre Wales were about to announce the production of my play, I read in the *Guardian* that Chelsea had spent her teenage years the UK. In Haverfordwest. And not only that, her mother is Welsh, so under British law, Chelsea is a British citizen.

And so, not only was I nearly an hour late for the meeting with National Theatre Wales, I also found myself telling John we were doing the wrong play. After recounting the Chelsea story, and the Welsh connection, John and I considered what we should do. I asked if anyone else was writing something on Chelsea for him and he said no. It was awkward. 'Then I suppose I'd better write it for you then.' I'm not sure how many other Artistic Directors in the world would pull a play from their programme days before it's announced and replace it with something that had not even been put down in an email. National Theatre Wales announced it had a play about the soldier at the heart of the biggest leak in history, a leak that has caused diplomatic earthquakes across the world, and would fuel the Arab Spring. The *Guardian* put it on page five, *The Times*, the *Independent* and the *Telegraph* all celebrated the announcement of this play that would finally shine some light where journalism had failed and get to the heart of this most gripping of international scandals. Little did they know that at that point, all I had was a fucking title. And so I went on the journey with NTW, via a pretty horrific workshop, to the *The Radicalisation of Bradley Manning*. In this play the internet forced me to consider the shifting identity of voices online, so I imagined the play as an ensemble. To locate the play firmly in the theatrical, and away from the journalistic, I decided every actor should play Bradley; this also helped give Bradley an everyman sense, and the feeling that this could have been any one of us.

Like many plays, *I'm With the Band* was conceived in the Traverse bar. Orla O'Loughlin had been head-hunted by the

Traverse Theatre and was making her mark on the home of new writing in Scotland. She was bemoaning the lack of plays about the (then) upcoming referendum on Scottish independence. I struggled to explain to her the hamstrung feeling Wales has over the issue: while on the one hand sympathising and encouraging a fellow Celtic nation to find autonomy, the idea of being left with England and Northern Ireland did not bode well. As I flailed around, I ended up describing the UK as a band, with Wales the lowly bass player. Orla suggested I write the play for the next festival. The play polarised opinion, and I experienced a fascinating degree of vitriol from all kinds of quarters. Some were indifferent, some were furious, all seemed to want to tell me.

Four months after *I'm With the Band* closed, *Protest Song* opened in the National Theatre's Shed space. I had met Ben Power a year earlier, and he talked about the space as a venue to open the National to people who would not normally get a chance there. We spoke about the Occupy movement which had just happened and I told him a story I'd heard about a rough sleeper who got swept up with the movement. Ben commissioned the play in October, I wrote it in November and in December he programmed it. I am desperately aware that that will probably never happen again in my lifetime. But I struck lucky meeting Ben and was at the right place at the right time.

I found *Protest Song* incredibly hard to write. I was suffering from burnout and I moved house to Liverpool during rehearsals. The original draft of the play was a stream-of-conscience monologue in the vein of *Under the Sofa*. The lack of innovation in form nagged me, and during a workshop with Rhys Ifans he suggested that he didn't want to do a play at the National about homelessness where the audience felt safe. It was a note imbued with integrity and he was exactly right. The National audience had no right to watch a play about homelessness that allowed them to walk past the rough sleepers in Waterloo afterwards. This play needed to be a confrontation. Danny had to have the freedom to challenge people in the audience. The play had to shift from a stream-of-conscience monologue to a conscious monologue. And it was this shift in form that had me bursting into tears in restaurants, screaming down the phone to my partner, and abandoning all responsibilities to family and friends as I failed to find the form. It was the stage management at the National that got me out of the worst professional crisis of my career. We were rehearsing in the Jerwood space, but halfway through week one Fiona and Alison managed to get us an afternoon in the Shed. Seeing Rhys on stage, delivering his story to the empty red chairs, it suddenly struck me how I needed to write the play. The play needed to be more than a confrontation, the drama between Danny and the audience *was* the drama.

I wrote and wrote and wrote for the next three weeks, aided by the fantastic dramaturgy of Polly Findlay and Rhys. I have a file on my computer that says '*Protest Song* cut stuff' which is three times the length of the final play. It is testament to the patience and professionalism of Rhys and Polly that they did not slap me each time I entered with 'a new bit'. My saving grace was that Polly and Rhys achieved an understanding that I've never seen before between director and actor. They would have conversations about a scene I'd written, that I would have no understanding of. They could finish each other's sentences, and evolve each other's ideas at a pace that left me bewildered and jealous. Working with a lapsed anarchist like Rhys also has its advantages. When there were some 'murmurings from upstairs' at the National about the extent to which we call Boris Johnson 'a cunt', Rhys was unfazed: 'They can say what they like, I'm on stage every night and I'm calling the cunt a cunt.' And the matter was settled. One show was populated with twenty or so Occupiers who staged an impromptu 'mic check' at the curtain call, and recounted the Initial Statement to an enthusiastic audience. It was an emotional, anarchic, communal end that was fitting for the show.

And so, thinking about the agonies of *Protest Song*, I have thought more about why I keep getting drawn to stories of resistance. Maybe this might be the work of the dreaded ego after all. Maybe the reason why I keep returning to ideas of resistance has its roots in my Welsh identity. To be Welsh is to feel permanently under siege. The first and oldest colony of the mighty English Empire, Wales has nearly a longer history of being governed than it does of self-determination. This has led to two significant national traits, shared with our Celtic cousins but I suspect felt most keenly by the Welsh. Owing to the fact the Welsh experience could not find expression in conventional power structures, the Welsh identity took up residence in culture, hence our normalising of rampant singing, poetry and dance. This trait is coupled with chronic national low self-esteem, which accounts for the unhinged passions the national rugby team can unleash that I have no immunity to, and our inability to write forewords for books. As a people, I suspect, moments of resistance in stories are where we make sense of the world, and maybe this is why I am continually drawn to them subconsciously. Perhaps being Welsh I am genetically programmed to root for the underdog. And maybe story isn't my God after all, but the underdog.

TIM PRICE

For Mark Jefferies

an inspirational performer
who planted the seeds of this book
in his classroom nearly twenty year ago

For Once

In memory of Martin Rutter

For Once was first performed by Pentabus Theatre at the Hampstead Theatre Downstairs, London, on 8 July 2011. The cast was as follows:

April   Geraldine Alexander
Gordon   Patrick Driver
Sid   Jonathan Smith

Director   Orla O'Loughlin
Designer   Anthony Lamble
Lighting Designer   Philip Gladwell
Sound Designer   Christopher Shutt
Assistant Director   Ben Webb
Production Manager   Chris Bagust

Characters

Sid, *seventeen, sporty, possibly wearing a beenie; blind in one eye*
April, *forty-five, schoolteacher, prides herself on her youthfulness*
Gordon, *forty-six, tendency to dishevel, big man about town*

(/) indicates when the next line should be spoken.

Scene One

A country kitchen.

The characters occupy the same space but are not aware of each other. It is as if they are in the same place but at different times. **April** *irons and folds shirts, and does the washing up.* **Gordon** *is on hold on a mobile, going through insurance documents and eating.* **Sid** *is mainly concerned with his laptop, mobile and walking around.*

April   I look at him. I look at the dog. I look at him.

Beat.

Even the dog is embarrassed. I throw myself at the dog, I'm not a doggy person, but I feel sorry for him. And probably, a bit sorry for myself. So I crawl across the floor towards the dog.

Eventually Sid joins us and we make some progress. I watch Sid pat his head and I think: this *isn't* how the books said it would be . . .

A little bottle of eye drops rolls out of Sid's pocket and I reach for them but Sid gets there first. I'm glad the dog's there, because I think I might cry.

Sid   Can I go now?

Gordon   Take the dog with you.

April *claps her hands excitedly, before stopping, embarrassed at* **Sid***'s underwhelm.*

April   Gordon sits on the sofa but I can't bring myself to sit down.

She swings her arms not sure what to do with herself.

Gordon   That went well?

April   I stop myself from smacking him on the head with the dog bowl, and give him a look instead.

Gordon   He's never liked dogs.

April   Why the hell did we buy him one then?

He takes his glasses off and starts cleaning them with his tie.

Gordon   All I know is, that boy is making faster progress than you want him to. It's time we jus . . . got on with our lives.

April   I want to answer, but I seize up. It's hard to imagine, but there's something about the way he sits on the sofa, cleaning his glasses, it's very threatening.

Gordon   We're on track! We are on track.

Beat.

Small steps. Small victories. Taking each day as it comes. Times like these you discover a lot about yourself, family and friends. And this place, it's not a town; it's a village with attitude.

Beat.

The cards, you can see for yourself, been a great comfort. I come down here quite a lot at night, read them all. Remind myself.

He reads a card.

This one's from my cousin. He runs a prison. One of the biggest in the country, Sunderland way.

Beat.

Very interesting fellow. He says when they fight, when the prisoners fight, they take privileges away from them; gym, library, all that. But when they've got less to do, they fight more, so really if they fight, they need more privileges. If that's what you're there for, to stop them fighting, give them stuff to do.

Beat.

That's what I'm like I think. Except I don't fight, I get familiar, take things for granted. Something like this pulls everything into focus.

Beat.

Things have never been so clear. April and I, some of our happiest times together have been in a crisis!

Beat.

Like when Sid swallowed a whistle! Thought he was going to die, put the fear of God up us, rushed him to the hospital, by the time we got there we were doubled up trying not to laugh; every time he breathed he . . .

Whistles a breath.

My boy.

Beat.

No, April and I, I think we're one of those couples, like the prisoners, get too familiar, and then something happens and by God we're glad we're there for each other. She is a blessing.

He reads another card.

Mark Trott.

Whenever **Gordon** *says 'Mark Trott' he always points in the same direction.*

Gordon   Runs the deli, he told me, he and his wife, once a fortnight, take a bath together.

He reacts.

I know for a fact he's on a water meter. And they've split up now, so what does that say?

Beat.

April and I have never gone in for that sort of thing thank you very much. We have a much more . . .

Beat.

Civilised relationship. Even now. There's been no histrionics.

Gordon *closes a card.*

Sid   I'm on Facebook for the first time in ages and trying to put the drops in my eye and it's going everywhere.

It feels like I'm plugging back into the Matrix after I've swallowed the red pill. Everything is fake now; only I haven't got any special powers to help me get through a conversation.

Luke, Owen and Alex are all offline.

Pause.

The webcam comes on and I see me but I'm all pixelated. Like in a film. I'm trying to fix it when:

April   SID? SID?

Sid   I wait for it.

April   SIDNEY?

Sid   There it is. The full name that she gave me.

April   Can you come down here please?

Sid   I love my mum. I do. I love her. I'd do anything for her. If she asked me to lift a car up with my bare hands I'd find the strength to do it. I'd like it if she asked me that. But she never asks for stuff like that.

Beat.

I go down to the lounge and I try really hard not to be a prick. But she starts talking and it's the same stuff it always is and I find myself making the least amount of noise possible. I'm embarrassed for her.

April   We've got something for you.

Sid   And in the middle of the room is a black lab. It's not a puppy, it's a proper dog.

April   It's yours.

Sid   It just sits there.

Beat.

I feel sorry for him. Mum tries to call him over and it takes ages.

April *makes all sorts of encouraging noises – underscore.*

Sid *is uncomfortable with* **April**'s *persistence.*

Sid   She'll get there in the end.

Beat.

Mum won't give up until she's found me a new friend.

Beat.

Gordon   Get up off the sofa and stroke the dog, Sid.

Sid   I get down and Mum joins me, she gives me some biscuits to give him and we kneel close and pat him.

Gordon   What are we going to call him?

Sid   Neil.

April   Neil?

Sid   Don't ask me why.

I can tell she hates it. I see them catch each other's eyes over the dog. It was a look I haven't seen since we played Monopoly when I was a kid. One of them would catch the other cheating. Cheating so I'd win, you know, forgetting to charge me rent or whatever. Mum saw Dad cheating again, and the dog was called Neil. Dad introduces himself to the dog as if they're on some committee.

Gordon   Hello Neil. I'm Gordon, Walker.

Beat.

Sid   Later on Mum shows me a dog gate in the utility room.
I look back at Neil in his square of the world and he seems
utterly pointless.

Gordon   That night April was off to some concert, I'm off
doing my own thing and Sid, well, he was too, bless him.
That's how our family works.

Beat.

We might be in the kitchen, I'll be listening to the radio, Sid'll
have his iPod on and April will be watching some foreign film
on her laptop, but we'll still be together, we just gravitate
towards each other.

Beat.

I used to quite like flat-hunting, in nearby towns, I wouldn't
buy or rent any or anything, I just liked keeping my toe in the
property market. I went as far as Bath once to look at a flat.
It's a lot like this place. Small size, big mouth!

Beat.

This flat, I walk around, and the living room has these little
French doors, and they look out over the town. Stacey, the
agent, opens the doors for me and we stand looking out
together. There isn't a street I recognise, or a shop I know.
I could be anywhere in the world. Before I know it, I'm
haggling with her and I haven't even seen the bathroom!
All on a blast of fresh air.

Beat.

I get her down to one eight five, and it's a bit embarrassing,
because I can see she's ready to put it to the vendor. I can't
buy it but I'm dying to hear what they'll say, I want them to
say yes, just to teach me a lesson, like when you feel a pain in
your chest and you want it to be a mild heart attack so you'll
finally stop eating cheese.

*

Sid   I'm at the fridge and Mum starts hugging me and crying. She's saying lots of stuff that I can't listen to but I know the rhythms. I don't know what to do to stop it. It's all I can do to hold her these days.

Um. When she hugs me. It's like she's celebrating? It's not her fault. I try so hard to put up with it, but it makes me nervous,

'I get nervous when she starts crying.'

Gordon   It's the whole fight or flight thing.

Sid   I don't want to fight or run away from Mum.

Even when she's chirpy and says things like:

April (*chirpy*)   Both drops before you go to bed now.

Sid   Whenever her voice wobbles Dad never ever looks at her, he looks straight at me as if he wants his stony face to take the place of her voice. Her voice wobbles because when she sees me, she sees the ghosts.

Beat.

Everyone saw the ghosts when they were alive. 'Where's the other two?' Me and Luke would get if uh, Owen and Alex were doing art. Getting our names mixed up, giving us crap nicknames like the four stooges.

Everyone knows which one I am now.

Beat.

I go round Luke's. His dad's on the council; runs a cheese festival. Luke used to call him the Big Cheese, we all did. Mrs Reeves hugs me but she's so small it's awkward; her head comes up to about there. We used to call her 'Travel Mum' – does the same job as a real mum, just more compact.

He manages a brief smile.

The Big Cheese shakes my hand, which puts me in some kind of groove. They're pleased at how sociable I am. So I start using their names mid-sentence:

'Well you say that, *Mr Reeves*, but if you dwell on things too much, it'll take over your life!'

'Thank you, *Mrs Reeves*, I will have a cup of tea.'

And on and on I go and I feel like I should be in fancy dress. I'm like a gap-year son believing his own lies that he never got lonely. And it hits me. Perhaps this is what everyone else does? Perhaps this is what adults do? I can just act happy. Perhaps I can do this with Mum?

April   I decide to get out of the house and go to Tesco's when I bump into Ronnie Trott. Ronnie's one of those women who wears wooden jewellery, swims in the river, that sort of thing? Immediately she starts over-sharing about Mark running off with the estate agent. Hence the pathetic basket.

She's telling me Tesco's is a designated 'red zone' because 'anything can happen' and I feel myself gripping a can of hairspray. All I can think of is Sid walking out of the room without turning back, and here Ronnie is wallowing in her misery: 'The Globe, the Buttery, I can't go anywhere, it's a bloody land-grab, April' and before I know it, I've squirted her in the eye with the hairspray.

'Jesus April!'

'The seal's broken the seal was broke!'

I try showing her but she can't see because . . . I've squirted her eyes with hairspray.

'Dean!'

I taught Dean art, he works here part-time.

'The seal was broken.'

Dean takes us to a staff toilet, where we watch Ronnie wash her eyes and I try to kill myself from inside. She's going to have a field day, plus she's probably allergic. Everything needs to be organic and reared in a stable relationship. I look around the room and for some reason I turn to Dean and say:

'So, what goes on in here then?'

'This is where people come to piss. Sometimes a dump. Depends.'

She winces with regret.

'Thank you! Dean. I get the picture. I thought this might be where you come to avoid work. It doesn't matter.'

Ronnie washes her eyes and makes little noises.

'There's an offer on oven trays,' says Dean.

She breathes deeply.

I look at him. And I look at Ronnie.

It strikes me that I probably hate her.

Gordon   Treasurer for the Cider Festival, Friend of the Castle, Vice-President of the football club, Town Hall Committee, Twinning Association Committee, Bread Walk Campaign Steering Committee, that one hasn't got a leader, *as such*, but it's probably me, and there are a couple of others I can't remember now.

Beat.

But the point is it's very hard to be a professional in this town and not be lassoed into running things. If this country goes to war again, they should run the war effort out of the castle, it'll be over in weeks I promise you. April and I were in town once, and we get stopped for the umpteenth time, outside the butchers.

April   Is there anyone you won't talk to?

Gordon   And I can't think of anyone.

Just because I don't collect grudges and vendettas for a hobby like her, she thinks I'm the one with the problem! I'm not the one who drives to Craven Arms for a prescription, because I've fallen out with the chemist. It has its benefits being the way April is – don't get me wrong, you don't want to get on the wrong side of her, that's for sure.

Beat.

When we were first married, we had dinner with a couple of my work colleagues; I think it was a works thing? And one of the fellahs, James, dead now, calls me 'Flash Gordon'.

April   'What do you call him?'

She holds a passive aggressive smile.

Gordon   Everyone shifts uncomfortably, because she's smiling, but with a sort of, *purpose.* If you get what I mean? 'It's a bit of joke we have in the office. His clothes are a bit boring that's all,' says James.

He smiles and then shudders at the memory.

I don't know where to look, James's wife looks at me, and April keeps smiling straight at him. She was relentless, she didn't stop until he turned bright red. She'd let him be loud and crass all night but when he displeased her, she was like Darth Vader! She humiliates him to a biological degree and then she turns to me and says:

April (*sweetly*)   Will you share a dessert with me, darling?

Gordon *shudders.*

Gordon   I still wake up sweating about it.

There's a lovely network here, I don't miss Birmingham. Lots of people in town, once a month they'll go to London, or Birmingham every other weekend. I never feel the need. And the last time I went to Birmingham I was in a bar, and I went to the toilet and when I pulled my trousers up, some bugger had swiped my wallet out of the pocket. Under the –

Makes action.

Here. It's doors open all hours. Took a bit of getting used to, it was important to April we bring Sid up in the country, like she was. We hadn't been here long and I was in the Blue Boar one night and a young farmer was drinking there. Got chatting, young fellah, but old, like farmers are. Like talking to a fossil.

Beat.

'Everyone here knows everyone else's business.'

He doesn't even look at me, he just says, 'If everyone knew everyone else's business, no one would live here. Specially the buggers from off!' I wrote it off as just a bit of friendly local hostility but now I think he was on to something.

April   Caught Sid with a bong once. He was on his way to a party; you can't call them barn dances, even though they're dancing, in a barn. It's a party. They were on their way to a party, and they were walking through town, the four of them. I was on my way to a meeting at the Assembly Rooms to see how we could get more young people to use the facility, and this lot were trying to persuade adults to buy them booze from the Spar.

I read an article about these drones in Afghanistan, how they find their direction not by satellite geo-positioning or anything, but by their distance from each other. That's how these four walked, if you watched them. Utterly, bloody directionless; but never more than two or three feet away from each other.

I see Sid, lolling behind.

'Sid!'

He turns, sees me, takes a bag off his shoulder and passes it to Luke before walking towards me. It's about as subtle as shouting 'I've got something in here and you're not gonna like it!'

With my best I'm-in-charge-of-the-yard tone I demand the bag from Luke. Usually he would have attempted charming his way out of it but I realise now he was far too stoned, and he hands it over.

Sid (*gritted teeth*)   Why are you trying to make me look like an idiot?

April   I'm not.

Sid   You're embarrassing me.

April   You're being ridiculous.

Sid   Mum, please.

April *holds something up to represent the bong.*

April   What's this?

Sid *shuffles his weight and looks at his shoes.*

April   Sid?

Sid   That? That's a . . .

April   What?

Sid   It's a . . .

April   What is it?

Sid   Well um . . .

April   Sid?

Sid   Bunsen burner. It's a Bunsen burner. Yeah.

April *looks at it in disbelief.*

April   As I try to look Sid in the eye I hear a very faint giggle from one of the other three. I look at Owen who judders as he tries not to laugh. Alex bites his fist and Luke turns his back to me to let out a giggle.

Sid   Science project.

April   If this is what you do in science, Sid, what the hell are you smoking at the weekends?

And the three of them step away and howl with laughter, clutching their tummies.

I look at Sid, unimpressed, but a smile creeps across his face and before I know it, I'm giggling as well.

'Bunsen burner!' shouts Alex and he goes down on his knees. Luke and Owen wipe tears from their eyes and have to lean on each other, Sid's caught between them and me, but he can't help it, I can't help it . . .

Sid *cracks up.*

April *cracks up.*

April   I've *never* seen them like this! It's so contagious, like watching babies laugh, and I can't stop myself . . .

She laughs.

It's like I'm part of the gang. Before long, we're all crying with laughter and I think –

She tries to compose herself, perhaps wipes tears.

– seeing me laughing makes them laugh even more which makes me laugh more and –

She laughs.

– I think I'm going to wet myself! And I'm holding a bong in the middle of town!

She tries to compose herself.

'I'd better put this away,' I say.

She laughs.

And that is it! They all hit the floor, now they *are* like four big babies, holding their tummies rolling around my feet and I can't –

She laughs.

Do anything with them!

She laughs and gathers herself together.

Finally, everybody calms down just long enough so they can get to their feet.

Beat.

They're still incapable of saying anything without descending into a giggling fit and there's a moment where we all look at each other and none of us can remember what we're doing. Alex says 'Party?' And they all sort of take their leave of me.

April   So you're off then are you?

Sid   Uh yeah. Yeah. Okay.

April   They start to drift.

'I'll take this with me.'

She raises the bong.

They just about manage a . . .

She gives two thumbs up.

Pause.

Sid resists the directionless pull just long enough to run back and hug me.

Beat.

In the middle of town.

Beat.

In front of all his friends.

She gives two thumbs up.

Gordon   There are things that will drive you a bit mad about this place.

Beat.

You will get to know everyone over time.

Beat.

But everyone in this town goes to other places all the time as well, so you can't go anywhere without bumping into someone you know. We went to Corsica. Who sits next to us in a restaurant?

He points to Mark Trott's deli.

Mark Trott's daughter.

Beat.

Go to Hay, Kiddie, Gloucester, someone will shout your name out. I was in a lay-by outside Keele, a lay-by, not a main thoroughfare, and I've got Dave Grimshaw tapping on the window telling me my driver-side brake light isn't working. Sid hates it, he's always complaining,

Sid (*underscore*)   Why don't we live in a city? / Or a town? Or a village near a town or a city, that would be alright, somewhere next to somewhere interesting. I'm not asking much.

Gordon   But he's only complaining because he can't get away with the stuff he wants to. Underage drinking, pot smoking, anything he shouldn't be doing, there's eyes everywhere. I told him:

'The more people who know you, the more you've got to be whiter than white. Keep up appearances.'

Beat.

That's why sometimes I book myself a little holiday and don't tell anyone. Not even April. I tell her I've got some work conference, Wednesday and Thursday night somewhere, and I go and book myself in somewhere for a couple of nights. Still go to work, but I go and sleep in the hotel or B&B, just to have a break. Get to know a new little area, a new little town, bit of peace and quiet, and get on with my own thing. I've stayed all over the Midlands, once every couple of weeks I'd have a night somewhere, just to have a little break. Plus it's nice to meet people who don't know you.

One night I was staying in Birmingham for a night or two. Just to have a break. Went into a trendy bar, loud music. All the time I'm thinking, why have I come here? I could go to the Feathers and plonk myself at the bar and speak to anyone who comes through the door. Why come here when I don't know anyone?

Beat.

I order a lager and it comes with a piece of lime in the neck which I can't get out. I try sitting at the bar, but the stools are so high I can't get comfy so I go and sit in the corner and wish I'd bought a newspaper because the magazines there aren't my kind of thing. That's what I love doing more than anything, a pint and a newspaper. Every bloke I know starts the newspaper from the back. I don't know why they don't put the sport on the front and news at the back? I was thinking, if I get chatting to someone, that's what I'll go on. Why isn't there a newspaper with sport on the front? I had my drink, and my corner, and my conversation ready. A couple of other guys over the other side of the room, they'd left their lime in the neck. So I left mine in too.

I spend about fifteen, twenty minutes, thinking about what I should do, and I think perhaps I should pop out and get a newspaper, so I've got something to do, so it doesn't look like anything. But then this young chap comes in with the side of his head shaved. He's got working boots on and tight jeans and I think, perhaps he might like a newspaper too? He's on his own. He might like something to read, and I'm going out. Seems daft.

He orders a drink and starts chatting to the barman. They look like they know each other, so I pick my drink up and I walk over to the bar and I'm trying to think, how are we going to sort this newspaper money situation out, I could just buy them I suppose?

'Alright mate?' he says.

I open my mouth but I'm not sure what to say.

'Just, you keep staring.'

Gordon *is speechless.*

Sid   Travel Mum and the Big Cheese are weirdly excited
and crying now and again. I put Neil in their kitchen and
I realise, not many young people have been round much. I
don't mind them dragging it out but I don't have much to
say. After a while, they tell me to go upstairs. On the way up,
I step past a picture of Luke stroking a dolphin and I think,
that dolphin's alive and Luke's dead.

Beat.

It catches me like when a bouncy ball hits you on the ear
in the schoolyard? Travel Mum puts her hand on my back.
She pats me. Everyone's touching everyone these days, it's
weird. Like I patted Neil not because I wanted to but because
I knew I should. I didn't want to pat him; I don't want her
patting me.

Beat.

Luke's room is bigger than mine. It's still a mess.

'Take anything you want. Clothes, games, anything. I'd
rather you have it than charity.' The Big Cheese stays by the
door eating a biscuit. I start to say something about not
wanting anything, but the Big Cheese won't hear of it. 'Luke
would have wanted you to have something. We want you to
have something.' And he winks, which makes me want to run
through the wall like in the cartoons leaving a Sid-shaped
hole.

I fiddle with his hifi.

He was the only boy in college to prefer CDs to MP3. He was
the only one who could afford them.

'It's lovely seeing you in this room again, Sid,' she says and she shrugged.

Pause.

You either have nothing in common with your mate's parents or everything.

Beat.

With that shrug I realise she's just as awkward and confused about all this as me.

I decide to tell Travel Mum about the time Luke rang me from France just to tell me he was happy. That's all he had to say. She'd want to hear about that phone call. What she didn't want to hear was what was now coming out of the stereo.

'Shut the Fuck Up' by STFU blares from the hifi. **Sid** *hangs his head in shame as the music plays for five to ten seconds.*

The music stops.

'I'll leave you to it,' she says.

Even from beyond the grave Luke was still making me look like a prick.

Gordon   I used to be an insurance rep, livestock and farming equipment, but I'm more deskbound now. I still try to get out on the road once in a while. Keep my hand in.

Beat.

Reps have a great life – the open road, no office politics, no irritating colleagues. It can get a bit lonely, but quite often you'll hit it off with other reps as you pass through, you've got so much in common.

Beat.

I'm at the bar having a drink.

'Andrew?'

But he doesn't hear me, and he heads into the restaurant. I thought I should probably let him have his dinner and I'll catch up with him later. But before I know it I'm standing at his table.

'Mind if I join you?'

Beat.

He has steak, I have scampi. We talk, I can't really remember what about, I think it was just work stuff, so that's fine.

Beat.

We finish dinner and he starts going on about emails he's got to send, and I'm in the middle of preparing some quotes for a new client, but when the waiter clears our plates I think sod it, and order another round of drinks. He rolls his eyes: 'We've been here before!'

Beat.

His room is massive. His firm books executive rooms and the difference is immense. Double sinks, broadband, mini-bar, it's big enough to just be called 'a bar'. We give that a bit of a hammering and by the end we're both a little 'tired and emotional' shall we say.

I wind him up about his pants. He's got boxes of pants stacked everywhere. Pants. In. Boxes. I open box after box, all different colours and styles.

'Oi, Del Boy, you got some kind of dodgy deal going on?'

But apparently his expenses cover 'sundries'. I take a box and open them while he fixes some G and Ts. 'Sloggies'. I look at them and can't help thinking how new they look compared to my pants. I don't think mine even come in boxes?

'April buys my pants.'

I'm so excited about his expenses, he shows me what else he can get: CDs, cinema tickets, underwear, clothes . . . you name it, he claims it.

'I can't believe all this,' I say looking at the stuff on the bed. And then I can't really remember what happened.

Long pause.

But I remember he insisted I take something, a CD or a pair of pants. I didn't want anything but he was so insistent. He said, 'I'm not letting you go until you take something.'

(*Reflective.*) Can't even remember what I took now.

Sid   In Luke's room, I catch myself in his mirror. It's warped in the heat and I look stretched between two worlds.

I curl up and think about the time we stopped speaking, and I used to see him around town. I think about how he was the only friend who sent postcards. I think about all the places I'm never going to see his handwriting on the back of.

Beat.

Mr Reeves insists on driving me and Neil home.

What no one tells you about having one eye is that it gets tired really easy. I was trying not to fall asleep when I realised he'd stopped. He turned to me and said, 'I want to set up an anti-speeding foundation in memory of Luke, Owen and Alex.' I feel my eye going to sleep. I try to fight it, but the car is really warm. I go for long blinks. When I close my eye, another me slips into Costa coffee.

(*Quickly.*) Owen shouts at the manager, it's turned nasty, I don't know if I should step in, I channel adrenaline, while everyone looks at us, like we're scum.

(*Slow.*) 'Are you okay, Sid?' The Big Cheese is looking at me.

'You look a bit pale,' he says. I tell him I'm fine, and concentrate on one of his eyes. He starts again, and it's only moments when my eye goes.

(*Quicker.*) 'Why don't you call the police? What are you gonna say? Excuse me, officer, these fuckers here aren't buying enough drinks,' says Luke. I laugh. I laugh because he said 'fuckers'. He doesn't care about winning the argument; he just wants to offend people. Luke sweeps the coffee off the table, next to us, I win bowling.

(*Slow.*) 'I want you to be the face of the foundation, as the only survivor of the crash.'

The crash.

Owen does his Velociraptor and we're laughing so much it turns us upside down. My foot kicks the back window out and my phone won't ring Mum because I haven't got any signal.

Long pause.

'I don't remember anything from that day.' He smiles, as if he understands. Sitting next to him on the way home makes me feel like somehow I've cheated the boys but I don't know how. Just as I get out he can't stop himself saying:

'The council want you, Sid. I can't raise the money without you attached.' I look at him the way Neil must have when my mum turned up to get him. What can I do in your world?

April I'm still reeling from the hairspray incident when I drive home and see Sid walking along one of the lanes with Neil. I pull over to give him a lift.

Sid I don't want a lift, I want to walk. Need the fresh air.

April So I roll alongside him for a few yards with the window down. I tell him about Ronnie and play up Dean's role. Lately, I tend to overplay any teen interaction I have.

'Do you think you'd like to move away now? We could move away if you want?'

He shakes his head and keeps walking.

But I'm determined not to let him out of my sight. I roll alongside him calling his name, telling him, I'm not going to let this drop when . . .

She strikes something to create a loud bang!

I don't know what happened but I'm covered in white powder and my face hurts.

Sid   Mum? Mum? Are you okay? The airbag's gone off.

April   I get out and realise I've rolled into the back of a parked car. I feel like I've been punched. Sid and Neil look at me like I'm the biggest bloody idiot they've ever seen. Their pity jolts me into action more than anything else.

We get back in the car and put Neil on the back seat. I drive home in silence.

As I pull the shopping out, Gordon joins us. Sid tries to explain, but I cut him off. I don't want Gordon involved and besides, I think the airbag flicked a switch in me.

Gordon   The May fair comes to town.

Beat.

I can't park near the house so I'm a little later getting in.

Beat.

April is in the shower, singing 'At Last' by Etta James.

Underscore: **April** *humming 'At Last'.*

Gordon   I unpack my overnight bag but I can't concentrate. I find myself sitting on the edge of the bed listening. She used to sing all the time when we first got together. Used to get on my nerves but . . . now. It's like a little postcard from home, and I ask myself why did I drink so much last night?

Beat.

April   You're quiet.

Gordon   And I know exactly how James felt under her gaze.

I open my mouth and out comes . . .

'Let's go to the fair.'

Sid   I tell the Big Cheese I'm going to walk the rest of the way with Neil. As we get near home Mum pulls up and she's so busy fussing that I'm not happy, and that we need to move away that she drives into the back of a Range Rover. Me and Neil get in and we help her get the car back home. She's flapping about the bumper but Dad's there, so I go upstairs and I'm not sure if Neil's allowed upstairs or not. So we both stop. I'm on the stairs looking back and he's in the hall looking up. It's up to us to make the rules. I check where Mum is and she's on the phone exaggerating to someone about the bump. I decide, if I tap my hip and he gets it, he can come.

He taps his hip, and smiles.

He likes upstairs.

Beat.

Later on she's back on track. And in counselling mode. She bought this book on grief from Amazon and every time she's finished a chapter she tries to get me to do stuff.

Beat.

Today, it's finishing sentences.

Beat.

I sit with my head on the kitchen table and with Neil at my feet.

April   It can be anything, Sid. What's important is, we don't hold back, do we?

Sid *shrugs.*

April   'I wish I had . . . '

Sid   I don't know.

April   Try, Sid, it'll help you.

Sid   I wish I had a gadget to tell me when to speak and when to look meaningful.

Beat.

I look away because I can't look at her and hurt her at the same time. She keeps the book on her lap and tries to thumb through it without me seeing.

April   Okay. Why don't you tell me what you want to talk about?

Sid *has nothing to say.*

April   Go on? It can be anything.

Sid   I look at her. Why does she want to own this? Of all things, she wants to get her claws into this.

'How about, my three best friends die, I'm half blind, I don't remember anything and my mum buys me a fucking dog? What's that about?'

April   I thought you'd like a dog.

Sid   'I've never wanted a dog in my life. When have I said, I want a dog? When have I ever said I like dogs? It's the last thing I want. It's the stupidest thing anyone's ever bought me in my entire life.'

I find myself reassuring Neil with my foot. Mum suggests I'm angry about other things, not Neil. I tell her I'm angry about the Big Cheese blaming Alex for crashing the car.

Beat.

April   How about we try some more sentences now?

Sid *would rather die.*

April   'The thing I miss about the boys is . . . '

Sid   I'm on the brink of walking out but I get the faintest, the faintest whiff, of a dog fart. In the middle of all this, Neil has decided to drop a stinker. And why not? He's amongst friends, he's had a nice walk, he's relaxed. I don't know why but breathing in his fart chills me out a bit.

'The thing I miss about the boys is missing the boys.'

April   I feel . . .

Sid   I feel left out.

I realise Mum doesn't care what I'm saying, but that I'm saying something is all that matters. It's like the reverse of her with me, I don't hear her but I know she's there. And for the first time in ages, I'm there with my mum.

When she kicks off later about some mud, I make sure she knows I appreciate her.

Gordon   I *hate* the May fair. The noise, the litter, it lowers the tone. But tonight I can't get enough of it. April doesn't know where to look; I buy candyfloss, fizzy pop. I see Sid and Luke with a bunch of girls.

'Ahoy!'

Sid *freezes with embarrassment.*

Gordon   See if . . . see if you can beat your old man on the strongman?

And I do a, a sort of a jig.

He is embarrassed.

Sid   Nah, we're waiting for / mates.

Gordon   Tenner if you can beat me?

'Deal!' says Luke and he swipes the tenner out of my hand. On the way to the stall he grabs my bicep.

'Don't fancy your chances, Mr W.' I can't take my eyes off April. We get to the strongman and she sidles up.

April (*side of mouth*)   'What are you doing?'

Gordon   Bit of fun, relax.

But as Sid peels off his jumper I think, I don't know what I'm doing. April doesn't want this, Sid doesn't want this, and I don't. Luke is like a pig in shit, with everyone watching. Sid hits the bell straight away. I go next and hit the bell, but it's not as loud as Sid's. We have two more goes each and the third time Sid is warmed up and nearly takes the bell off. Whereas my third time, I'm exhausted and don't even ring the bell. I can barely hold the hammer.

April   Well done, Sid! My big strong boy.

Sid   Another go, Dad? Double or quits?

Gordon   No / thank you.

Sid   Go on. I'll only use one hand.

Gordon   I want to say, 'Well done, have fun' . . . but I say:

'Have a bit more grace in future, Sid.'

He looks at me and his smile fades. April is speechless. She gives him another note and tells him to go and buy some chips. He rejoins his friends waving the money.

April   What was that about?

Gordon   I don't know. Just a bit of fatherly advice, I can advise my son if I want can't I?

And I find myself pulling her by the hips and kissing her. I don't know what's wrong with me, perhaps it's all the riled-up teenagers but tonight I have a real appetite for her.

April   Stop it. I'm. People can see. Gordon!

Gordon   I can see she's thrilled though.

'What do you want? Choose something? Anything.'

April   Oh, I don't want any of this old rubbish.

Gordon   I grab her from behind and kiss her neck, it's like she's one of the fairground attractions.

'I want to win something for you, tell me what you want and I'll win it for you.'

April   It's crap!

Gordon   Let me win something for you.

Beat.

Anything.

April *slowly points at something.*

April   I want that one then.

Gordon   A bloody reindeer!

Beat.

After three goes, April loses patience.

April   Come on. Let's get a cup of tea.

Gordon   I want the reindeer.

April   Forget about the bloody reindeer, you'll never get it.

Gordon   I buy another two goes.

April   Gordon. I am bored.

Gordon   I take aim and –

April *huffs.*

Gordon   I take aim again and this time she says –

April   I'm going to find Ronnie.

Gordon   I'm trying to win you something here?

But she walks off through the fairground through all the lights. In my head I follow her, and we buy some tea and put whisky in it and we run behind a trailer and kiss. But all I do is turn to the man and say:

'Keep giving me darts till I'm the winner.'

*

April   After inspecting the car, Gordon 'helps' unpack. In Gordon's world, helping means moving things around until he finds something he can open and eat immediately.

I open the fridge and the light comes on and it's the first time I realise how dark it is in the kitchen. I stand there, looking at the fridge holding an Edam cheese and I have no idea what I'm doing. There's a fridge full of food, I don't know if it's fresh or old, I don't know if I should be pulling things out or putting things in, I don't know if I've bought this cheese or just pulled it out. I know I should be at the fridge, but why I don't know.

With the cheese in my hand I look at Gordon.

'What I am doing with this?'

Gordon   You've had a shock with the airbag, why don't I run you a bath? Have some peace and quiet.

April   Why am I holding this cheese like an idiot?

Gordon stops leaning and straightens up, alarmed at my tone. I stand there trying for the life of me to work out why I have a cheese in my hand; it's like the most complicated sum in the world. I focus and concentrate and just stare at the cheese. No matter how hard I try, I can't do it. For a second I think I'm having a stroke.

And then I hear a voice; in the distance it's not clear at first but the more I concentrate the better I hear it. I look at Gordon and from his face I can see that the voice is actually mine.

'If it wasn't for Sid I'd leave you.'

Sid   Neil and I are walking around the lanes and I see the Big Cheese going into his house. I tie Neil up and I'm banging on his door. The Big Cheese answers and he's holding a scotch egg. How quick can you get in the house, take your shoes off and get a scotch egg?

When **Sid** *speaks as the Big Cheese he holds the scotch egg to his chest.*

He's all trying to get me to come in and stuff.

'Nah. I've, I've uh got Neil with me.' He like leans out of his house –

Sid *does this.*

He sees Neil. 'Well. What can I do for you, Sid?' 'I think the speeding foundation's a fucking crap idea.' I walk around when I talk to him, but I don't care.

He walks around.

'The boys would have hated it. Especially Luke.' 'I'm sorry you think that, Sid, but I don't agree.'

He points a finger at the Big Cheese.

'I know them, you don't.' 'I know you're upset, Sid, so let's calm down. What do you suggest would be a fitting tribute?'

'Fitting tribute? There is no fitting tribute,' I say. 'I don't want a fitting tribute.' The Big Cheese blinks. 'We have to do something.' I realise I've been a bit out of line with him.

It's just normally, in this situation Luke would have said something sarky, Owen would have tried to calm everyone down, Alex would have been looking the wrong way and I would have waited till the fighting started. But now it's just me, and I've got to weigh up all my feelings all the time on my own. I don't know what to do. He tries again. 'We have to change something so this never happens again and no one has to go through what we have.' 'I don't know.'

'What would you like to change?'

'Why don't you get the council to get Pizza Hut to come here? Or a bowling alley? Or a McDonalds? McDonalds would be good, somewhere we can go that doesn't chuck people out for making a coffee last three hours.' 'Your three best friends die. And you want a McDonalds?' Even I get how stupid that sounds. Before I can think I'm at it again.

He searches for the words.

'The reason we're all killing ourselves driving to Hereford or Kiddie is because there's fuck-all for us in this town. It isn't Alex's fault. It's yours. It's shit being a kid here. But you won't do anything about it because you'd rather some cunt from London come here and spend twenty quid on a cheddar than open a place for us.' 'I'm sorry, Sid, that's not true.' 'You lot love tourists more than kids and that's why all my mates are dead and I'm half blind.' 'That's not true at all, Sid, why don't you come in and we'll talk some more.' I see my reflection in his glasses and I look tiny. 'I've got the dog,' and I turn around.

Beat.

I untie Neil. I don't wanna wave to him but I do and he raises . . .

Beat.

He raises his scotch egg to me, the prick.

April   Sid managed about ten minutes of counselling. The idea of being alone with Gordon sends me into a panic so I throw myself into some marking, he knows not to disturb me when I'm marking. I don't mark a single book, but when he comes in from the garage I act like I'm heavily into it.

Gordon   No serious damage done.

April   I've got a lot to get through.

I watch him through the corner of my eye and he looks around for something to do. Something to be near me. He starts to load the dishwasher. And he does it just as I like to do it, glasses and cutlery first. I stop marking and look up and there he is tensed up trying to pull the drawer out further without making any noise.

April   Gordon?

Gordon   Yes.

April   I want to tell him why I said what I said.

Long pause.

'Big plates at the back.'

He obeys quietly and I feel sorry for him. But before I can do anything, Sid comes back from one of his walks with Neil. Even though he's like a yo-yo he moves so silently and inoffensively these days. He heads to his bedroom. For some reason I decide to make a big song and dance about the mud they've walked into the corridor, so I start, huffing and puffing.

Standing at the bottom of the stairs, Sid doesn't move as I get on my hands and knees and start scrubbing. My spine chills as he doesn't go up the stairs but goes into the kitchen. He comes into the corridor, dunks a cloth in the bucket and starts scrubbing the carpet behind me.

No, no, don't bother, I'll do it.

And I push him off the stain he's scrubbing. He straightens himself on his haunches.

Sid   I can do it.

April   No you can't.

Sid   It's my fault.

Pause.

April   I want my lazy son back. My stroppy boy who'll happily watch me scrub up his mess while he plays on his Xbox. I don't want a son who understands consequence.

Beat.

'You're not well. I'll do it.'

He starts again, twitching his head like a bird. He does this when he's trying to focus. As I crawl over to Sid, Gordon comes in.

Please stop.

Pause.

Please stop.

Sid   It's okay.

April   Please.

Sid   I don't mind.

April   I don't want you to do this.

Sid   It's coming off, see.

April   I need you to stop, you're making it worse, just leave me alone to clean my carpet. I wish everyone would just leave me to clean my carpet the way I want to.

Sid *is confused.* **April** *is ashamed.*

Gordon   Let your mum do the carpet.

Pause.

Sid   I'm old enough.

April *closes her eyes in pain.*

Gordon   I know. Just, let's leave her.

April   I don't look up as Gordon ushers Sid out of the corridor.

Gordon   I'll run you a bath.

April*'s heart sinks.*

Sid   Neil and I stand by the river at the bottom of the Linney.

Beat.

I see myself in the water. That's me now. That's me. A one-
eyed boy with three friends missing. I throw stones and mud
and sticks in. But in this town's water, that's all I'll ever be.
A one-eyed boy with three friends missing.

April I light candles, put some music on and sink into the
bath. As I unwind, the music acts as a thermal to my thoughts
and they float around the night of the crash like a glider.

Beat.

I sit alone at the Symphony Hall and watch the couple in
front share a drink. Anthony sings under a gauze sheet, and I
cry through every song, I'm so perfectly alone. I think I'd like
to paint him; this woman trapped in a six-foot New York
man's body.

The steam from the bath escapes like a puff of white powder,
and I'm suddenly aware of a lump in my mouth, and an ache
in my shoulder. The stiffness reminds me of sleeping in chairs
and feeling hospital jet-lagged. I sink under the water to hide
from the truth that I avoid the other boys' mothers now.

Reaching for the razor, Ronnie Trott carves up the town to
avoid seeing Mark and his new fling and I think I can't avoid
my lounge.

I lather up my soap and I rub the bruise inside my mouth with
my tongue, and think; no one knows I'm hurt. I close my eyes
and float towards Sid cleaning my carpet and I wonder . . .
I wonder if Neil can sniff out who Gordon's sleeping with?

I refill the bath with fresh hot water and imagine if it was red.

Beat.

'He had to climb over his friends to get out,' the officer says.
We were so lucky.

Beat.

Halfway through a song, the sheet falls from Anthony, and everyone cheers even though I'm alone and cold, in the car park, holding a photo of my family and The One We Take To America is in Gordon's boot. Below the waterline I try to escape but it's as if a sheet falls off me, and now I can see.

Beat.

The tap drips and it's like it's applauding me: it's not me who's trapped. It's Gordon. I'm not angry with him for trying to leave. I'm angry with him for trying to stay.

Gordon   'What's the most amount of cash I can withdraw on my account?'

Beat.

I look at Katie the teller, and she can see I'm on some kind of mission. Only I don't know what it's for.

Beat.

I drop the money into a holdall of Sid's and leave the branch.

Beat.

Two hours later I'm standing in a purpose-built flat in Smethwick with a letting agent. 'Where do I sign?'

Beat.

I sit on the bed next to the holdall and look around the furnished flat. My new flat. I walk around getting to know the IKEA-trite furniture. It's soulless, and for some reason I feel completely at home. I lie back on the bed with my hands tucked behind my head.

Beat.

This is different to the B&Bs; this is going to be quiet. Anonymous. No April, no Sid, no cider festival, no parking campaigns, no town hall meetings, no pub, no May fair. Just me. Peace and quiet.

He pulls a phone out and puts it to his ear.

Andrew?

Beat.

Gordon.

Beat.

Walker.

Beat.

I've done it.

Beat.

(*Hopeful.*) Where are you?

Beat.

You think. You think you might like to come over? I'll stock the mini-bar. Or, fridge, as we call it in Smethwick.

Beat.

He hangs his head.

Okay.

He hangs up.

April   For the first time in years I feel like drawing.

Beat.

I rub a face on the steamed-up mirror.

Gordon   On the drive home, I list all the things I'm going to pack. Shirts, trousers, underwear, toiletries, slippers.

I need the big suitcase down, the One We Take To America. Some favourite books and DVDs and I know exactly which photograph I'm taking. The three of us in Tenby.

I pull into the driveway, and the boys are in the garage lifting weights. It's the last time I see them together.

Beat.

Sid stands over Owen as he bench-presses, Sid's the guru when it comes to anything sporty, everyone defers to him.

Beat.

I watch them for a while. Alex, such a thoughtful young chap, calls out to the boys to pack it in, he sees me waiting to put the car in.

'It's fine; it's fine lads, you carry on.'

'Just getting the guns pumped for the girls in town Mr W,' shouts Luke and shows me a bicep.

'As long as that's all you're pumping, Luke.'

And the boys guffaw, Sid springs into action and takes the bar off Owen.

You've never seen four boys like it. Like puppies, from the same litter. I don't think they had any secrets between them.

Beat.

Sid   Mum's gone to see Anthony and Johnsons in Birmingham. She's left cottage pie.

Gordon   Good good. I'd forgotten.

I want to tell Sid everything, I want to say I can't do any more for you.

Beat.

I salute the boys as they pull off for the last time, music blaring, Alex's exhaust pipe blowing.

I hear a surge of laughter as they vanish around the hedge.

And I think.

Long pause.

I think: thank God they've gone.

Sid   At the riverbank, a gentle breeze takes me back to a morning not long before.

Beat.

Alex picks me up first on the way.

'What the fuck's with the gay hair?'

'It's not gay.'

He fiddles with his hair.

(*To himself.*) It's not gay.

Luke gets in.

'Sid's hair's gone gay.'

He punches Alex on the leg.

Luke says:

(*Camp voice.*) 'Well, I think it's lovely.'

He leans back and gives Luke a dead leg.

'Don't you start!'

Alex laughs and bangs the steering wheel. 'Football kit! Shit!' says Luke.

'Fucking hell,' says Alex and we turn around and head back to Luke's. Outside his I say:

'Luke, mate.'

'What, mate?'

'Get us a beenie, mate.'

We pick up Owen, and he starts telling us about who he was Facebooking last night. He's rubbish around girls but get him online and he's a genius.

Beat.

I roll down the window, I'm not sure why. But with the beenie on, the banter and the boys, I want the whole town to see us. I want the whole town to lean out of their little houses and see us. Just see us, for once.

Gordon   I look at the paraphernalia and wrack my brain; when did I agree to this?

April   I think we should get Sid a dog. I think he needs a friend.

Gordon (*distracted, reading paper*)   Oh yes.

April   Do you think it's a good idea?

Gordon (*distracted, reading paper*)   Uh-huh.

There's a basket, a dog bowl, dog gate, dog toy, dog food. And in front of me, in the middle of the lounge, is a panting dog.

Sid looks like he's on camera, he doesn't know what to do with his arms, and I want to pick up all the stuff, and the dog, and throw it all out the front door and say to Sid:

'It was a crap idea, you do what you want. Whatever you need to do we'll do too.'

But I don't. I say:

'Get up off the sofa and stroke the dog.'

Pause.

Sid's patting him like he's bouncing a ball and I find myself gathering all the dog stuff together, putting it all in the basket so it's easy to carry to the car when this goes pear-shaped.

Beat.

I pick up the dog gate and the mechanism swings open and the way I'm holding it, it sort of frames Sid, April and the dog, like they're in a photo. And I remember speaking to a fireman, who was there at the scene. He said Sid surviving was a 'miracle'. My boy.

'Uh, what are we going to call him then?'

Sid   Neil?

April   Neil?

Gordon   Neil it is! Welcome Neil, I'm Gordon, Walker, this is April, and this is Sid and this is your new home. Hey?

And I stroke the dog like I find him adorable.

Long pause.

Because what's better? Lying to get what you want; or lying so people you *love* can get what they want?

Sid   The breeze dies and Neil lets me know it's time to go by circling around and not saying anything. Just as Mum does. And I think of her in the kitchen, in her own little square of the world wringing her hands, and I realise without me around she feels pointless. Just like I feel with the boys gone. But it's worse for her, because she can't grieve what isn't dead. I've been a ghost to her ever since the crash.

Scene Two

Sid *is offstage.*

April *folds shirts and puts them on the table.*

Gordon *is on the phone with some paperwork on the table.*

Gordon   Yes.

Beat.

Yes, it's a VW Polo.

Beat.

The integrity of the bumper is fine, there's no damage that I can see. My wife was driving.

Yes, she drove into the back of a stationary vehicle.

Beat.

Yes. It's just that the airbag has been decommissioned. Commissioned – I'm not sure what the right term is. The airbag's gone off.

Beat.

No. I don't mind.

He picks at some food.

Yes. Hello. I was telling your colleague, my wife was driving our VW Polo earlier today and bumped into a stationary car. And the airbag has been decommissioned or commissioned, what's the right term?

Yes.

It's gone off. The airbag went off.

Beat.

The bumper doesn't need replacing but obviously the airbag does and I can't see anything referring to it in our policy.

Beat.

Okay, I'll hold.

Yes?

Beat.

Hang on.

He gets some of the paperwork together.

It's Alpha Zebra one three nine nine Lima Papa.

Beat.

Walker.

Beat.

He sees **April** *stack up his shirts into a pile.*

Gordon   Uh. Sorry?

Beat.

Yes.

He goes through some more paperwork, but he can't stop watching **April** *fold shirts.*

Gordon (*to* **April**)   What are you doing?

April *ignores him.*

Gordon   VW Polo.

Beat.

Yes I'll hold.

He eats something and looks at his paperwork. **April** *watches him.*

Silence.

April   Do you remember that purple pashmina Sid gave me for my birthday?

(*In response to* **Gordon**'s *reaction.*) The / shawl.

Gordon   The wrap thing, yes.

April   I've been looking for it for months, haven't I?

Gordon   Yes, we couldn't let on, we thought you'd lost it.

April   I turned the house upside down looking for it didn't I? The last time I wore it we went to that picnic-in-the-park concert in Berrington Hall, do you remember?

Gordon   Yes.

April   That's the last time I wore it.

Gordon   Do you think we left it there then? It's probably gone by now.

April   The night of the crash at the hospital I was stood outside making phone calls and I got cold. I was walking back and forth trying to stay warm and it hit me. I knew exactly where that pashmina was.

April *pulls a suitcase out,* The One We Take To America, *and puts* **Gordon***'s shirts in as she speaks.*

Gordon   Where was it?

Beat.

April   Folded up, under the plastic sheet. In the boot of your car.

She picks up a photograph of the family, places it on his folded shirts and closes the suitcase.

Gordon *fills with dread.*

He puts his head in his hands.

April   I saw it. I saw your packed suitcase.

Gordon   It's . . . I can / explain.

April   Don't you dare stay with us because of what happened to Sid.

Gordon   I . . . It's. I can make it.

He censors himself as **Sid** *enters the room oblivious to the weird atmosphere.* **Gordon** *can't take his eyes off* **April***, who turns her back to both of them.*

Slowly it dawns on **Sid** *that something is the matter.*

Sid   Is everything okay?

Deafening silence from his parents.

Gordon   Everything's fine.

He waves his phone.

We're just, just a bit shaken up about the airbag. Aren't we love?

Very long silence as **April** *stares at the floor, unwilling to hurt* **Sid**, *unable to lie any more.*

Gordon   Where's Neil?

Sid (*looking at* **April**)   Basket.

April *can't look at either of them.* **Sid** *is really unnerved.*

Gordon   Where've you been then? Give him a good walk, did you? Neil.

Sid *is torn between* **Gordon** *and* **April**.

Sid   Um . . . yeah.

Gordon *is out of conversation.*

Sid *watches* **April**. *He turns to* **Gordon**, *points to* **April** *and indicates 'What's up with her?'*

Gordon *can't begin to explain.*

Sid *turns to his mum, he thinks about leaving . . . but stops himself.*

Sid (*to* **April**)   I was wondering, Mum . . . if, if you could help me, with my eye?

April *turns, and sees* **Sid** *looking at her.*

After some fumbling, **Sid** *gets his drops out and holds them towards her.*

April*'s knees weaken and she has to steady herself. This is the best present she could have wished for.*

April   Yes. Yes all right.

She takes the drops from **Sid***'s hand.*

April *and* **Gordon***'s eyes meet momentarily.*

Sid *tilts his head back; she attempts to administer the drops but it's unsuccessful. They shuffle around each other, it's awkward.*

April   Hang on. Sit down.

Sid *obeys and takes a seat.* **April** *stands behind him and holds his face close to her body.*

She looks down at him while he looks up at her.

Gordon   Do you uh, do you need some light? To see.

April *looks at the room lighting, it's not good enough.*

April   That might help.

Gordon *pulls down the pendant light above the table so it stretches down and he angles it over* **April**'s *shoulder to light* **Sid**'s *face.*

April *sits down on the bench, and she indicates for* **Sid** *to rest his head on her lap.*

April   Come here.

Sid *stretches out and lies on his mother's lap.*

Sid (*to* **April**)   Remember that time you knocked your sewing box over and the needles went all over the carpet, and he comes in and says, 'I'll get my magnet.'

April *and* **Sid** *laugh.*

In perfect silence, **April** *administers the drops.*

Sid *blinks.*

April *looks at* **Sid**'s *eye for a while – she's evidently avoided looking at it for so long.*

She applies another drop, **Sid** *blinks and the job is done.*

April   Do you want me to keep this safe?

Sid *nods.*

April *looks around briefly for somewhere to put it but doesn't want to disturb* **Sid**. *Without a second thought* **Gordon** *offers a hand and* **April** *instinctively gives it to him.* **Gordon** *puts the drops in his pocket and* **April** *returns to looking at her son.*

Gently, **April** *wipes the solution from* **Sid***'s face.*

Gordon *puts his hand on* **April***'s shoulder.*

April *kisses* **Sid** *on the nose.*

Lights down.

The End.

Salt, Root and Roe

For Chloë

Where once the mermen through your ice
Pushed up their hair, the dry wind steers
Through salt and root and roe.

Dylan Thomas

Salt, Root and Roe premiered in a production by the Donmar Warehouse at Trafalgar Studios, London, on 10 November 2011. The cast was as follows:

Iola Hughes   Anna Calder-Marshall
Anest Owen   Anna Carteret
Menna Hopkins   Imogen Stubbs
Gareth Rowlands   Roger Evans

Director   Hamish Pirie
Designer   Chloe Lamford
Lighting Designer   Anna Watson
Composer and Sound Designer   Alex Baranowski

Author's note

Salt, Root and Roe owes its production to the faith and tenacity of Hamish Pirie. As director, Hamish has, at various stages, invested financially, professionally and personally in this play. His commitment to writers, and new writing, is unshakable and this author owes him an eternal debt of gratitude.

Characters

Iola Hughes (*pronounced* YO-LAH), *seventies, identical twin, lived in North Pembrokeshire all her life, on a smallholding most of her life, slightly more countrified than her sister.*

Anest Owen (*pronounced* ANN-EST), *seventies, identical twin, lived in North Pembrokeshire all her life, in the city of St David's most of her life, slightly more urban than her sister.*

Menna Hopkins, *forty-five to fifties, daughter of Anest. Neurotic, in cheap, nondescript clothes.*

Gareth Rowlands, *forty-five to fifties, local policeman.*

(/) *indicates when the next line should be spoken.* (–) *indicates an interruption of thought.*

The phonetic pronunciation and English meaning of Welsh words and phrases is specified, directly after the first instance of each word or phrase, in the form [PRONUNCIATION – *English meaning*].

Translations of Welsh words and phrases which appear in the play text are also included on pages 249–50.

Thank you

Hamish Pirie, Michael Grandage, James Bierman, Miriam Green, Jo Danvers and all at the Donmar. Anna Carteret, Anna Calder-Marshal, Imogen Stubbs, Roger Evans, Lisa Jen, Bob Blythe, Niamh Cusack, Sian Phillips, Laura Cotton, Len and Elspeth Cotton, Richard, Branwen and Dafydd Cotton, William John Cotton (Poppin), Janet Davies, Grace Griffiths, Robert Davies, Phil Davies, Chloe Moss, Menna and Philip Price, Matthew Maryline and Sophia Price, Mark Jefferies, Gary Marsh, Nicky Lund and Katell Keineg.

Scene One

Underwater.

Sounds of the sea.

Light on **Iola** *and* **Anest** *in heavy coats, tied together by a skipping rope.*

Anest Inside a limekiln.

Iola You can play.

Anest You can play games.

Iola Imagine you're back.

Anest In your mammy's tummy.

Iola In your mammy's water.

Anest You are water.

Iola And you.

Anest At the same time.

Iola Like in the beginning.

Anest With God's face peeping.

Iola Pressing the tide.

Anest Observing us alive.

Iola To the shore of lives.

Anest Like in the beginning.

Iola To the land alone.

Blackout.

Scene Two

A stone cottage on the northern coast of Pembrokeshire, the most westerly part of Wales, facing the Atlantic Ocean.

Cardboard boxes fill the room.

Menna *stands in the middle of the room with latex gloves on. Facing her is* **P.C. Gareth Rowlands**.

Gareth   Scratch my nose?

Menna   No.

Gareth   Hold my hands like this?

He holds his hands.

Menna   No.

Gareth (*clears throat*)   Clear my throat?

Menna   You might need to do that anyway.

Pause.

Gareth   Wink. I could wink? (*Off* **Menna***'s reaction.*) No. Text? I could text you before?

Beat.

I'm / sorry, that's ridiculous.

Menna   No. Something in the moment. Something only we know.

Gareth   Pull my ear?

Menna   No.

Gareth   Have you got any ideas? I can only think of winking now.

Menna *can't speak.*

Gareth   There must be something.

Menna   It doesn't have to be big. / It doesn't have to be −

Gareth*'s radio crackles with a voice: 'India Whisky Uniform'. He walks offstage.*

Gareth   Receiving, go ahead . . .

Menna *watches* **Gareth** *go off. She circles the room before pulling her phone out and dialling.*

Menna (*to phone*)   Hi.

Beat.

Nothing.

Beat.

Nothing.

Beat.

I love you.

Beat.

No, nothing.

She becomes self-conscious when **Gareth** *appears at the door holding a box.*

Menna   Call later, bye.

She hangs up.

Anything?

Gareth *shakes his head.*

Gareth   They've got, Guess Who?

He puts it down.

It's just there.

After putting it down, he taps it.

Peter?

Menna   Hm?

Gareth   Peter?

Menna   Yes.

Menna finds herself leaning on something. Immediately she gets some sanitiser out and sanitises her gloves.

Menna   Yes, that was Peter. Um, it's the furniture. It's the furniture that's bothering me.

Gareth   Okay.

Menna   It's final.

Gareth   Hm?

Menna   There's nowhere to sit.

Seeing a bench leaning up against something, **Gareth** *pulls it down.*

Menna   It's a garden bench.

Dusting the bench with his hands, **Gareth** *sits on it.*

Gareth   Don't read anything / into anything

Menna   I don't need to read anything into anything, I've got the words right here.

She pulls a letter out of her handbag.

I just want you to be honest with me that's all, Gareth, we're – I'd hope you know – we're old friends and I'd hope you'd just, be honest.

She waits for **Gareth**'s *honesty.*

Menna   Can you be honest / with me Gareth?

Gareth   Honestly, Men –

Menna   I don't want any training / speak.

Gareth   Honestly, I'm not saying anything. It's been so long since anyone bloody trained me for anything, for anything, listen, until we know either way none of this – it's pointless. Alright?

Gareth *wipes part of the bench clean and indicates for* **Menna** *to sit.* **Menna** *declines.* **Gareth** *takes his jacket off and puts it on the bench.*

Gareth   How's that?

She sits down.

Boys coming down?

Menna   Haven't told them. / I'm not telling them. Not yet.

Gareth   Nothing to tell yet.

Silence.

Menna   How are the girls?

Gareth   Out of my house, thank God. I miss them but I don't miss the two-hour showers and all the beeping.

Menna   Peter's one for two-hour showers.

Gareth   What if I tell you to sit down? / Would that work?

Menna   Might already be sitting.

She puts her head in her hands.

Gareth   Come on, let's play Guess Who.

Beat.

Pass the – you'll go mad otherwise.

Menna   I don't want / to.

Gareth   Neither do I but it's all we've got.

Pause.

Menna   It's not really appropriate, is it?

Gareth   Who says?

Menna *doesn't know,* **Gareth** *fiddles with the game.* **Menna** *gets up and goes to the window.*

Gareth   I can't remember how to play myself.

Menna *looks out the window.*

Menna   What do people do?

She indicates – this – situation.

(*Off* **Gareth**'s *reaction.*) I'm being – aren't I? / I am.

Gareth   Best try not to think about that.

Menna   I can't / do anything.

Gareth   I know it's hard.

Menna   I can't stop thinking about it so perhaps we just talk about it; how would you do it?

Gareth   I'm not even going there.

Menna   We're just chatting.

Gareth   We're not just chatting.

Menna   Gareth.

Gareth   I'm not / talking about this.

Menna   I want to know.

Gareth   I'm not here / for this.

Menna   What the hell are you here for if . . .

Gareth *isn't sure what to say.*

Menna *turns her back on him.* **Gareth** *stares at her. He tries to say something but nothing comes out.*

He fiddles with the game; he lays out some cards on the floor, but can't bring himself to play the game. He puts his head in his hands. He can't look at her, so he looks long and hard at Guess Who.

Gareth   Cliffs, are popular.

He returns to the board with new purpose.

Menna   Thank, good. Good.

Beat.

Gareth   I have no idea what I'm doing.

Menna   You uh, you pick one.

Gareth   What?

Beat.

Menna   You're meant to, pick one. Each. One face each.

Gareth *looks at the laid-out cards. He picks one, yet still isn't sure what to do. Exasperated* **Menna** *approaches, she sweeps up all the cards and shuffles them.*

Menna   Didn't you play this with the girls?

Gareth   Yes, but when they were . . .

Checks box.

One to six? Yes, I was drinking a lot of whisky.

Menna *offers him the pack;* **Gareth** *takes one.*

Menna   Put it in the little holder.

He puts it in the holder.

That's how you play it.

She hands the pack of cards back to him. **Gareth** *occupies himself with the game. Perhaps one caddy won't go down flush, and so he fiddles with it.*

Menna   How's Eirwen? [EYE-R-WHEN.]

Gareth   Fine, yeah. Doing a lot with the, uh, with the church these days. Very involved. I steer clear.

He hands her a card.

Menna   Oh my God, he looks like Auntie Iola. [YOLA.]

Gareth *looks.*

Menna   Can you believe that?

Beat.

When she was younger.

Gareth   Yes.

Menna   I can't believe that.

She looks at the card for an age.

Gareth   Choose another card. Choose another card.

Menna *takes another card off* **Gareth** *and puts the one of Iola in the pile.*

Gareth   Does yours have a beard?

Menna   No –

He starts flicking faces down.

– she doesn't.

He flicks even more faces down.

Menna   Does yours have a moustache?

Gareth   No.

She looks at the faces.

Flick all the ones with moustaches down.

She starts flicking the faces down, she then checks her mobile.

You done?

Menna   Hang on.

Gareth   Flick the moustaches down.

She flicks a couple more down and stops.

Does, yours, wear glasses?

Beat.

Menna   What am I doing?

Gareth   Look at the one you've chosen, say yes or no if she's got glasses.

She looks at the card.

Menna   Should we be driving around or something?

Gareth   We'll play one game, and then when there's a winner I'll radio through, see what's what.

She accepts this.

After I've won, mind.

Menna   This is all my fault.

Gareth   No it's not.

Pause. **Gareth** *realises he hasn't got many faces left.*

I think perhaps we should try and draw the game out. Okay, you can't ask a question about their description.

Menna   I don't understand.

Gareth   Does yours look like the kind of person who'd have a tracker mortgage?

Menna   Um . . . well. I don't. I don't know.

Gareth   What would you say?

Menna   No, I don't think she would.

The game slows down, **Gareth** *mulls over his faces, he weighs up every face. He flicks down one.*

Then he flicks another.

Gareth   Your go.

Menna   Um . . . Uh . . . I can't think of anything.

Beat.

Gareth   Hm . . . Can he fold maps? How about that?

Menna   Okay.

Gareth   Can he fold maps? Hmm . . . No, I don't think he can.

Menna *flicks some faces down.*

Gareth   Does yours look like the kind of person to have a litre of petrol in the boot for emergencies?

Menna   No.

Gareth   Right . . .

He confidently flicks some faces down.

Menna   You know the kind of people to keep petrol / in the boot?

Gareth   Absolutely. Your go.

Menna *and* **Gareth** *start to smile.*

Menna   Um . . . I can't think of any again.

Gareth   Does yours look like the kind of person who sticks her tongue out when she parallel parks?

Menna *and* **Gareth** *share the joke.*

Menna   I do that.

Gareth *puts his helmet on a hook.*

Gareth   I know.

Menna*'s attention is drawn to the helmet on the hook.*

Menna   That's it.

She points at the helmet.

That's it.

Gareth   What?

Menna *points to the helmet.*

Gareth   That?

Menna   That'll work.

Gareth   That'll work?

Menna   That'll work.

Pause.

Gareth *gets up, picks up the helmet. He looks at* **Menna**, *puts it on the hook.*

Gareth   There?

Menna   Yes there.

Beat.

Put your helmet on the hook when you come in and that's how I'll know she's dead.

Gareth   That's it?

Menna   That's it.

Long pause.

Gareth   Well, that's something.

Menna   You must think we're crazy.

Gareth *gets a hip flask out and takes a swig.*

Gareth   Not at all. Seen it all before. When I started, Bob Socks said to me, he was the old sergeant, there wasn't anyone he hadn't arrested. He said to me – 'You can never ever underestimate how effing mental the general public are.' And I'm not saying this is 'effing mental' you know, but . . . I'm just saying.

Beat.

The stuff we see. Men frothing at the mouth. Women biting each other. Kids fighting and (*censoring volume*) shitting through drink and drugs. We don't even cover Haverfordwest. Probably always been like that, but we never saw it, did we? When we were kids? But it's going on. Behind all those closed doors there's no end of nonsense.

Beat.

'Behind closed doors, that's where you'll find the infinite chaos of human desire.'

Long pause.

Menna   Bit grand.

Gareth   Bob Socks again. Man was a poet. And it's true. Nearly everyone round here's got themselves in a situation they don't know how to get out of. And then it's the drinking and the fighting. Not their fault half the time. It's living by the sea.

Menna   What do you mean?

Gareth *offers* **Menna** *his hip flask. Hesitating,* **Menna** *takes it but spends an age cleaning it.*

Gareth   You know.

Menna   What?

Gareth   You were brought up by the sea. You know what it's like.

Menna   I don't.

Gareth   Okay.

Menna   No, explain what you mean.

Gareth   I don't know, I just thought you'd understand; I don't know what I mean. I don't, I just thought. I don't know, it's just living by the sea, isn't it?

Menna   I don't understand what you mean.

She takes a swig from the whisky.

Gareth   It's an ocean, isn't it? You know. I don't know. Offers hope. That's why everyone's pissed all the time and the kids are sniffing glue and shagging. Going to church. Drives people mad. Farmers topping them –

Menna *gets up and runs out of the room.* **Gareth** *runs out and follows after her.*

Offstage, sounds of **Menna** *throwing up.*

Gareth   There there. Get it up.

Opposite, **Iola** *and* **Anest** *enter, carrying a plastic shopping bag each with pebbles in.*

Menna *continues to heave.*

Iola *and* **Anest** *look at each other, confused at the sounds offstage. They each pull a pebble out and hold them aloft ready to attack the intruder.*

Gareth *(offstage)*   That's better. Whoa! Quite a lot there.

Menna *(offstage)*   Sorry. Thank you. Sorry.

Menna *comes into the room wiping her face with a towel. She freezes, and* **Gareth** *bumps into her.*

Anest   Menna?

Menna   Auntie Iola!

Anest   Were you just being sick?

Menna *sweeps* **Iola** *up in her arms.*

Gareth *(under)*   India Whisky Uniform, missing persons have just returned home.

Anest   What's going on?

Gareth *(heading offstage)*   Station command. Yes, missing persons have arrived home, two-fifteen. At Gwaelod y Garth, cottage.

Menna   What the hell is all this about?

Anest   What about?

She pulls a letter out of her pocket and hands it to **Anest***.* **Anest** *starts to read it.*

Iola *(to* **Anest***)*   I'm sorry.

Menna   There's police out looking for you. Do you know how much trouble you've caused? They've had helicopters out. Where the hell have you been?

Anest   The beach. / Collecting pebbles.

Gareth *re-enters.*

Menna   I had that in the post this morning. / Peter and I nearly had a heart attack.

Iola   Has this caused you a lot of bother, Gareth?

Gareth   Don't / worry about that.

Menna   They've had helicopters out / for Christ's sake!

Gareth   We're just glad you're safe. I'm going to have to speak to both of you individually though. (*To* **Iola**.) You first / Mrs Hughes.

Iola   There's no need, Gareth.

Menna   I'll be having a word with her, Gareth, don't you worry.

Gareth   Mrs Hughes, I'm sorry to be so formal and all that, but I have to tell you we have reason to believe you intend to take your own life and I'm duty bound to try to prevent you. And you, Mrs Owen . . .

Anest   I was going to help her.

Legs going from under her, **Menna** *sits down on the bench without checking for dirt.*

Blackout.

Scene Three

The cottage.

Anest *pulls dresses out of a box and presses them against* **Menna**, *who is wearing latex gloves.*

Menna   I'll never get in that.

Anest   Yes you will, I should know, I made it. Made them all.

Menna   No.

Anest *puts another dress to her.* **Menna** *looks at it, and is confused.*

Menna   No I don't think so.

Anest   What's wrong with it?

Menna   It's just. I don't know the colour? I think I'm more. I think my colour's green.

Anest *puts a green dress next to* **Menna**.

Menna   I don't know, perhaps not green. Maybe red.

Anest *puts a red dress next to* **Menna**.

Menna   I don't know. It might be a bit much.

Anest *puts a patterned dress next to* **Menna**.

Anest   What about something patterned then?

Menna   What do I look like?

Anest   You look like. You look lovely.

Menna *is sorely tempted. She puts the dress away.*

Menna   No I won't. I'll leave it / thanks, Mam.

Anest   You haven't got any whatyoucall, just pick something for tomorrow / and I can pack it all away.

Menna   I don't want to pick anything Mam! I'm not wearing any of those, okay?

Anest *smells one of them.*

Anest   They're clean.

Menna   I'm just not wearing them, okay, can we drop it?

Anest   How long are you / staying for?

Menna   Do you want me to go?

Anest   No, I'm thinking of you, you haven't got any clothes to wear. Does Peter know / about this?

Menna   Everyone knows about this, everyone. The whole county was out looking for you, it was on the radio. It'll be in the papers. I don't even want to think – I'll never forgive you for this.

Beat.

Peter and I have been out of our minds with worry. Lucky Gareth was on the phone and I had someone down here.

She looks at her phone.

I should ring Peter.

Anest   She shouldn't have / written to you.

Menna   If she hadn't written to me, I wouldn't be here and it would be too late, because you're going to bloody –

Stiffly and slowly, **Iola** *enters carrying a pillow, blankets, sleeping bag.*

(*Under breath.*) – help her.

Iola   This is one of those whatyoucallit . . . let me see. Organic / pillows.

Menna *takes the pillow, which is stiff and curved, and the blankets and sleeping bag off her.*

Menna (*impatient*)   Ergonomic.

Anest   Yes. And some thick warm socks there for you, put them on.

Menna   What's all this?

Anest   Put / them on.

Iola   Blankets. Sold the spare beds.

Menna   There's no beds?

Iola   There's one bed. We sleep in that.

Menna   Where am I – What if you have visitors?

Anest   Ty Felin [TEE VE-LIN – *Yellow House*] is empty, why don't you go there?

Looking around the room, **Menna** *realises she's going to have to sleep on the floor.*

Menna   What am I going to sleep on?

Anest   He's done the changeover so it's clean, you haven't got to worry about that.

'Clean' rings a bell with **Menna***. She is tempted. She looks at her mum and aunt, and the floor.*

Menna (*stiffly*)   No. No . . . it's fine.

She looks around the room, disgusted.

Anest   You can have your own bed. You've got the money. / Just round the corner

Menna   I'll.

Beat.

It just needs a clean, that's all.

Anest   Peter won't want you / sleeping on the floor.

Menna   Peter doesn't have to know. And if you've sold your spare beds and I want to stay here then I'm going to have to sleep on the floor, aren't I? Sorry it's just.

Pulling a plastic sheet from her handbag, Menna places it on the floor before kneeling on it. She gets a dustpan and brush and starts sweeping the floor.

Iola   Are these blankets enough?

Menna *continues sweeping.*

Menna   They'll / be fine.

Anest   She's going to need another blanket.

Menna   This is / fine, stop fussing both of you.

Anest   There's some in the box by the toilet.

Menna   This is enough.

Iola *heads out of the room.* **Menna** *has her back to* **Anest**. **Anest** *reaches out to touch* **Menna** *but pulls back.*

Slowly **Iola** *enters with another blanket.*

Iola   This one.

Anest   That one.

While **Menna** *sweeps an increasingly bigger area,* **Anest** *starts to make a makeshift bed out of blankets and sleeping bag.*

Iola   Nice yna fe? [UN A V-AIR – isn't it?] Where did you make that? / Did you make that? You –

Anest   I can't remember.

Iola   – shouldn't give that away.

Taking blanket in hand.

Look / at that.

Iola *starts putting teabags in the teapot.*

Anest   I don't / know.

Iola   It was with the rest of the whatyoucall . . .

Iola *picks up* **Menna**'s *phone.*

What's this?

Menna (*to* **Iola**)   My mobile. Are you giving your stuff away?

Back to the task in hand, **Iola** *puts the mobile in the teapot and starts swilling it around.*

Anest   Well. Can't stay here, can I? (*Off* **Menna**'s *reaction.*) I'm not going to stay here.

Anest *avoids* **Menna**'s *eye.*

The clunking in the pot draws **Iola**'s *attention.*

Menna (*coldly*)   Where were you going to go?

Anest   The Willows, I think.

Iola   Oh!

Menna   The nursing home.

Anest   I've heard very good / things about it so −

Iola *looks into the teapot.*

Menna   We have room, you didn't think, you didn't think to come to Bristol?

Iola   Oh no.

Anest   I don't know, Menna, it's not important is it? I haven't thought it through.

Iola *gasps.*

Menna   Peter would go along with anything I said. The boys have moved − is this about me?

Iola   I put your phone in the teapot.

Menna *isn't sure how to respond. She goes over to the teapot and puts her hand in; it burns. She gets a tea towel and wraps her hand and gets it out.*

Menna   Oh Auntie Iola.

She fiddles with it, trying to get it to work.

Iola (*worried*)   I'm sorry dear, is it new? (*Confused.*) I don't know how that happened.

Anest   It'll be fine in a minute.

Bemused, **Menna** *looks at* **Anest** *and* **Anest** *wills her to be fine about it.*

Menna (*sighing*)   It's fine.

Iola   Is it working?

Menna   Yes. It'll be fine. It's a, waterproof phone. Got a waterproof app / on it so . . .

Iola   Oh good. I'll make a fresh pot. I don't know where that thing's been!

Iola *takes the teapot out to the kitchen.*

Anest   Do you want something to eat?

Menna *looks at* **Anest** *and then back at her phone. She goes over to a bin and drops the phone in.*

Menna (*looking around*)   I'm not cooking here.

She stands in the sleeping bag and zips it up as she speaks.

I know you think / I'm pathetic.

Anest   Menna.

Menna   No, and you might be right. Okay? But – I don't care what you want and I don't care what she wants, I'm going to put an end to this nonsense, and I don't care if you don't want to take me seriously and I don't care if I've got to clean every surface and buy back all your furniture then I will. It's – I will.

Blackout.

Scene Four

Underwater.

Sounds of the sea.

Iola and **Anest** *stand a little closer.*

Iola   If you ever see a horse.

Anest   With his hooves the wrong way round.

Iola   He won't be broken.

Anest   Plenty have tried.

Iola   Ceffyl Dwr yw e. [KE-FILL DOOO-R EWE-E – *He's a water horse.*]

Anest   A water horse.

Iola   Full of mischief.

Anest   You can mount him.

Iola   But you go where he goes.

Anest   Back to the sea.

Iola   Or river.

Anest   Or waterfall.

Iola   That's where he comes from.

Anest   And it's where he's going.

Iola   Like every one of us.

Anest   His hooves give him away.

Blackout.

Scene Five

The cottage.

Restless and wearing gloves, **Menna** *can't get comfy as she tosses and turns in her makeshift bed while reading an iPad or Kindle.*

Creeping, **Iola** *enters.*

Iola (*hissed*)   Do you want a game of cards?

Menna   What?

Iola (*hissed*)   Cards? Do you want a game?

Menna (*checking clock*)   It's two in the morning.

Iola   It's. I can't sleep.

Menna   I'm sort of in the middle of something.

Iola *heads over to* **Menna** *and climbs into bed with her, holding a skipping rope.*

Iola   What's that then?

Menna   It's like a book in a computer. Why've you got a skipping rope, Auntie Iols? [YOLS?]

Iola   Oh, what you call? Um. Anest ties us. When we sleep. I end up out in the yard. I was in the yard and the milkman said, 'Getting a start on the potatoes, Mrs Hughes!'

She laughs.

Pause.

Reading something, are you?

Menna   It's about a woman who goes travelling and explores, food, spirituality and love. I'm on the food bit.

Iola *leans over and looks at the iPad / Kindle.*

Menna   Okay. Okay. Let me turn this off and we'll have a game.

Iola   All the years Albie was alive, never read a book. Read a newspaper cover to cover, or a magazine. But a book? Duw, duw. [DUE DUE – *Good God.*] Like I was asking him to put his hand in the fire.

Menna *tries to get a bit more space between herself and* **Iola**.

Iola   Newspaper though. *Telegraph. Western Herald. Western Mail.* Read them all.

Menna   I don't buy / newspapers now.

Iola   Forty years, never argued. No cross words. Ti'n pwdu nawr [TEEN POODY NOWR – *You're sulking now*] he'd say?

Menna   What's / that? Sulk?

Iola   He'd say . . . 'Yes, you're in a sulk, Iola.' He'd say, 'No matter, we'll be talking this evening.'

She laughs.

Laughing at me. All through the way. 'We'll be talking this evening.'

Menna *smiles.*

Menna   Shall we play?

Impatiently, she takes the cards off **Iola** *and starts to shuffle.*

I'll do it.

Iola   Gin rummy.

Menna   You'll be no use tomorrow.

Iola   I'm no use anyway. Oh, tablets.

She picks up a bottle of tablets.

Oh. I'm going mad.

She cackles.

Menna   Don't say that. How come you're not tired?

Iola   I don't know. Get confused. There we are.

Beat.

Put something down and then; can't remember what I'm doing.

Menna   Everything's got its place in our house. Nothing ever goes missing.

Iola   There we are.

Menna *starts dealing the cards out. As they talk, they play cards.*

Anest *enters but isn't seen.*

Iola   How are the boys?

Menna   I haven't told them if that's what you're thinking.

Long pause.

Peter is worried sick, he wanted to come down here, but I said no, 'You hold the fort.' And besides he's got so much work on, he can't get away from his drawing board.

Beat.

You know Mam could go to jail.

Long pause.

Thought about that?

Iola   They say we're yn y felan. [UN AR VELAN – *in the doldrums.*]

Menna   What's that?

Iola   Fallow. Like. It's like a fallow field. Nothing grows. What you . . . Families get it. There we are. Too many lambs die, Albie'd say, 'Ry' ni yn y felan Iola.' [RUN NEE UN UH VAIR IAN YOLA – *We're in the doldrums.*] It's like doldrums. Doesn't translate ti'n bod. [TEEN BORED – *you know.*] Whole families get it.

Anest *stands out of sight and watches* **Menna** *and* **Iola** *play cards.*

Menna   And we've got it?

Iola   So they say.

Menna   Explains a lot.

Iola *looks at her cards.* **Menna** *bristles as she gets back in the game.*

Iola   Oh.

Menna   What?

Iola   Hang on . . . what you call . . .

She looks at cards.

Uhhh . . . iawn. [YAW-N – *okay.*]

Iola *picks up a card and spends an age making up her mind.* **Iola** *picks a card up, puts it down, and picks up another.* **Menna** *reflexes, because* **Iola** *has broken the rules, but then lets it go.*

Menna   Nathan's got a new girlfriend. Scottish, very glamorous. Brogan. When they're all in the dining room, she comes into the kitchen for little chats. Helps me whatever I'm doing, she's very good at following instructions, she's delightful. Part of me hopes they'll never get married, so she just stays as she is.

Beat.

She had this scarf on, and it was a tartan. Her clan. They fought in . . . I don't know, some battle. I tried telling her about Grandad but I couldn't remember.

Beat.

What was it about Grandad, so I can tell her?

Iola   Nothing to tell.

Menna   Yes there is.

Iola   What you want to know? He used to fart something rotten.

She cackles.

Anest *leaves.*

Menna   No. What's the story? He was half merman wasn't he? That's what they used to say.

Iola *laughs.*

Iola   I don't know.

Menna   Yes you do.

Iola   Well that's what he used to say. He went back to the sea. They called him back. He heard the bells of Cantre Gwaelod [CAN-TRA G-WHY-LOD – *the Lowland Hundred*] and climbed over.

Menna   Cantre / Gwaelod is that . . .

Iola   The city under the sea. And the fishermen hear the church bells. A warning, see.

Menna   For what?

Iola   Storm, with the undercurrents. The bells still ring.
Some people say it was um . . . oh. Whatyoucallit?

Pause.

Oh. Hang on now.

Menna   Capsized.

Iola   No.

Beat.

When they walk.

Menna   He went for a walk?

Iola   Yes. You know, on the waves.

Long pause.

Menna   Your go.

Beat.

You can pick up.

Iola *picks up.*

Menna   I don't understand. He walked on the sea.

Iola   Fishermen see. With the weather, hot on their heads
they have twmwyn haul. [TOOEY-MIN-HIGH AL – *sunstroke.*]
What you call . . . um . . . let me see. Sunburn . . . suntroke.

Menna   Sunstroke.

Iola   Yes, sunstroke, and then the waves, whatyoucall . . .
They think are hills. They think it's land, see. And they step
off the boat and . . .

Menna   They think they're on land?

Iola   'Cause of the whatyoucall . . .

Menna   Sunstroke.

Iola   Sunstroke isn't the right word. / Calenture!

Menna   Do you think that's what happened?

Iola   When now?

Menna   With your dad.

Iola   Duw. [DUE – *God.*] I don't know.

Menna   What do you think though?

Iola   I don't, I don't know. Years ago now.

Menna   Come on, Auntie Iols.

Pause.

Iola   Be nice if he was still swimming around.

Menna   Like a merman.

Iola *laughs.*

Iola   Mermen don't drown, ti'n gweld? [TEEN GW-ELED – *you see?*]

She laughs, and **Menna** *laughs with her.*

Iola   Borrowed he was, see. 'I'm borrowed, girls, make a fuss of me now, because tomorrow they might want me back,' that's what he'd say. He was borrowed from the sea. And one day we'd have to give him back. That's why he never went with us to the beach, said he was scared we'd give him back. After he died I was scared of the sea for years. Thought some big fish would come and take me to the bottom and ask me lots of questions. That's why we never went in the sea.

She chuckles.

Menna   You and Mam never went in the sea?

Iola   Once he died that was it. Never again, neither of us. Drove our mam mad, she loved swimming but she couldn't get us to go in. We didn't go back in till you came along.

Menna   What was the story with you two?

Iola   Found us in a lobster pot.

She laughs.

Menna   That's right.

Curious, she gets up.

Isn't the pot here?

Iola   I don't know. Somewhere.

Menna   I'd love to show Brogan that, that would be lovely.
Where is it?

*She looks around the room. She looks at a box. Tentatively with her
fingertips she tries to open the box by having as little contact with it as
she can.*

Menna   You wouldn't have thrown that out.

Iola   Your mother might have.

Menna   No, no! You wouldn't have thrown that out. I
remember it said, what did it say on it?

*With less care, she opens another box, her desire for the pot overcoming
her fear of dirt.*

Iola   I can't remember.

Menna   It had your names on it and some lovely Welsh
on it. What was it?

Iola   Trysor y Mor. [TRUSS OR UH MORE – *Bounty of the sea.*]

Menna   What's that?

Iola   Treasure. Sea treasure. Bounty of the sea.

Menna *opens more boxes with increasing fervour.*

Menna   Where is it?

Iola   I don't know.

Menna *opens more boxes, pulling stuff out.*

Iola   Come and play cards.

Menna *opens more boxes.*

Iola   Menna.

Beat.

It's just a pot.

Menna   It's not just a pot.

She rips open another box.

What is all this crap? None of it is important.

Iola   You'll wake Anest.

Menna   I don't care! I want to show her something about my family.

She keeps looking. **Iola** *goes to join her and help, she looks inside a box.*

Iola   It's just an empty pppp. PP / ppp PPppPP PPP pPPuuPPPP PPPppp pppPPPPppp –

Menna   Auntie Iols.

She goes to her and takes her arms.

Iola   p Pp / Ppppppppp – PP-pppp p – pp –

Menna   Stop it. Stop, shh shh . . .

Iola *gasps, moves away from* **Menna** *and retches.* **Menna** *helps her and grabs a blanket to catch* **Iola***'s vomit.*

Menna   I'm here, I'm here.

Iola *recovers, exhausted, breathless, and rests in* **Menna***'s arms.*

Iola   Sorry.

Menna *kisses her.*

Weakly **Iola** *smiles,* **Menna** *holds her tight.*

Blackout.

Scene Six

Underwater.

Sounds of the sea.

Anest *and* **Iola** *are closer together.*

Iola   The water.

Anest   The milk.

Iola   The electric.

Anest   The gas.

Iola   The phone.

Anest   The TV.

Iola   The cat.

Anest   The neighbours.

Iola   The windows.

Anest   The post.

Iola   The money.

Anest   The savings.

Iola   The papers.

Anest   The scandal.

Iola   The stories.

Anest   The law.

Iola   The shame.

Anest   The find.

Iola   The loss.

Anest   The gain.

Iola   The pain.

Anest   The worry.

Iola   The detail.

Anest   The thought.

Iola   The thought.

Blackout.

Scene Seven

The cottage.

More boxes are stacked around the cottage. Standing in the middle of the room, carrying a table, is **Menna**, *wearing gloves, and* **Gareth** *in civilian clothes with a rucksack.*

Gareth   Where's it going?

Menna   Over here.

They walk the table to the corner of the room and put it down.

That was well timed, I never would have got this in.

Gareth   I was just passing. So I thought. Come see you. And Mrs Hughes.

He looks around.

Peter?

Menna   No, no, I spoke to him last night, he says hello. But. It's best he stays at home. He's got a lot of work on.

Gareth   You could do with a hand down here.

Pause.

Menna   He's amazing. He's. He's so good, with the boys. He's just, not very good with things like this, he'll admit that himself. Which is fine. He's good at little things. Detail.

Gareth   Architect's eye.

She goes into her handbag and pulls out a little bottle.

Menna   He got this little bottle made, and engraved for me last Christmas.

Gareth   'Soul mate'. What is it? Perfume?

Menna   Sanitiser.

Gareth   I bought Eirwen a North Face jacket for Christmas.

He picks up **Iola***'s big coat. He puts it on. He opens it up; there are lots of extra pockets sewn in.*

Enough pockets?

Menna   They don't like carrying handbags. Scared of hoodies.

Gareth   In St David's?

Menna   Power of the *Daily Mail*.

Gareth   You know, when I was a kid, I'd see them around town and I'd be asking my mam, 'Can I have a twin? I want a twin.'

Menna   Think we all did that.

Gareth   Got a bit obsessed, they'd make anything look interesting. Shopping. Be brilliant with a twin. Waiting for a bus, there's two of you. Going to bed. Could do with one, make cleaning more fun, wouldn't it? Two of you together, never be lonely.

Menna   Yeah.

Gareth   Still can't walk past a lobster pot without thinking . . .

He rubs his hands.

'this could be the one'.

Menna   You remember that?

Gareth   Yeah. Lobster pots.

Menna   I used to tell myself I was one of them. That we were three twins.

Gareth   Triplets.

Menna   I wanted to be a twin.

Beat.

Gareth   I brought some clothes round – Eirwen sent me round with some clothes.

He pulls some things out of his bag. **Menna** *is surprised.*

Beat.

Gareth   Thought you wouldn't have had time to pack. What with the; and everything.

Beat.

It's – / Told her you were staying for a few days.

Menna   Oh. That's. She's too thoughtful, Eirwen! She is.

Gareth   I've got *no* idea if you're the same . . .

He points at **Menna***'s body.*

Menna   Okay.

Gareth *pulls out lots of colourful, slightly bohemian, patterned dresses. He pulls out a pair of knickers.* **Menna** *takes them out of his hands.*

Menna   That's great, I'll go through these and yes. I'll tell her thank you, when I see her.

He hesitates.

Gareth   Yes.

Menna   She's so thoughtful, / she puts me to shame.

Gareth   Yes.

Menna   Perhaps I should ring her? I can't ring her. Iola boiled my phone / in a bloody teapot.

Gareth   No worries at all.

Menna   I want to thank her.

Gareth   It's fine.

Menna   I'll pop round. Is she in tonight?

Beat.

Gareth   Actually, best not to thank her.

Menna   What if I bump into her?

Gareth   Just don't mention it, I'll pass on your thanks.

Menna   I'll be wearing her clothes.

Pause.

Gareth   She doesn't know I've brought these over.

Menna*'s confusion is matched by* **Iola***'s, who enters in a dressing gown holding a bag tight to herself.*

Iola   Anest?

Menna   Menna. Gareth's here.

Gareth   Hello!

Iola *goes to the window and looks out.*

Iola (*under breath*)   Starlings are coming, starlings coming from Coed y Brenin. [COID UH BREN-IN – *King's Wood.*]

Menna (*side of mouth*)   What's she on about?

Gareth (*side of mouth*)   Starlings carry foot and mouth. (*To* **Iola**.) Do you want me to go out and fire a gun, Mrs Hughes?

Iola   Iawn. [YAW-N – *Good.*] Thank you bach. [BA-CH – *little one.*]

Menna   We haven't got any animals and you haven't got a gun.

Gareth (*winking*)   Been on a course, haven't I? (*To* **Iola**.)
Gotta keep an eye on them haven't you, Mrs Hughes? Rats of
the air.

Iola *looks around and clutches her bag tight to her chest.*

Gareth (*to* **Menna**) Do you want me to stick around?

Menna   No, it's fine.

Gareth   I'll . . .

Indicates, 'head off'.

Leave it to me Mrs Hughes, I'll sort them out.

Gareth *leaves.*

Iola   Have I eaten?

Menna   Yes. We had cheese on toast. Rarebit.

Beat.

Do you want to go back to bed?

Iola   I don't want to go back to bed. I don't want to go back
to bed.

Menna   Perhaps you should.

Iola   I don't want to.

Menna   I think it might do you good.

Iola *smashes a plate on the floor.*

Deciding to leave **Iola** *alone,* **Menna** *picks up some of the plates and
puts them into a cardboard box.*

Menna   Perhaps I'll put these in here. Keep them safe.

Iola   It was – Albie will be home soon.

Menna   Albie used to like Gareth. He used to joke about
us / getting married all the time?

Iola   You're not having my money.

Menna *wobbles.*

Menna   Iola?

Iola *starts putting money in a teapot.*

Menna   Auntie Iola, I don't think you should put that there.

Iola *carries on.*

Menna   I'm not after your money.

Iola   Where's Anest?

Menna   She's in town, / she won't be long.

Iola   Don't lie to me! Where is she? She's – why are you lying to me? She should be here!

She grabs some more plates and stares at **Menna** *threateningly.*

Iola   She should be here.

Menna   Okay.

Iola   Where's Anest?

Menna   She's in town. But I'm here. I'm here because you wrote to me. / I'm here to –

Iola   I've never written to you.

Menna *goes into her purse and shows* **Iola** *the letter.*

Menna   That's your handwriting. Look.

Beat.

You're telling me, you love me, look. But you're in too much pain. Look here. Can you see your writing?

Iola *looks at the letter.*

Menna   You're telling me how much pain you're in. And you want it to stop. And you're going to miss me.

Beat.

Iola   It's. Um . . .

Beat.

I've forgotten who this is.

Menna   Anest's girl.

Iola *and* **Menna** *stare at each other through the fog of confusion.*

Anest *enters with some shopping.*

Anest   What's going on here?

Anest *puts the shopping away while listening to* **Iola***, perhaps even moving* **Iola** *to pass by her.*

Iola   She – I caught her. She's been here since – because she thinks I'm – because Albie's not in. Well, I'll tell you, bach, I'll be here the sun will be setting on you long after you – this place is mine, you've got.

She points at **Menna***.*

Iola (*threatening*)   I'm not on to you.

Anest   Is that right?

Iola (*to* **Anest**)   I caught her. Lying to me! Looking at me straight.

Menna (*to* **Anest**)   Shall I, shall I call the doctor?

Anest   There we are then.

Iola (*to* **Anest**)   Straight in my face!

Menna   She's distressed.

Iola *throws a plate at* **Menna***'s feet.* **Menna** *retreats across the room.*

Anest   Hey! Dyna ddigon! [DUH NA THI-GON – *That's enough!*]

Pause.

Menna   Um . . . Uh . . . What's the number? I'll go to the phone box.

Anest *goes to* **Iola***, who is staring at* **Menna** *aggressively.*

Iola   You're a lying / bitch.

Menna   Mam? / We need to do something. It's not fair on her.

Anest   Dere mewn, dere. [DER-AH MEWN – *Come here, come.*]

She takes **Iola** *in her arms.*

Menna   She needs a doctor. She might be having a haemorrhage or something.

Anest (*whispered in her ear*)   Canu nawr. [CANI NOW-R – *Sing now.*] Sing with me. You love to sing.

Beat.

Ignore her.

Beat.

Look at me now. Forget her.

She kisses **Iola** *on the cheeks and holds her in her arms.*

Anest   '*Aderyn du ai blufyn sidan,*' dere. [DARE-EH – *come.*]

She kisses **Iola** *on the face and sways with her.*

Anest   '*Ei big aur ai dafod arian,*' dere.

She holds on to **Iola** *and sways gently.*

Iola *and* **Anest** (*meekly together*)   '*Ei di drosta i i Gydweli*'

Iola *looks at* **Menna***.* **Anest** *turns her so she's looking at* **Anest***.*

Iola *and* **Anest** (*together*)   '*Isbio hyntyferch wy'n charu.*'

Iola *clasps her hands, like she would as a young girl in Eisteddfodau, and steps forward.*

Iola   '*Un, dau tri pheth syn anodd I mi,*
     Sef rhifor, ser pan fo hi rhewi,
     A chodi llaw I dwtsh a'r lleuad.'

She reaches to touch the moon.

'*A deall meddwl f'annwyl gariad*'

She touches her heart.

'*Llawn iawn ywr môr o swnd a chregyn*
Llawn iawn ywr wy o wyn a melyn
Llawn iawn ywr coed o ddail a blode
Llawn iawn o gariad ydwyf inne.'

'*Aderyn du ai blufyn sidan, ei big aur ai dafod arian*
Ei di drosta i i Gydweli
I sbïo hynt y ferch wy'n ei charu.'

Anest *claps enthusiastically,* **Menna** *is slow to start clapping.*

Anest   Ardderchog! [AR-THERE-CH-OG – *Excellent!*]

Iola *breaks into a shy, broad smile.*

Anest   Why don't you go and check on the chickens?

Iola *leaves.*

Anest *starts to pull money out of the teapot and put it into* **Iola**'*s bag.* **Menna** *joins* **Anest** *at the table.*

Menna   Where are the chickens?

Anest *gets on her hands and knees and starts sweeping up broken china.*

Anest   We don't have any, but she doesn't remember.

Anest *sweeps the china.* **Menna** *goes to a box, pulls out one of* **Anest**'*s dresses and presses it to herself. She breathes in the smell from it.*

Blackout.

Scene Eight

The beach.

The three women walk along the beach, **Anest** *and* **Menna** *either side of* **Iola**. **Menna** *is wearing gloves.*

Menna   Come on, over here. Nearly there. Nearly there.

They approach a blanket, a hamper of food. A bucket and spade. Beach umbrella. **Menna** *is supremely pleased with herself.*

Anest   Have you done this? (*Off* **Menna**'s *reaction.*) You shouldn't have.

Iola   We haven't been down here for years. / It's like a charabanc, isn't it?

Anest   We were here yesterday.

Menna   I thought we could all do with getting out – getting out, and getting some fresh air. And having some, having a nice time.

Iola   We're old women.

Beat.

Menna   I know that.

Anest   I'm not sitting down.

Beat.

Menna (*sarcastic*)   Do you want me to pass the food up to you?

Anest   Okay.

Menna   I'm not doing that. Look. Come on. We can. We can all. We all need.

Beat.

Leisure.

Beat.

What's the point of living down here if you don't go and see the sea once in a while? Let's – Lower down; let me lower you down.

Menna *goes to* **Anest**, *who refuses her hands.*

Anest   We'll never get up. She'll never get up.

Menna *goes to* **Iola**, *who mistakes her approach for a hug.* **Menna** *reciprocates.*

Menna   Come on, Auntie Iola do you want / to sit down?

Anest   No! She'll never get up.

Menna   I'll pull / her up.

Anest   You could hurt her / or yourself.

Iola   Eh! Don't you bloody whatyoucallit / now.

Anest   What?

Iola *takes* **Menna**'*s hands.*

Iola   I've killed bulls, I can sit on some bloody sand.

Menna *takes* **Iola** *by the hands.* **Iola** *sits down with an 'oomph'.*

Beat.

Menna   Mam?

Beat.

Come on.

Iola   Old bopa! [BOR-PAH – *Old spinster!*]

Finally **Anest** *concedes and* **Menna** *lowers her down gently.*

The women communicate the novelty of sitting on the floor together to each other.

Menna   Right, so we've got, hummus, dips, pastrami sandwiches, chicken and mayo, crisps, some quiche from the deli, sliced beef.

Silence.

Anest   She doesn't eat much.

Menna   Have a little bit of something.

Beat.

Anest   Have you got any ham?

Menna   Pastrami? (*Off* **Iola**'s *reaction.*) No, okay. Um. Try some quiche?

Anest   Have a little bit.

Iola   A little bit then.

Menna *hands her a small piece of quiche.*

Menna   Mam?

Anest   I'll have some quiche as well then.

Iola *drops her quiche all over herself.*

Iola   Oh Damo.

Menna *springs into action and cleans it up.*

Menna   Why don't you have some hummus, it's easier.

Iola   What, *is*, hummus?

Beat.

Menna   Um? Chickpeas. Chickpeas? Pulses? Beans. Mashed beans. With lemon and I don't know what else.

She offers some to **Iola***, who looks at it before shaking her head.*

Menna   Here. Here's some bread. Try that.

Silence as all three eat their underwhelming picnic. **Anest** *carefully puts her quiche to one side.* **Iola** *eats some bread and hands it back to* **Menna***.* **Menna** *sees that not much of the food is going to be eaten.*

Menna   Are you sure there's nothing else you'd like?

Iola   It doesn't matter.

Anest   No, it's lovely. (*To* **Iola***.*) Mam used to like it down here, didn't she?

Iola   Used to swim.

Struggling to hide her irritation, **Menna** *starts to pack the food up.*

Iola   Every day if she could, till she was fifty ti'n bod?

Anest   No.

Iola   Ie! [YEE-EH – *Yeah!*]

Anest   Pan odd hi'n byw gyda' chi? [PAN OATH HE'N BUE GU-DA CHEE – *When she lived with you?*]

Iola   Ie, wir. [YEE-EH WEER -*Yes, for sure.*]

Menna   Don't start with the Welsh.

Beat.

Iola   Yes, Albie went with her once, he stood by the fire. 'Not doing that again,' he said.

She laughs.

In the blue / pool.

Anest   She didn't go in the blue pool.

Iola   Yes. She did.

Menna   I'm sorry I didn't get this right.

Beat.

But I just want you to know, I am a good host. When Peter was, a bit more social, his partners would rave about my hosting. So – that's all I'm saying.

Silence as everyone feels embarrassed. **Iola** *reaches over to the hummus and pastrami and puts the pastrami into the hummus and is about to eat it.* **Menna** *grabs it from her.*

Menna   No no, it's okay.

Iola   I should / try it.

Menna   No no, it's fine.

Iola   It looks nice.

Menna   Really! It's fine.

Beat.

It's just a . . . bloody picnic.

Beat.

Anest   We're just old.

Beat.

We enjoy sitting on the sand.

Looking at the picnic and then the twins, **Menna** *has to make a decision whether to kick off or kick back. She kicks back and takes her shoes off.*

Menna   Remember the hopscotch wars, Mam?

She marks out some squares in the sand.

See if I've still got it.

She starts to hopscotch and fails, but bursts out laughing. **Anest** *and* **Iola** *join in laughing.*

Menna   I haven't done this in years!

She tries it again, and sees **Iola** *and* **Anest** *giggling together.*

Menna   Have I lost it, Auntie Iols? / What you reckon?

Iola   Very good.

Menna   Come on then, you two. Let's see if you can do it.

Iola   No, / we can't do that.

Anest   No, we're not doing that.

Menna   Come on.

Anest   We'll fall / over.

Menna   One / go, that's all I want.

Iola   Break / our necks.

Menna   You used to play it with me all the time, Auntie Iols, / you and Uncle Albie.

Iola   I'm weak now.

Menna   Come on, you old farts.

Iola   Ready to die now.

Comfortable with this, **Anest** *returns to looking at the sea.* **Menna** *stands in front of* **Anest**.

Menna   Mam?

Anest   No / thank you.

Menna   You're not ready to die, are you?

Anest   I am not playing hopscotch.

Menna *hopscotches away from them. She throws a shell on to the markings and then plays hopscotch.*

Menna   Oh Mam! Come on, watch me! It's boring on my own.

She helps **Anest** *to her feet. And then* **Iola**. **Menna** *scoops up the picnic and dumps it out of the way.*

Menna   Think we've had enough of that. Right, you throw it, I'll do it.

Anest *throws the shell.*

Menna   Five, okay.

She hopscotches, avoiding number five.

Iola   Da iawn bach! [DAR YA-WN BAR-CH – *Well done little one!*]

Anest   Very good!

Menna   Now you try it, Mam.

Beat.

Anest   No.

Menna   One little hop. One teeny tiny hop.

Anest *goes to the start of the grid.*

Menna   Are you ready?

Anest   No.

She braces herself.

I'm, not going to get in there.

Menna   Swing your arms.

Anest *swings her arms and nothing happens.*

Beat.

Everyone bursts out laughing.

Anest   I can't!

She swings again and still fails to jump, causing more hilarity. Third time lucky and she jumps! All three cheer and whoop with utter delight.

She stops.

One more go and then I'm done.

She goes back to the start and manages two hops and then stops.

Menna   Come on, Auntie Iola? You next.

Anest   Yes. (*Off* **Iola***'s reaction.*) Have / a go.

Iola   No. No I'm too old.

Anest *puts* **Iola** *at the start of the grid.* **Iola** *looks isolated.*

Menna   Try it! One little hop.

Anest   Swing your arms.

Iola *tries but nothing happens.*

Menna   You can do it.

Iola   No. I can't do it.

Beat.

What's the time now?

Seeing **Menna***'s disappointment,* **Anest** *steps towards* **Iola***.*

Anest   I know.

She faces **Iola** *and holds her hands.*

Anest   Try now.

Holding **Anest***'s hand,* **Iola** *braces herself for a hop.*

Anest   Now look at me. Just look at me. Hold my hands, don't look at the floor, just look at me. I'm here. Ready?

Iola *starts to smile with nerves.* **Anest** *chuckles.*

Anest   Come on.

Iola   No.

Anest   Menna, come and take Iola's hand.

Menna *goes and takes* **Iola***'s hand and holds her under her armpit and* **Anest** *follows suit.*

Anest   Un . . . [EEEN – *One.*]

Anest *and* **Menna**   Dau, tri! [DYE, TREE – *Two, three!*]

And with the help of **Anest** *and* **Menna***,* **Iola** *manages a hop! The threesome whoop and laugh with joy as they do it again and* **Iola** *hops again.*

Iola   I'm playing hopscotch!

Menna   That / was amazing Iola!

Anest   See / you can do it.

Iola   I can do it if I hold your hand! / Keep me steady.

Menna   See you've / got plenty of, plenty of life in you . . .

Iola   I didn't think I could do that. Fi'n teimlo'n saff yn dy ddwylo di tin gwbod. [VEEN TAME-LO'N SAPH UN DUH THWEE-LO DEE TEE'N GOO-BORED – *I feel safe in your hands, you know.*]

Menna   What's that?

Anest   Safe in my hand. Just needed me, didn't you?

Iola   I was always better than her at sport.

Menna   Were you now?

Iola   I'm the / stronger twin.

Anest (*mocking*)   'Stronger twin'.

Menna *and* **Anest** *laugh.*

Anest   Why don't you go and find some more pebbles for us?

Menna   What is it with you two and pebbles?

Iola *heads off.*

Anest   We can keep an eye on her.

Beat.

Menna   There's plenty of life left in her.

They both watch **Iola** *for a moment.*

Menna   What's she doing now?

Beat.

Anest   Picking up something.

Beat.

Pebble.

Menna   I haven't spoken to Peter today.

She looks at **Anest** *with shock.*

Menna   I don't think I spoke to him yesterday either.

Anest   There's a phone box by the uh . . . the –

She indicates in the distance. **Menna** *looks at it.*

– life boat.

Menna   I should ring him.

She looks at the box.

Not having a mobile, see.

She bites her lip and stands up and stares at the phone box in the distance.

Anest   I'll watch the things.

Beat.

Menna.

Menna   Yeah.

She picks up her purse and opens it to get some cash out. She pulls out the little bottle of sanitiser, she reflexively goes to take her gloves off and squirt a hand but stops herself. She looks at the bottle.

Anest   Not going?

Menna *isn't sure what to say.*

Anest   Go later.

Menna *puts the bottle back in her purse. She pours herself a glass of wine, leans back and relaxes.*

Menna   Is it weird that I'm glad Iola boiled my phone?

Anest *chuckles.*

Anest   Come here, push your hands in the sand with me.

Anest *takes one of* **Menna***'s gloves off and pushes her hand into the sand.* **Anest** *pushes her own hand into the sand.*

Anest   I'm glad you came.

Menna   Me too.

They play with the sand.

It's funny how this beach is sandy and Newgale's pebbly.

Anest   You know why Newgale's pebbly?

Menna   No?

Anest   There was a fish that swam around Ireland protecting it, and a dragon that stood on the edge of Wales protecting it and the two eyeballed each other every day. And then one day the fish swam too close to Wales, and the dragon lost patience with him so he dived into the water to deal with the fish once and for all, except they got so caught up in the fight, they didn't realise they'd sunk to the bottom and they both drowned. And all the pebbles that washed up on Newgale are the scales from the dragon and the fish as a warning.

Menna   I wish Tom and Nathan could hear these stories. The only thing they were taught the sea is good for is bloody slavery.

Silence.

Anest   I like the idea of them at the bottom of the sea together. Sounds like they had a lonely life before.

Menna *brushes sand from her hands.*

Anest   He's the one, whatyoucall, with the germs.

Menna   What?

Anest   Peter's the one who's fussy about germs.

Menna   It's none of your business, Mam.

Anest   If your father was here / you'd listen to him.

Menna   Well he's not, is he?

Silence.

So drop it.

Anest   There we are then.

Beat.

Menna   She's been good today.

Anest   Yes, I suppose.

Menna   Much better.

Anest   It's a good day.

Menna   I don't understand how she can write such a beautiful letter, and then forget about it.

Anest   Some days she's fine and others, she's just awful.

Menna   She doesn't even recognise me sometimes.

Anest   She hasn't forgotten who I am yet, but, it's coming.

Pause.

One time. The time I knew it was whatyoucall – serious . . . little things had been happening for a while. But this time. I'd been somewhere. On the bus. Must have been town. Was it town? Must have been. And, she forgot. She just, forgot.

Menna   What happened?

Anest   She rang neighbours, the shop, Gareth; she told them I'd gone missing.

She plays with the sand.

Menna   They found you though?

Anest   Gareth's wife.

Menna   Eirwen.

Anest   Eirwen saw me in town. Drove me home.

Menna   That's good then. Was she upset?

Anest   Yes. She, hit me with a poker.

Menna   What? She hit you?

Anest *touches her arm to indicate where.*

Menna   Were you alright? I didn't know about this? How come I didn't know about this?

Anest   Eirwen sort of, whatyoucall, smoothed it. Looked after my arm. It was all over in a minute.

Beat.

Menna   Mam, I don't want you being hit. Has she hit you
since?

Anest   Don't give her the chance.

Menna   I'm not having that.

She puts her arm around **Anest***.*

Anest   It's okay.

Menna   She could have seriously hurt you.

Anest   She was lonely. I'd never seen it in her eyes before.
I would have let her hit me all day if she'd stop looking at me
like that.

Silence.

Menna   No.

Beat.

What if – ? I think.

Beat.

I think, what if I came down here?

Beat.

To live. Just for the time being.

Anest   What about Peter and the boys?

Menna   They've moved out, Peter's fine.

Anest   No . . . What about work?

Menna   I'll – well; I suppose I'll quit.

Anest   You can't / do that, no.

Menna   Yes I can. I can do, anything I want.

Beat.

Sorry I snapped.

Anest   You didn't snap.

Menna   Be nice to be back down here.

Beat.

You won't be alone, Mam.

Anest   Don't move down here.

Menna   Why not?

Anest   I don't want you to.

Menna   Don't play the martyr.

Anest   Please . . . I just.

Menna   I'm going to look after you. The boys have moved /
out, work's just work.

Anest   I don't want you to.

Menna   Well, you haven't got a choice.

Anest   Please.

Menna   No, I'm in charge now.

Anest   I lied.

Menna   About what?

Beat.

Mam?

Anest   When I said I was going to the Willows.

Menna   Where were you going?

Anest   I know what she was doing, posting her letter early,
she wanted you to come down here, so I couldn't. So I had
to tell you whatyoucall. Face to face.

Menna   What are you talking about?

Anest   Every time I tried to write. I couldn't get to the end of anything. I couldn't bear to think of you with all this and Peter just, *staring* at you from across the room. Every time I tried to write anything I couldn't get past that.

Menna   What are you saying, Mam?

Anest   You mustn't think this is anything to do with you.

Pause.

I want to die with her.

Blackout.

Scene Nine

Underwater.

Sounds of the sea.

Iola and **Anest** *stand in light, closer to each other.*

Iola   There was a cow.

Anest   Dad?

Iola   The size of a house.

Anest   It's me.

Iola   A drought.

Anest   And Iola.

Iola   And then suddenly.

Anest   Tied.

Iola   Heaven opened.

Anest   Together.

Iola   Clover clover everywhere.

Anest   We're here.

Iola   And they ate.

Anest   At last.

Iola   And they ate.

Anest   See.

Iola   And they ate.

Anest   Together.

Iola   And they ate.

Anest *gasps.*

Iola   Until one cow.

Anest   Harry.

Iola   Blew up, to the size of a house.

Anest   Menna.

Iola   Under the ribs.

Anest   Iola.

Iola   But not too low.

Anest   Nathan.

Iola   Is a piece of flesh.

Anest   Tom.

Iola   Ripe for a knife.

Anest   Harry.

Iola   A careful cut.

Anest   Iola.

Iola   And out it comes.

Anest   Menna.

Iola   Down she comes.

Anest   Menna.

Iola   The cow balloon.

Blackout.

Scene Ten

The cottage.

In silence, **Iola** *and* **Anest** *sit at a table with bowls of soup.* **Menna** *sits in the middle with her head in her hands watching* **Iola** *and* **Anest**.

In silence, like a perfect dance, **Iola** *and* **Anest** *grind pepper and salt mills, swap them, break bread, pass butter, break kitchen paper and start to eat.*

Anest (*reproachful*)   Menna.

Menna   I'm eating, I'm eating.

She pushes her soup around but doesn't eat a thing. She watches them – isolated.

Does, anyone come and sit with you? If Mam needs to do anything.

Anest   No. I don't like leaving her and she doesn't like being left.

Menna   I could ask Eirwen?

Anest   I don't need to go anywhere.

Menna   I know! But I might want to go somewhere. I might want to go; buy a bed. I can't keep sleeping on that thing.

Beat.

Anest   Perhaps you should stay in Ty Felin?

Menna   I think I'll go to Haverfordwest.

Anest   Okay.

Menna   Will you come with me?

Anest   Okay.

Menna   Tomorrow.

Anest (*including* **Iola**)   The three of us could go.

Iola   What?

Anest   Haverfordwest.

Iola (*spitting*)   Below the line.

Anest   She hates Haverfordwest, isn't she comical?

Menna   Yes. Or I could get Eirwen to sit with her, it's no, you know. / I'll ring Gareth.

Anest   No, we'll all go. Girls' day out.

Beat.

How about that?

Beat.

Menna   Yeah, why not?

The twins break some more bread between them.

Unless.

Beat.

If you don't want to go, Auntie Iols.

Anest   She'll be fine.

Menna (*discreet*)   I don't want to force her.

Anest (*discreet*)   She'll be fine.

They eat in silence.

Menna   If you don't want to go, Auntie Iola.

Iola   Um?

Anest   She won't want to stay.

Menna   Auntie Iols?

Anest   She won't want to.

Menna   I just thought if she didn't want to go she doesn't have to go. / Then she doesn't have to go.

Anest   She won't want to be left behind. Do you?

Iola   I don't want to be left behind.

Silence.

Menna   Good.

The twins break some more bread, and perhaps exchange mills. Snapping, **Menna** *goes over to the bin and gets her phone out.*

She takes it apart and tries drying each part.

Anest   Be nice, the three of us.

Silence.

Iola   I hate Haverfordwest.

Blackout.

Scene Eleven

In water.

Sounds of the sea.

Iola   Anest?

Anest   Yes. I'm here.

Iola   Are you thinking about Dad?

Beat.

Anest   Yes.

Iola   Tell me about Dad.

Anest   He was borrowed.

Iola   That's right.

Anest   Borrowed.

Beat.

From the sea.

Beat.

Couldn't live on the land.

Beat.

Couldn't die in the sea.

Iola *chuckles.*

Iola   Make a fuss now girls eh!

Anest   Make a fuss of me now!

Beat.

Iola   Not here long.

The twins chuckle.

Blackout.

Scene Twelve

Bedroom in the cottage.

Iola *lies on the bed.*

Menna *enters, wearing gloves.*

Menna (*hissing*)   Mam.

Beat.

(*Hissing.*) Mam?

Iola   Hello?

Beat.

Hello?

Menna (*hissing*)   Shh! Sh! Sorry.

Iola   Menna?

Iola *sits up.*

Menna   Where's Mam?

Iola   In the toilet. She's gone to have a try.

Menna (*hissing*)   Don't get up. I'll. I'll speak to her in the morning. Don't get up.

Iola   What's the matter?

Long pause.

Menna   I can't, sleep.

Iola *taps the bed.*

Menna   I'll speak to her in the morning.

Iola *taps the bed.* **Menna** *sits on the bed with* **Iola**, *who yawns.*

Iola   Been eating cheese?

Menna   No.

Iola   Do you want me to sleep on the bench?

Menna *shakes her head.*

Iola   Been lovely having you down.

Beat.

I never meant to upset you bach.

Menna   You two drive me insane. I wish fucking Peter was here.

Iola   He's busy.

Menna   How did Dad and Uncle Albie put up with you two?

Iola   Glad to get rid of us half the time! 'Go on!' he'd say,
'Up your sister's! Get out from under my feet you are.'

She chuckles.

I'm glad you came down.

Menna *wipes a tear.*

Iola   There there now.

Menna   I can look after you.

Iola   When we'd have a horse go lame, or a cow go barren.
Always having still births you know, awful sad for her. You
know we'd give them some time. Whatyoucall see how they
go. But we'd have to see to them, in the end. If you've got
livestock you've got deadstock. It's just the way.

Pause.

Menna   Mam's not ill though.

Iola *hugs* **Menna***.*

Iola   She is a stubborn cow though.

Silence.

Menna   Will you talk to her?

Iola   I'm the one with this whatyoucall, tumour. And it's
bloody miserable, God knows it is. But, I'm glad it's me.
Because it must be hell the other way round.

Menna   I shouldn't have come up here.

She gets up and starts walking away.

Iola   Where are you going?

Menna   I'm going to try and ring Peter, go back to bed.

Iola   He'll be asleep.

Menna   It's fine go back to bed.

Iola   I'm not tired. I think I'm due a tablet.

She gets out of bed and starts looking for something.

Menna   What are you doing?

Iola   I've got so many, Anest tells me.

Menna   You've taken them. I helped you.

Iola   Have I? Oh I'm no use.

Menna   I'm sure. Go back to bed.

Iola   I'm sorry you have to put up with this.

Menna   Stop apologising, it's fine.

Iola   Don't worry about me now. I'll be, I'll just wait for Anest, she won't be long.

Menna *hesitates.*

Menna   Try and sleep.

Iola   Yes. Did I take the big ones, the red ones?

Menna   Yes, you took all of – Where's the box?

*She gets a large tablet box out and sits with **Iola**.*

Menna   You took hang on, what's today's date?

She looks at her watch and then opens a box.

See, empty. All of them gone.

Iola *looks at the box.*

Iola   Pathetic yna fe?

Menna *kisses **Iola**'s head.*

Menna   Go to bed.

*She gets up but **Iola** doesn't move.*

Iols.

Iola   Look at all these. Never taken a tablet before in my life.

Menna *rejoins* **Iola**.

Silence.

Menna   Nothing to feel bad about.

Iola   I have to take them standing up I've got so many.

Menna *takes the tablet box from her.*

Menna   Come on. Let me brush your hair and then you have to go to bed.

She gets a brush. She puts a mirror in front of **Iola**, *stands behind her and starts brushing.* **Iola** *hums 'Aderyn Du'.*

Menna   What's? What's . . . that song about?

Iola   Eh?

Menna   The song. What's the words mean? My Welsh is awful.

Iola   Aderyn du [A DARE IN DEE] / is blackbird.

Menna   I know that.

Iola   It's a uh, boy singing. Singing to a blackbird; in a tree. He's got. He's full of love, but it's whatyoucall, lonely. He's asking blackbird to fly on his behalf to his calon − [CAL-ON − *loved one*]

She taps her heart.

− in Cidwelly [KID WHERE-LY] and find out what the . . . Understand the . . . whatyoucall what's going. If she feels the same ydw e? [UH-DOO-EH −*you see?*]

Menna   So he sings to the blackbird?

Iola   That's it. Can't take it any more.

Menna   What?

Iola   Being in love and being alone.

Menna *stops brushing* **Iola**'s *hair and looks at her reflection.*

Iola   Let me . . . what is it now? Oh . . . I'm terrible. Silken plumed . . . Silken plumed, golden beaked, silver tongued blackbird. Will you please tell her to let me know that she loves me?

Menna   Sounds so happy though.

Iola   Uhmm . . . Everyone thinks that. All the Welsh songs are beautiful but they're bloody miserable ti'n bod. That's the Welsh for you. See a bloody tragedy. Like a family drowning a young girl for falling in love with the wrong man and they bloody sing a song about it. Sing a song so it doesn't sound so bad. Put a brave face on it. It's hope that kills you in the end.

Slowly **Menna** *stops brushing* **Iola**'s *hair, and* **Iola** *gets ready for bed.*

Put my coat on if you're going to the phone box.

Menna *looks at her reflection.*

Blackout.

Scene Thirteen

Bedroom in the cottage.

Offstage sound of a storm.

Iola *sits in a chair.* **Menna**, *wearing gloves, helps* **Anest** *strip a bed and remake it with fresh sheets.* **Iola** *has been ill in bed.*

Anest *and* **Menna** *work together to make the bed up.* **Menna** *approaches* **Iola**.

Menna   Come on, Auntie Iols. Clean bed now.

She helps **Iola** *get into bed.*

Iola   Anest?

Anest *reflexes.*

Menna   I'm here. It's Menna.

Anest   Did too much yesterday.

Beat.

That was the worst she's been.

Beat.

Poor dab.

Menna   Why don't you try and get some sleep?

Anest *doesn't move.*

Anest   I'll stay with her.

Menna   I can stay with her.

Anest   You must be shattered too.

She sits on the bed and strokes **Iola***'s face.*

Menna   I'll stay with her.

Anest *doesn't move.*

Menna   Mam, leave her, she's tired.

Anest   She's fine.

Menna   If she can fall asleep, we're all better off.

Pause.

Anest   She likes to know I'm here.

Menna   You could be Jeremy Clarkson and she wouldn't know.

Beat.

Perhaps it's time she got used to you not being here.

Anest   She sleeps better with me.

Menna *starts to clean the floor.*

Anest (*to* **Iola**)   Ti'n eisiau panad? [TEEN EYE SHY PAN ARD – *You want a cup of tea?*]

Menna   Mam? Why are you moithering her?

Silence.

Anest (*to* **Iola**)   Ti'n eisiau panad?

Menna   Mam. She doesn't want a cup of tea.

Anest *refuses to look at* **Menna***.*

Menna   Mam.

Anest   I know what she likes? / Ti'n eisiau panad?

Menna   Talk to me, Mam, talk to me while I clean the floor.

Anest *watches* **Menna** *cleaning.*

Menna   Anything.

Anest   I don't know.

She touches **Iola***.*

Anest   I think she's hot.

She starts to fold back some of **Iola***'s sheets.*

Menna   Of course she's hot, she's been ill, everyone overheats when they're sick, it's normal don't fuss.

Anest   It's not / fussing.

Menna   You have to stop.

Anest   We've had, a terrible night.

Menna   *She's* had a terrible night. *She* needs some rest. Come out of the bed, Mam.

Beat.

Mam.

Menna *holds out a gloved hand to* **Anest**. **Anest** *considers it, she's caught between* **Menna** *and* **Iola**.

Anest   Leave us.

Menna   Mam.

Anest   I want to spend some time with her.

Beat.

For me.

Beat.

Wasn't sick over there.

Iola   Anest?

Menna   I've got a clean bit now, haven't I? And now I can see how dirty this place is.

Beat.

Anest   You won't get it clean.

Menna   I will.

Anest   We're not frightened of a little bit of dirt.

Menna   I'm cleaning it for you! I'm doing all of this for you! So this place is clean, so we can look after Iola and not be rolling around in dirt.

Iola (*to* **Anest**)   What's the matter? Anest?

Anest   No one's asked you to clean the floor, you started doing that yourself, so don't come here saying you're on your hands and knees, no one's asked you to do that.

Menna   And no one's asked you to spend every waking minute with her but you're doing it. I'll stop cleaning if you get out of the bed.

Beat.

Mam.

Beat.

Mam?

Beat.

Mam, I'm talking to you.

Iola   Anest?

Anest   I'm here. Shh now?

Beat.

Menna   Mam!

She walks around to get into **Anest**'s *eyeline.*

Menna   Mam I'm talking to you.

Anest *ignores her.*

Menna   Mam!

Anest *continues to ignore her and comfort* **Iola**, *with whispers.*

Anest   Shh now.

Iola   It hurts.

Anest *kisses* **Iola** *and whispers to her.* **Menna** *sits on the end of the bed.*

Anest   I'm here, see.

Iola   Anest. Pen tost. [PEN TOSSED – *sore head.*]

She holds her head in pain.

Anest   Shh now.

Menna *sits on the bed, totally isolated from the twins.*

Iola *groans in pain.*

Menna *can't take it any more. She walks out.*

Iola   Anest?

Anest   I'm here. Shh shh . . . nawr. [NOWR – *now.*]

Beat.

Load of stuff and nonsense.

Beat.

Eh? Stuff and nonsense.

Pause.

Iola   You're not Anest.

Anest *freezes.*

Anest   It's me? Fi sy yna. [VEE SEE UN AH – *It's me here.*]

Iola   Where's Anest?

Anest   It's me.

Beat.

Listen to my voice.

Beat.

Iola, it's me.

Iola   I want Anest.

Anest   It's me.

She crawls towards **Iola**.

It's.

Anest *crawls to* **Iola** *and puts her forehead to* **Iola**'s *forehead and holds her head in place. They hold for a while.*

There.

Beat.

Can you see me?

Beat.

See?

Beat.

It's me.

Beat.

Me.

Iola   I don't.

Anest   Look.

Beat.

Look hard.

Iola   Um.

Anest   Can you see me?

Long pause.

Iola   Oh.

Beat.

Uh.

Beat.

Um.

Beat.

Blackout.

Scene Fourteen

The cottage.

Offstage sounds of a storm.

Soaking wet, **Gareth** *is wearing civilian clothes and a baseball hat. He puts the hat on the hook.*

Menna, *wearing gloves, is pacing around, soaking wet also.*

Gareth   What's all this about? In this weath – Have you got a towel?

Menna *indicates a towel.* **Gareth** *towels his hair and sits down.*

Gareth   You're soaked / too.

Menna   Had to walk to the phone box. Where's your stuff?

Gareth   What / stuff?

Menna   Uniform / all that stuff.

Gareth   I was in my / pyjamas.

Menna   I thought you'd come with all your stuff.

Gareth   Why? You said it was an emergency?

Menna   A police emergency.

Gareth   I got here as quick as I can.

Beat.

So.

Beat.

Menna   Will you, will you, arrest my mam?

Gareth   What for?

Menna   You said it was against the law, to help Iola, well, they plan to help each other. They're both going to do it, so I want you to arrest them both. It's a crime you said. Assisted.

Beat.

I can, testify. They plan to commit a crime you need to arrest them both.

Gareth   There's nothing I can do to stop them.

Menna   You can arrest them.

Gareth *sits down.*

Gareth   This, isn't a police thing.

Beat.

If *you* can't persuade / them then I've . . .

Menna   I've never persuaded my mam to do anything.

Beat.

Please?

Beat.

So that's / it then?

Gareth   They're not going to listen / to me.

Menna   They will if you arrest / them.

Gareth   I am not arresting two women in their seventies.

Beat.

Why don't you take them home? Peter's in all day; he can keep an eye on them.

Beat.

You need to be a bit more, delicate about stuff.

Menna   Really.

Gareth   I'm just saying.

Menna   No, thanks, that's good advice.

Menna *goes to a box and pulls out some crockery.*

Gareth   You're welcome.

Menna   Eirwen made Mam some casseroles, here's the plate.

Gareth   I can get them another –

Menna *drops it on the floor so it smashes.*

Menna   Take it now.

Gareth   What are you doing?

Menna *goes back to the box and pulls out another dish.*

Menna   Showing my appreciation.

Gareth *startles towards her.*

Menna   Don't you come near me.

Stepping back, she holds the crockery in the air.

You . . .

Menna *holds the crockery threateningly.*

Gareth   Men?

Menna   What kind of people see an old lady get hit by a poker, and don't tell anyone about it?

Gareth   Well.

Menna   What's the matter with you?

Gareth   It's not as simple / as that

Menna   Yes it is simple! / You pick up the phone.

Gareth   She didn't tell me / for ages.

Menna   Why didn't she tell you? / Isn't she the biggest gossip around?

Gareth   We're not together any more. Okay?

With crockery over her head **Menna** *lowers it.*

Gareth   We're sort of, not . . . Dr Matthews told me about the poker so.

Menna   You're not together?

Gareth   We sort of are. She's still living at home. She's started seeing someone else, / from church.

Menna   I don't understand.

Gareth   Hoping it's just a fling.

Menna   You're still living together?

Gareth   I don't know, Men. Hoping it'll fizzle out. That was a good dish / that was. Deep, for . . .

Menna   My mam wants to kill herself!

Pause.

My mam wants to kill herself.

To deflect the silence, **Gareth** *gets his hip flask out and takes a swig.*

Menna   Who is it?

Gareth   The fucking organist.

Silence.

There's a joke there somewhere about the size of his organ and mine but . . .

He exhales.

Silence.

I don't know. She's so nice about it. And thoughtful. It doesn't seem so bad. I think it's just a little. Funny little thing and / it'll go away.

Menna   She's a fucking . . .

She is exasperated.

Gareth   She still cooks and we eat together, most nights. Pretty much the same. It's not too bad really. It's not as if, I don't see her.

Beat.

Sometimes, we watch *Strictly* together.

Beat.

Gets us chatting.

Beat.

That and the dog.

Long pause.

And it seems like it's fine really. You know.

Beat.

And then I go to work, and I see some. I see some horrible.
I see some really sad stuff you know? People's homes burned,
stuff like that. It's really sad. I'll get a call, like someone's
home has burned and, find myself, sort of looking forward
to it.

He takes another swig.

Can't all be like you and Peter.

Menna   He's not. He's not easy to live with.

Gareth   He's not shagging a fucking choir leader is he?

Pause.

Menna   No, he wouldn't do that.

Gareth   Exactly.

Menna   He couldn't.

Gareth   Because he's got an ounce of decency, that's why.

Menna   Every couple of months, he'll gather up our clothes
in an oil drum in the garden and set fire to them. And I watch
from the kitchen. He burns my clothes, that's how scared he
is of germs. He could never have an affair.

Waves gloves.

This is him.

Beat.

Forgotten what clothes I like. I just look at price tags.

Beat.

Spend a fortune on bleach.

Gareth   Fucking hell.

Menna   He's so scared of contaminating me, he never touches me, ever. That's how I know he loves me. He can't leave the house, even when I had Iola's letter and I was going out of my mind, he said, 'I'll hold the fort.'

Long pause.

You know what? I can't be fucking bothered.

Gareth *offers his hip flask to* **Menna** *who takes a swig from it.*

Gareth   You want to get a dog. Down the beach with the dog, nothing better.

Menna   We were there today. Got the pair of them to play hopscotch.

Gareth   Bet that was interesting.

Menna   It was.

Beat.

Couldn't stop thinking, I was watching them hopscotching and I couldn't stop thinking even if Iola dies; at least I've had a break.

Gareth   So, shall I go home and get my handcuffs?

Menna *laughs.* **Gareth** *pats her thigh and takes a swig of his whisky.*

Gareth   Keep, buggering on.

She sees his hat on the hook. She picks it up and presses it to his chest.

Menna   Go home, Gareth.

Beat.

Gareth   Yeah.

He hangs his head and looks at his shoes.

I don't want to.

Menna   I know.

She gives him a kiss on the cheek and **Gareth** *pulls her tight to him for a hug.*

He holds her tightly before letting her go.

Gareth *wipes his tears, puts his hat back on and exhales loudly as he tries to gather himself.*

He takes a moment, straightens himself and heads back into the storm.

Menna *stands alone – with a new purpose.*

Blackout.

Scene Fifteen

The cottage.

Anest *stands in the corner of the room.* **Iola** *in the other corner.* **Menna** *enters and immediately senses something is wrong.*

Menna   What's going on?

Anest   She doesn't recognise me.

Menna   What? Course she does.

Anest *shakes her head.*

Menna   Iola. Who's this?

Iola   It's . . . Um . . .

Beat.

I do know.

Awkward chuckle.

I do know.

Beat.

Um . . . how embarrassing.

Menna   It's Anest.

Iola   Anest.

She lets out an embarrassed laugh.

Neither **Menna** *nor* **Anest** *are convinced.*

Iola   Anest. Of course.

Menna   Who's /Anest?

Anest   Menna, please.

Menna   She's your sister.

Iola   Uhm . . .

Beat.

I'm sorry.

(*To* **Anest**.) I'm sorry. I do know.

Menna   Who am I?

Beat.

Who do you think I am?

Beat.

Iola   The council.

Menna   The council.

Iola   The girl from the council.

Beat.

Um. Sorry.

Menna   I'm not from the council. I'm Menna.

Iola   Sorry. Menna. Okay.

Iola *is agitated and starts looking around the room.*

Right. I'm sorry.

Beat.

Menna from the council.

Menna   You've taken your tablets.

Iola   Yes.

Menna (*to* **Anest**)   She shouldn't be out of bed. (*To* **Iola**.) Do you want to go back to bed?

Iola   No. I'm . . . just trying to think.

Beat.

Menna   It'll come back to her.

Beat.

It'll come back to her now, I promise.

Anest   I don't think it will.

Iola   Hang on. Whatyoucall . . . um . . .

Menna   You know that Anest is your sister.

Anest   She doesn't know.

Beat.

I can see.

Beat.

Menna   See what?

Anest   She's . . .

Menna   What?

Anest   She's lonely.

She can't bear to watch **Iola** *wandering around the room any more. She goes to* **Iola** *and tries to hug her,* **Iola** *recoils.*

Anest   Iola. It's me.

Iola *doesn't recognise her.*

Anest   It's me. Please.

Iola *carries on looking for something.*

Menna   What's the matter, Auntie Iols?

Iola   I don't know.

Menna   What are you looking for?

Iola   Um . . .

Menna   I can help.

Iola   It's uh, private.

Menna   I'm family.

Beat.

Okay, I'm from the council.

Iola   Where's my money?

Menna   What money?

Iola   I have money saved.

Menna   Is it in the bank?

Iola   I had it right here.

Menna *and* **Anest** *share a look.*

Iola   Where is it?

Menna   Let's help her look, shall we?

They start to look around.

You keep some in your bag.

Iola   It's not in my bag.

Anest *goes to* **Iola** *and touches her shoulder.*

Anest   You keep your money in your bag.

Iola   How do you know?

Anest   Because I put it there for you so you don't lose it.

Iola   Have you stolen / it?

Anest   No! No one's stolen anything.

Iola   She's trying /to steal my money.

Menna   No she's not! No one is, this is just you getting confused.

Iola   I'm watching / you!

Anest   I put it in your bag to keep it safe for you.

Menna   See?

Iola   She's a fucking liar.

Anest   Menna.

Menna   She hasn't taken anything, she's been with you the whole time. She never leaves your side, I don't know how you can be confused.

Pause.

Anest   Iola / please.

Menna   This is Anest, Iola! Anest, / she's been looking after you.

Iola   She's a fucking thief. You wait till Albie gets hold of you, / you fucking cunt.

Anest   We need help, / we need Dr Matthews.

Menna   Let's just see if we can deal with / this on our own.

Anest   She's never not known me.

Iola   I know what you said.

Anest   What? What did I say?

Iola   You're a fucking. A fuck. I fucking. Trying to steal / my money!

Anest   I'm not trying to steal, Iola.

Iola   You are I can see you. I'm not. / I'm I'm. This is my money.

Anest   I'm not doing anything!

Iola   You're trying to steal from me.

Anest   I look after / you.

Iola   I DON'T KNOW YOU! And I've never seen you before in my life.

Menna   Auntie Iols, no one / is trying to upset you okay?

Iola   I know what she's after. I know she wants / to get her hands on my money.

Anest   I don't want your money.

Iola   You do. I caught you.

Anest   I don't. What do I want money for?

Iola   You. It's greed! You . . . I have to. I'm watching you. Fucking.

Anest   You've never had money! You had to borrow from me and Harry all your life. / Why do you care now?

Iola   Get out of my house!

She pulls a poker out and points it at **Anest**.

Menna   No!

She rushes between them to protect **Anest** *and wrangles the poker from* **Iola**.

Menna   Give me the poker.

She takes it.

Iola   I'm not I'm not I'm not. This is. Shh. Shh. I'm shh.

Menna   It's okay.

Iola   I'm shh. I'm not. I'm being pushed around! You
fucking dis – I'm / a dis – fucking you!

Menna   Calm down. It's okay.

Beat.

Calm down.

Beat.

Why are you worried about money?

Iola   I keep. I have to keep it; for my niece.

Menna   Perhaps you should sing to her, Mam?

Anest   No.

Menna   Um . . . uh . . . you like um. You like puzzles, and
she hates them, but you make her help you.

Beat.

You like, you like jam and she likes marmalade. Um. You
can't tie balloons because of your fat fingers and she hasn't
got any puff so, you blow the balloons and she ties them.

Beat.

She likes the sun, you always get too hot. You wanted
children and she had me. She cries at weddings even though
she says she won't, and you've always got hankies. You used
to go to each other's houses on laundry days to help. And
we'd all make the beds together.

Iola *looks pacified.*

Menna   See. And you like, collecting pebbles, look at these.

Anest   She's not with us.

Menna   Yes she is.

Picking up a pebble, **Menna** *shows* **Iola**.

Look, you're always finding these and keeping them as ornaments around the house.

Menna *shows* **Anest** *and* **Iola** *some pebbles.* **Iola** *picks one up and looks at it.*

Menna (*to* **Anest**)   See, she knows. (*To* **Iola**.) Don't you? Smooth aren't they? You fill bags –

Iola *strikes* **Anest** *across the face with a pebble.* **Anest** *staggers back and blood pours from her face.*

Menna   Mam!

Anest *groans in pain.*

Menna   Let me see.

She looks at **Anest**'s *wound and gets a hand towel to stem the blood.*

Menna   Let me see.

Anest *groans.*

Menna (*to* **Iola**)   What the fuck is wrong with you! (*To* **Anest**.) Let me see, Mam.

Menna *looks at* **Anest**'s *face. She stems the bleeding with a hand towel or cloth.*

Anest *groans.*

Menna *sweeps around the room picking up all the pebbles. She snatches the pebbles from* **Iola**'s *hand and hides them.*

Menna   Does that hurt?

Anest *winces.*

Menna   It's okay.

Anest *winces.*

Menna (*to* **Iola**)   Stay over there! (*To* **Anest**.) I'll get the doctor out.

Iola   I'm dis – I'm a I'm a I'm a dis. I'm a. Watching. I'm watching.

Menna *starts to clean* **Anest***'s face of blood.*

Anest *winces.*

Anest   Rather she was dead than this.

Menna   You don't mean that.

Anest   I do.

Beat.

I do.

As **Menna** *cleans* **Anest***'s face, she gets upset.* **Anest** *reaches and comforts* **Menna***.* **Anest** *and* **Menna** *hold each other and cry.*

Menna   I'm sorry.

She kisses **Anest***. She gets up.*

Menna   Auntie Iols, we're going to have to put a plaster on Mam, and then we're going to take you to see the doctor.

She pulls out some things from a box.

There's a first-aid box here somewhere, isn't there?

As she searches she pulls out an ornamental lobster pot with shells stuck on. It has 'Trysory mor' written on it.

She looks to **Anest** *on the floor and* **Iola** *– who is in her own world.*

Initially she puts the pot back in the box.

A moment.

She decides to try one last time. Tentatively she approaches **Iola** *with the pot.*

Menna   Iola.

She sits on the bench with it.

Look.

Iola *is unsure what to do.*

Menna   Come and look.

Iola *approaches.*

Menna   This mean anything to you?

Iola *touches it.*

Menna   Every shell has a story. Doesn't it? Can you remember any?

Iola   Whatyoucall . . . um . . .

Menna   Put your hand on the shells.

*She puts **Iola**'s hand in hers and runs it all over the pot.*

Your dad used to say he found you in this, didn't he? Can you remember anything he told you?

Beat.

What did he used to tell you?

Beat.

Iola   That we were special.

Pause.

Menna   Mam. Come here.

Anest   No.

Menna   Come here.

Beat.

Please.

Anest *sits next to **Iola** and **Menna** on the bench.*

Menna   Tell us about the pot.

Anest   I don't know.

Menna   Mam. Please just talk to her.

Anest *struggles before composing herself.*

Anest   When our dad, went missing; we stuck a new shell on here for every night he didn't return. Then we ran out of space.

Beat.

We'd just bring a shell, or pebble home.

Slowly it dawns on **Iola** *who* **Anest** *is.*

Anest   Brought so many home Mam made us put them in the garden. We'd play with them and sometimes they'd make us cry, but we were always on the, look out. Nice pebble. Nice shell.

Filling with shame and confusion, **Iola** *can't look at* **Anest**. *She just looks at the pot.* **Iola** *touches* **Anest**'*s wound,* **Anest** *winces.*

Iola *holds on to the pot as a sob escapes her.*

She takes **Anest**'*s hand.*

She sits crying holding her sister's hand for a moment.

She takes **Anest** *in a hug.*

She cries in **Anest**'*s shoulder, as* **Anest** *comforts her.*

Iola   I want to die.

Anest   I know. I know.

Iola *cries and* **Anest** *comforts her.*

The twins hold on to each other tighter than ever before and cry. **Menna** *stares at her gloved hands. She peels off her gloves, one by one, and throws them away.* **Anest** *sees this and catches* **Menna**'*s eye. They share a half-smile.*

Blackout.

Scene Sixteen

The beach.

The sound of waves in the distance.

Menna *is not wearing gloves; she is wearing one of* **Anest**'s *dresses and is carrying a bag of pebbles.*

Anest *and* **Menna** *are either side of* **Iola**. *They walk along the beach,* **Anest** *and* **Iola** *in their big coats.*

Menna   The stone circle. Up on the path. That wasn't there when I lived here, Auntie Iols?

Iola   What now?

Anest   The doctor put them there for tourists. Nonsense ti'n bod. They look ancient but they've only been there since two thousand and six. People love a story don't they? Same as all that bloody merman nonsense.

Menna   Grandad?

Anest   He had another family over in Ireland.

Menna   What?

Anest   They all did. She probably put her foot down one day and never let him back.

Iola   Nonsense.

Anest   What's more likely, he's a cheating bastard, or part-fish?

The threesome walk.

Iola   Are you okay Menna?

Menna   Yes, I think I might.

Beat.

I think I might get some chickens.

Anest *takes a pebble out of* **Menna**'s *bag.*

Menna   Where can I get chickens?

Anest *gives the pebble to* **Iola***, who puts it in one of her coat pockets.*

Anest   Coed Y Brenin will, sell you a couple of hens.

She pulls another two pebbles out and puts them in her own pockets.

You'll probably need to get someone in to fix the whatyoucall.

Beat.

Run.

As they walk and talk, **Anest** *goes into the bag and pulls out more pebbles, putting them into her own pockets as well as handing them to* **Iola***.*

Iola   And a dog. / Need a dog.

Menna   I don't want a dog.

Anest *hands some more pebbles to* **Iola***.*

Anest   You'll need a dog.

Menna   What for?

Iola   Foxes. Go for the chickens.

Anest   Yes, you'll need a dog.

Iola *and* **Anest** *continue to fill their pockets with pebbles.*

Anest   Get a proper dog. Not a bloody poodle / or anything.

Iola   Na!

Menna   I'm not going to get a bloody / poodle, Mam.

Anest   I know what you're like.

Menna   I won't get a . . . poodle.

The plastic bag is empty and the reality hits **Menna** *although she fights her emotions. She scrumples the bag up.*

Long silence.

Menna (*fighting tears*)   What kind of dog . . . *should* I get then?

Anest   A collie / or something.

Iola   Border collie.

Menna   Border collie, right.

Iola   Damp nose and a clean bum!

Menna   Damp nose and clean bum okay.

Pause.

Anest   Anything else, love?

Menna   I – um . . . I, know how to work the oven, don't I? Yes.

She cries as **Anest** *hugs her.*

Anest   Dwi'n caru ti. [DO EEN CARRY TEE – *I love you.*]

Menna   Dwi'n caru ti hefyd. [DO EEN CARRY TEE HE-FID – *I love you too.*]

She sobs into **Anest***'s shoulder.* **Iola** *puts her hand on* **Menna***'s back.* **Menna** *turns and hugs* **Iola***.*

Menna   I love you, Auntie Iols.

Iola   Caru ti bach. [CARRY TEA BACH – *Love you, little one.*] You know, I used to be so intelligent.

As the twins leave **Menna***,* **Iola** *turns around with her finger in the air.*

Iola   Give the chickens, seashells; helps them make the eggs.

Beat.

Still have my uses!

Menna *holds her hands to her mouth as the twins leave and* **Anest** *pulls a skipping rope out of* **Iola***'s pocket.*

Iola *waves as* **Anest** *ties it around* **Iola***'s waist and then her own.*

The sound of the waves increasing, as used in the underwater scenes.

The twins are alone.

Anest *and* **Iola** *now hold each other tightly.*

Anest   Cold.

Iola   Over soon.

Anest   Can't see.

Iola   Don't let go.

Anest   I won't.

Iola   Keep going.

Anest   Oh! It's so cold.

Iola   Have you tied us? / Are we tied?

Anest   Yes, yes we are.

She holds **Iola** *tight. Lights darker, sound of waves louder.*

Iola   Don't let go.

They hold hands.

Anest   Let's not be scared.

Beat.

Keep walking.

Beat.

Keep walking.

Lights darker, sound of waves louder.

Iola   It's cold.

Anest   I know.

Beat.

I know it's cold. But, if you tell yourself it's not cold. It's not cold.

Iola   It's not cold.

Anest   Not cold.

Slowly, the twins smile.

Iola   It's not / cold.

Anest   It's not cold.

The twins laugh.

Iola   It's not cold, is it?

Anest   It's not cold.

Iola   It's quite nice actually.

Anest   It is. It's nice.

With broad smiles the twins walk into the waves together.

Sound of waves increases.

Lights down on the twins.

Blackout.

The End.

Welsh Words and Phrases

Ti'n bod / Ti'n wybod – You know?

Yna fe – Isn't it?

Ty Felin – Yellow House. In small villages, houses are known by names rather than numbers.

Ceffyl Dŵr yw e – He's a water horse.

Dyna ddigon – That's enough.

Dere – Come.

Eisteddfodau – Cultural events, where singing, poetry, dance and music are performed in Welsh. Schools, communities and counties hold them, with the National held once a year.

Ardderchog – Excellent.

Bopa – Aunt.

Ydw! – Yes.

Pryd hi'n byw gyda' chi? – When she lived with you?

Ie, wir – Yes, it's true.

Da iawn bach – Well done.

Bach – Little one (term of affection).

Calon – Heart / love / girlfriend / boyfriend.

Ie – Yes.

Dwi'n caru ti – I love you.

Dwi'n caru ti hefyd – I love you too.

Duw, duw – Good God.

Ti'n Pwdu nawr – You're sulking now.

Yn y felan – In the doldrums.

Cantre Gwaelod – The Lowland Hundred – a Welsh city under the sea.

Trysor y Mor – Bounty of the sea.

Twmwyn haul – Sunstroke.

Iawn – Okay / Good.

Coed y Brenin – Kingswood.

Canu nawr – Sing now.

Ti'n gweld – You see.

Fi'n teimlo'n saff yn dy ddwylo di ti'n gwbod – I feel safe in your hands, you know.

Un – One.

Dau – Two.

Tri – Three.

Aderyn du – Blackbird.

Ti'n eisiau panad? – Do you want a cup of tea?

Pen tost – Sore head.

Fi sy yna – It's me here.

The Radicalisation
of Bradley Manning

For my parents

The story I tell happened in a time
we cannot understand.

Jorge Luis Borges

I will officially give up on the society we have
if nothing happens.

Bradass87

Courage is contagious.

Billy Graham

The Radicalisation of Bradley Manning was commissioned and produced by National Theatre Wales. It was first performed on 12 April 2012 at Tasker Milward V C School, Haverfordwest, and then toured to Cardiff High School and Connah's Quay High School, Flintshire. The cast was as follows:

Matthew Aubrey
Harry Ferrier
Gwawr Loader
Kyle Rees
Anjana Vasan
Sion Daniel Young

Director   John E. McGrath
Designer   Chloe Lamford
Lighting Designer   Natasha Chivers
Sound Designer   Mike Beer
Multi-Platform Designer   Tom Beardshaw
Emerging Director   James Doyle-Roberts

Characters

in order of appearance

Marine 1, *guard at Quantico brig*

Bradley Manning, *fourteen to twenty-three, US soldier, accused of leaking the largest amount of classified material in history – to be played by every member of cast*

Chorus, *see Author's Note*

Mrs Stokes, *fifties, inspirational history teacher*

Mark Pritchard, *fourteen to seventeen, Welsh teenager, class charmer*

Gavin Hope, *fourteen to seventeen, Welsh teenager, class thug*

Lisa Williams, *fourteen to seventeen, Welsh teenager, class beauty queen*

Anthony Edwards, *fourteen to seventeen, Welsh teenager, class whipping boy*

TFL Worker, *any age, Londoner*

Commuter 1, *any age, London worker*

Commuter 2, *any age, London worker*

Commuter 3, *any age, London worker*

Lady Gaga, *American popular music star*

Customer, *any age*

Tina, *Bradley's colleague in the US service industry*

Brian Manning, *fifties, Bradley's father*

Waitress, *any age*

Drill Sergeant, *instructor for US basic training*

Recruit 1, *fellow recruit of Bradley's to the US military*

Recruit 2, *fellow recruit of Bradley's to the US military*

Recruit 3, *fellow recruit of Bradley's to the US military*

Reporter, *news reporter for Syracuse.com at Proposition 8 rally*

Tyler Watkins, *twenty, gay student, Bradley's first love*

Marine 2, *marine at Quantico brig*

Marine 3, *marine at Quantico brig*

Marine 4, *marine at Quantico brig*

David House, *twenty, President of Builds, hackerspace at Boston University, one of the few people allowed to visit Bradley at Quantico*

Kyle, *twenty, hacker*

Alison, *twenty, hacktivist*

Commander Browning, *marine in charge of Quantico brig*

Soldier 1, *soldier stationed at the Discharge Unit, awaiting dismissal from the army*

Soldier 2, *soldier stationed at the Discharge Unit, awaiting dismissal from the army*

Soldier 3, *soldier stationed at the Discharge Unit, awaiting release from the army*

Private Miles, *Bradley's 'battle buddy', assigned to Bradley at the Discharge Unit to help with the stress of transition from army to civilian life*

Sergeant, *Sergeant at Discharge Unit tasked with recycling Bradley back into the army*

Intel Officer 1, *fellow intelligence analyst of Bradley's at Forward Operating Base Hammer*

Intel Officer 2, *fellow intelligence analyst of Bradley's at Forward Operating Base Hammer*

IFP, *Iraqi Federal Police*

Nidal, *Iraqi Federal Police*

Major, *translator in charge of Bradley's Division*

Deaf Counsellor, *US military counsellor*

Blind Counsellor, *US military counsellor*

Mute Counsellor, *US military counsellor*

Commander, *US military commander in charge of Forward Operation Base Hammer in Iraq*

Author's Note

Throughout the play there are stage directions for the Chorus. These are just suggestions. All direction for the Chorus should be discovered by the director and cast in rehearsal. The Chorus should be on stage at all times, and should serve the story by creating the subtext of the scene – through physical language as well as by bringing fluidity to the transitions between time and space. The cast should seek to blur the lines between characters and choral personalities, so that the Chorus serves as a five-headed monster, holding the play together by pulling it apart.

Throughout the play there are directions when a new cast member should start playing Bradley. Again these are just suggestions and should be discovered by the director and cast.

/ *indicates when the next line should be spoken.*

/ / *indicates the next following line should also interrupt.*

– *indicates an interruption by another thought or character.*

It is suggested lines between angle brackets < thus > are delivered chorally. How that manifests itself is for the director to discover.

Scene One

March 2011.

Bradley *on 'Prevention of Injury' watch in Quantico brig.*

On Screen: Wales is a radical country. The internet is a radical space. Both have a history of fighting corrupt concentrations of power. For Wales, the fight is over. For the internet, it's only just begun . . .

In this story Bradley Manning's school years have been imagined. Everything else is true.

Darkness.

Bradley *lies in a smock on a bench.*

Marine 1 (*offstage*)   Detainee 4335453, are you okay?

Beat.

Bradley   What?

Marine 1 (*offstage*)   Answer affirmative or negative. Are you okay?

Beat.

Clanking sound of door opening . . .

Scene Two

Present day.

Chorus 1   Bradley Manning is a traitor.

Chorus 2   Bradley Manning is a hero.

Chorus 3   Bradley Manning is a f***ing a-hole.

Chorus 4   Bradley Manning is a soldier.

*Now **Chorus** speaks at the same time, over each other, getting louder and louder trying to be heard.*

Chorus 5   Bradley Manning is a sign of the times.

Chorus 6   Bradley Manning should fry!

Chorus 1   Bradley Manning is going to die in jail.

Chorus 2   Bradley Manning is not going to get a fair trial.

Chorus 3   Bradley Manning is a human rights issue.

Chorus 4   Bradley Manning is being held in inhumane conditions.

Chorus 5   Bradley Manning is an intelligence analyst.

Chorus 6   Bradley Manning should not have enlisted.

Chorus 1   Bradley Manning needs our help.

Chorus 2   Bradley Manning is only a boy.

Chorus 3   Bradley Manning caused the Arab Spring.

Chorus 4   Bradley Manning is gay!

Chorus 5   Bradley Manning was tortured.

Chorus 6   Bradley Manning was held in Kuwait.

Chorus 1   Bradley Manning's glasses were taken from him, which is a contravention of his human rights.

Chorus 2   Bradley Manning is a whistleblower.

Chorus 3   Bradley Manning is innocent.

Chorus 4   Bradley Manning is not a machine.

Chorus 5   Bradley Manning is a hotheaded loner.

Chorus 6   Bradley Manning is twenty-three.

Chorus 1   Bradley Manning is meh . . .

Chorus 2   Bradley Manning is in chains twenty-three hours a day.

Chorus 3   Bradley Manning is a communist.

Chorus 4   Bradley Manning should never have gone to Iraq, whose idea was that?

Chorus 5   Bradley Manning took an oath to serve his nation, and abide by the rules and regulations of the armed forces.

Chorus 6   Bradley Manning is a complex character deserving of our compassion.

Chorus 1   Bradley Manning was tired of being a victim.

Chorus 2   Bradley Manning's personal and sexual issues inform his decisions.

Chorus 3   Bradley Manning was let down by those above him, and if this is anyone's fault it's the army. And don't ask don't tell.

Chorus 4   Bradley Manning was witness to war crimes.

Chorus 5   Bradley Manning went too far.

Chorus 6   Bradley Manning is the WikiLeaks guy, right?

Chorus 1   Bradley Manning was recycled.

Chorus 2   Bradley Manning is our Dan Ellsberg.

Chorus 3   Bradley Manning has security clearance.

Chorus 4   Bradley Manning was the kid who got all aggro on *The X Factor*, right? Right?

Chorus 5   Bradley Manning sounds like a real cool guy, at least before they sent him crazy in detention.

Chorus 6   Bradley Manning knew when he leaked all of those records he had a pretty good idea he was going to pay for it down the road. He still did it. That's not cowardly.

Chorus 1   Bradley Manning is a fucking hero no matter how a trial plays out.

Chorus 2   Bradley Manning is just a dumb kid, and his actions really haven't changed anything.

Chorus 3   Bradley Manning worked at Starbucks.

Chorus 4   Bradley Manning didn't know what was in the cables he leaked.

Chorus 5   Bradley Manning's commentators have presumed he's guilty.

Chorus 6   Bradley Manning is guilty of nothing at this time.

Chorus 1   Bradley Manning saw what looked like a pattern of wrongdoing.

Chorus 2   Bradley Manning's case serves to illustrate how badly designed US military networks are in terms of supporting information compartmentalisation and secrecy silos.

Chorus 3   Bradley Manning is a dickhead of colossal dimensions.

Chorus 4   Bradley Manning is rotting in the brig.

Chorus 5   Bradley Manning is too trusting.

Chorus 6   Bradley Manning is alleged to have released extensive US military and government materials to WikiLeaks. These show how the US and many other governments so often say one thing in public, another in private, and yet a third through their actions.

Chorus 1   Bradley Manning needs a bullet in the fucking head.

Chorus 2   Bradley Manning is no hero and neither is Julian Assange.

Chorus 3   Bradley Manning's actions are down to his frustrated sexuality and personal isolation.

Chorus 4   Bradley Manning is why we don't have gays in the military.

Chorus 5   Bradley Manning is still a soldier.

Chorus 6   Bradley Manning hadn't read hardly any of the stuff he leaked.

Chorus 1   Bradley Manning is a transvestite.

Chorus 2   Bradley Manning discovered his company was run by the mob.

Chorus 3   Bradley Manning is now left with the sinking feeling he doesn't have anything left.

Chorus 4   Bradley Manning is not allowed to hold a gun any more.

Chorus 5   Bradley Manning is woken every twenty minutes.

Chorus 6   Bradley Manning's prison guards are being targeted by Anonymous.

Chorus 1   Bradley Manning likes Pi Day.

Chorus 2   Bradley Manning leaked footage of another botched job by your shitty and unprofessional military.

Chorus 3   Bradley Manning is a little squirt who betrayed his country and has risked the lives of all of us. This has been a lesson in what happens when you let homos in the army.

Chorus 4   Bradley Manning wants to work in the prison library.

Chorus 5   Bradley Manning is bipolar.

Chorus 6   Bradley Manning heads our reader poll for who should win this year's Nobel Peace Prize.

Chorus 1   Bradley Manning worked at Abercrombie and Fitch.

Chorus 2   Bradley Manning is not a piece of equipment.

Chorus 3   Bradley Manning has an iPhone.

Chorus *moves into position so that* **Mrs Stokes** *stands in front of a classroom of kids.*

Chorus 4   Bradley Manning is moving to a less harsh detention centre.

Chorus 5   Bradley Manning wants an air purifier.

Mrs Stokes   Bradley Manning is Welsh!

Scene Three

October 2001.

Tasker Milward V C School.

Mrs Stokes   So I don't want to hear any bullying or joking about his accent. He can play for Wales, so he has as much right to be here as any of you. Bradley?

The entire room looks at **Bradley** *who stands in the corner of the room holding a piece of paper – his timetable. Ad lib* **Class** *muttering and talking.*

Bradley   Um . . . I don't know if I'm in the right period.

Class *sniggers at his accent and 'period' – some imitate.*

Mrs Stokes   Bradley, within this room you will find people you will love and people you will hate, I know I do. Mr Pritchard, / I assign Mr Manning, // it is your duty to get him to his next class and to make sure no one sticks his head down the toilet until at least Thursday.

Mark   No no no no! Not me.

Gavin   Bummers!

Mrs Stokes   Bradley what do you know about the Norman invasion of Wales?

Bradley   Who's Norman?

Class *erupts into hilarity.*

Lighting state change.

Class *continues to laugh in silence as* **Mark** *walks* **Bradley** *around the room – an opportunity for* **Mark** *to pick out audience members as fellow pupils.*

Mark   Okay! Quickest way to Tesco's is through the lady's garden. Stick with us TASK boys, avoid the ERM lot. Back here's the wasters. Don't lend him anything. She cries when she has her period. His dad got caught with a rent boy. England supporter.

Beat.

Hard (**Gavin**). Wanker (**Anthony**). Psycho (**Lisa**). Stokesy's alright, for a teacher. Keep hold of your bag and don't take a shit in school.

Sequence over: **Class** *noise returns, normal lighting.*

Mrs Stokes   Settle down! Bradley, you'll get up to speed in no time. Having defeated King Harold in 1066, why did William the Conqueror build Chepstow Castle in 1067, Mr Pritchard?

Mark   He wanted a palace.

Mrs Stokes   Mr Hope?

Gavin *shrugs.* **Class/Chorus** *is permanently harassing, giggling and talking to each other to grotesque degrees, isolating* **Bradley**.

Mrs Stokes   Anyone? Ms Williams?

Lisa   Was it? Was it because . . . right, was it because he wanted to get away from where they'd just had a fight? Where was it?

Anthony   Has / tings.

Lisa   Hastings! I thought it was somewhere else then for a second. So, because he'd won there, did he want to like get far away from there so, they couldn't come back at him. I don't know where's Hastings?

Mrs Stokes   Mr Manning? Hazard a guess?

Silence.

Bradley   I, don't know.

Mrs Stokes   Why does it look like we're going to invade Afghanistan?

Bradley   The Taliban are / hiding bin Laden.

Gavin   Ye-haw!

Mrs Stokes   Thank you, Mr Hope. Throughout history the invaded countries have changed, but the reasons stay the same. *Strategy* drives America to invade Afghanistan, and *strategy* . . . drove William the Conqueror to build a fort at the edge of Wales.

A piece of paper hits the back of **Bradley**'s *head.*

Mrs Stokes   Through / military might and intermarriage // the Normans went on to take control of Wales.

Bradley (*under*)   What was that for?

Mark (*under*)   Don't.

More paper flies at **Bradley**. **Lisa** *throws paper.* **Anthony** *throws pieces of paper at* **Bradley**.

Bradley   What the fuck?

The frenzy of throwing stops as **Mrs Stokes** *turns.*

Mrs Stokes   What's going on? Bradley?

Silence.

She turns her back again.

'The Mailed Fist', as it was known, gripped Wales following the Norman Conquest.

More paper flies, **Anthony** *throws some paper and it hits* **Mark**, *who takes umbrage at* **Anthony** *joining in.* **Mark** *stands up to throw paper at* **Anthony**, *but* **Mark** *becomes the target and gets totally plastered by the rest of the* **Class**.

Mark *is overwhelmed until* **Bradley** *joins in, steps in front of* **Mark** *and defends him, hurling paper back at* **Anthony**.

Mrs Stokes *turns around and the* **Class** *immediately reverts to good behaviour. But* **Bradley** *is too slow. He is left standing alone pelting paper at* **Anthony**.

He realises he's alone.

Mrs Stokes   Bradley Manning. See me after class.

Bradley   It wasn't just me.

Mrs Stokes   You are the only one I saw.

Bradley   I'm not lying.

Mrs Stokes   You were the only one I saw.

Bradley   But that's / bullshit. I'm not lying.

Mrs Stokes   I won't ask you again.

Bradley   But –

Mrs Stokes   I won't tell you again.

Bradley   WHY WON'T YOU LISTEN?

Scene Four

August 2010.

Quantico brig.

Marine 1   Contravenes regulations.

Beat.

No exercise.

Bradley   I'm / just –

Marine 1   No exercise.

Bradley *stops exercising.*

Bradley   I am still a soldier.

Marine 1   No exercise.

Bradley   Who's in charge here?

Scene Five

7 July 2005.

King's Cross Station.

Rolling screens say 'All trains cancelled'.

Bradley *is wearing a rucksack.*

TFL Worker   I am, you have to leave.

Bradley   Can I use your phone?

TFL Worker   It's not working, mate, you have to leave.

Bradley   Excuse me, can I use your phone? Is your phone working?

Commuter 1   I can't get through. / There's no dial tone.

Commuter 2   They take down the mobile networks when stuff like this happens.

Bradley   Stuff like what?

Commuter 2   Bombs. Bloke over there said it was two separate lines. Don't sound like gas. / You on your own, mate?

Bradley   I'm trying to get the embassy. I've got a flight to the States tomorrow.

Commuter 2   Can't see any planes leaving London.

Commuter 1   Here, have some water.

Bradley *and* **Commuter** *share water.*

Commuter 1   My wife's in Paddington. I think there's an internet café over there/ I'm gonna try and email her.

Bradley   I need a phone. Are there any phone booths anywhere? I just need to make a call.

Commuter 3   There's no phones working.

Lady Gaga *hands* **Bradley** *a telephone.*

Bradley   Um, Dad? Have – have you seen the news? Turn on the news.

Beat.

What's it say? I'm at, I'm at King's Cross Station, I'm meant to be getting a new passport and then flying home tomorrow but there was this explosion and smoke and – what's the news saying?

Beat.

Oh my God. How many?

Beat.

Was there one on a bus? What's going – My phone doesn't work, everyone's being really kind – Oh my God, oh my God. Have they said who it is? Is it al-Qaeda? I could've – what?

Beat.

I'm okay. I felt the explosion in my feet. I was that – It was underneath me. I could have been on one of those subways, Dad, I could have – hang on. The boards are changing. It's changing. Everything's changing. Hang on, I'll tell you what it says.

('I'm running away.')

Oh.

('I'm running away from Wales because I'm a coward.')

Um. They're not saying. They're not saying. They don't have any new information.

('Like you.')

It's just . . . saying random things. Dad. Can you call Mom for me? She's – I don't want her worrying about me. She'll be worried about me. I don't want her worrying.

('Mom needed me, and I abandoned her. Just like you did.')

I'm in the middle of a fucking terrorist – Can you just call her? Please? Call her. Thank you.

('I have to show her I'm nothing like you.')

I'm fine! I've just – I was really close that's all.

('By making something of my life.')

I'm uh . . . I don't think my flight is uh, is . . . is going to be, running either so . . .

('I have to do something special.')

Yeah.

('For her.')

Yeah. Are you gonna call Mom?

Scene Six

October 2001.

Tasker Milward V C School.

Mrs Stokes   I won't be calling your mother this time, Bradley, but you do seem to have a problem with authority. Do you have a problem with authority?

Beat.

Why were you arguing with me?

Bradley   Because it's not fair.

Mrs Stokes   Who are you to say what's fair and what's not?

Bradley   Who are you to?

Pause.

Mrs Stokes   Think you've just answered my first question there, Bradley.

Beat.

Listen. This is a new school. New teachers. New classmates.

Beat.

You're already at a huge disadvantage. You're American; you've joined late; you're not a big lad. You don't need to add a bad attitude to that mix.

Beat.

How's things at home?

Bradley *shrugs.*

Mrs Stokes   Okay, next time you feel yourself filling up with anger, I want you to take a deep breath. Once you've taken that deep breath all your anger will go away and you'll have clarity. You'll know what you should do next, and I guarantee it will never be lash out.

Beat.

Will you try that for me?

He nods.

Mrs Stokes   Who threw the first paper ball?

Bradley   Gavin, miss. Is that everything?

Scene Seven

April 2006.

Bradley *in a McJob.*

Customer   Yes, just the soya latte.

Bradley   Flat white soya latte?

Tina *hands the cup to* **Bradley** *who hands it over to the* **Customer**. **Chorus** *performs service industry jobs, and ensures* **Bradley** *and* **Tina** *have the right props.*

Customer   Thank you.

Bradley   Sorry for the . . .

Customer *has left.*

Bradley *yawns.*

Tina   So where you living now?

Bradley   I was at my dad and stepmom's for a while, didn't really belong there, so I got my own place in Midtown. Landlord's kind of a crappy.

Tina   Okay.

Bradley   I'm just doing this till I get my own tech company up and running. Last place was a fucking joke. I'm not here long so, it's okay.

They start folding shirts.

Tina   Everyone's just here for the summer.

Bradley   Yuh.

Tina   What's that supposed to mean?

Silence.

You think I want / to work here for ever?

Bradley   No.

Beat.

I didn't mean that.

Beat.

I don't know what I meant.

Silence.

They stand at a counter with a factory line of burgers on it. **Tina** *puts the lid of the bun on and passes it to* **Bradley***, who closes the box.*

Beat.

Bradley   I'm not being mean.

Tina   You are.

Bradley   Forget it.

Silence.

Tina   My friend lives in Midtown, whereabouts?

Bradley   Uh, Brady Arts District, around there.

Beat.

I'm just saying. I've lived in the UK. I've built websites. I practically nursed my mom on my own. I'm sorry if that's made me want to do something with my life.

Tina *squirts the surface with a cleaning product, he mops the floor.*

Bradley   These people don't. So I have nothing in common with them.

Beat.

If that makes me mean. Then fine. I'm mean.

Tina   You haven't tried talking to everyone.

Bradley   I have.

Tina   Really?

Bradley   Yes. Most of them.

Tina   Most of them.

Bradley   They don't wanna do anything with their lives. I can tell. There's no rush. I can't get out of here quick enough.

Tina   You look down on / people, Bradley.

Pause.

Bradley   Maybe I do. They deserve to be looked down on, if they think this is all they're good for.

They put headsets on.

Tina   Jason said he saw you sleeping in your car.

Beat.

Bradley   I was doing a double shift.

Tina   He's seen you a few times. (*To headset.*) I'm just putting you through to our policy support team, sir. Please hold! (*To* **Bradley**.) You sleep in your car.

Beat.

Bradley   I don't, sleep in my car.

Tina   You're always the last to leave and you have a toothbrush in your drawer.

Beat.

Bradley   I'm a hard worker.

Tina   Everyone's seen you brushing your teeth in the toilet.

Beat.

Bradley   That doesn't mean anything.

Tina   You look down on everyone and walk around telling everyone we're all stupid but you're the one who's homeless.

Beat.

Bradley   I share a place in Midtown.

Tina   I thought it was your *own* place? (*To headset.*) Yes, sir, we're just waiting for one of my colleagues who's on another line. Sorry for the delay.

Beat.

I don't care if you sleep in a dumpster. Just don't act like you're smarter than everyone else. It'll bite you on the ass. You sleep in your car, and work a crappy job. You can't look down on *anyone*. You're just as trapped as the rest of us.

Scene Eight

September 2010.

Quantico brig.

A clunking sound.

A plate of food is slid under the door.

Bradley *approaches it. He looks at* **Tina**.

He picks up his food, sits next to **Tina** *and eats in silence.*

Scene Nine

August 2007.

An American diner.

Another **Bradley** *sits in a diner opposite* **Brian Manning**, *his father.* **Brian** *is played by the whole* **Chorus**.

Bradley *fiddles nervously with a napkin.*

Bradley   Thanks for meeting me.

Brian   You ate yet? I think I'm going for pancakes. You think pancakes?

Bradley   I'm good.

Brian   You eat yet?

Bradley   I haven't got any / money so –

Brian   I can buy you breakfast, Bradley.

Bradley   Pancakes are fine.

Brian (*to* **Waitress**)   Two pancakes, both with maple syrup.

Brian   I ain't eat here before.

Bradley   It's good. It's / good.

Silence.

Brian (*about the napkin*)   Stop that.

Silence, as **Bradley** *puts the napkin down.*

Brian   You not going to ask how your stepmom is doing?

Bradley   How is she?

Brian   Doing just fine.

Beat.

Getting new carpet. House is a mess.

Silence, as **Bradley** *starts fiddling with the napkin again.* **Brian** *takes it off him.* **Bradley** *takes a deep calming breath.*

Bradley   I uh. I asked to see you today, Dad, because uh . . .

Brian   Where you living now?

Beat.

Bradley   I'm staying. I'm with friends. Around.

Chorus *acts as* **Waitress**, *who brings over two pancakes.*

Bradley   Thank you.

Waitress *becomes a* **Brian**.

Bradley   I wanted to ask you. If uh, if you know, if you could help. If you had. If you could help, me pay my way to go to college.

Two Brians   You been looking at schools?

Bradley   MiT, BU.

Silence.

I'll work. I'm working crappy jobs now, but I need to be going someplace else otherwise, all I am is someone who works crappy jobs. And living, you know, / with nowhere.

Brian   Where are you working now?

Bradley   I was at Abercrombie and Fitch. Looking for something else. In between.

Brian   You think the world owes you a career. Well, it doesn't. / Your mother took you to Wales and you lost all sense of reality.

Bradley   This is not because Mom took me to Wales when you walked out on us.

Silence.

Brians (*three Brians*)   You watch your mouth.

Silence.

Eat your pancakes.

Beat.

You want to go to college.

Bradley   Yeah, major in computer sciences.

Silence.

Brian   You think that's going to fix everything?

Bradley   Ye / ah.

Brian   Well it's not.

Bradley   Are you going to help me or not?

A fourth **Brian** *counts out some money and puts it on the table.*

Brian   Take that money. Meet me here tomorrow with a résumé, a clean shirt and tie. We head on down to the military recruitment centre together.

Bradley   No, Dad, I'm not joining the army! I want to go to college!

Brian   When you were a boy all you wanted to do was join the army.

Bradley   I want to go to college.

Brian   What's your problem with the military?

Bradley   I don't have a problem with the military, Dad, it's the government / I have a problem with.

Brian   You get three square meals a day. A roof over your head.

Bradley   I don't know why I thought you'd help.

Brian   You can work with computers in intelligence. They've got the best hardware. You get three square meals, roof over your head and a skill base. And here's the thing. After four years' service, they pay for you to go to college.

Bradley   They pay you to go?

Brian   To any school you want. Ivy League. And they pay you a wage. You have to wait but you're getting life experience and money in your pocket.

A fifth **Brian** *joins and physically leans on* **Bradley**.

Brian   Get your degree and get the hell out of there, with a degree and military credentials.

Silence.

Bradley   I could go to MiT?

Brian   You go where you want. For free.

Silence.

Bradley   I'm five-two and I weigh a hundred / and five pounds.

Brian   You ain't going in for infantry. Basic will be tough.

Bradley   I'm gay. I'm not allowed to be open and in the military.

Beat.

Brian   Life's about compromises. D'you wanna be a man and join the army, or do you want to be gay and work in Starbucks?

Beat.

Brian *offers him the money.*

Bradley *takes it.*

Bradley   Where do I go?

Scene Ten

September 2002.

Tasker Milward V C School.

Mrs Stokes   The front please, Bradley, take the hot-seat. Today! We are learning about the Merthyr Rising of 1831!

Reluctantly, another **Bradley** *goes to the front of the* **Class** *and sits down.*

Mrs Stokes   A popular rising where the workers took control of the town. A time when revolutionary ideas threatened the status quo. The first time the red flag of revolution was raised in the world.

She leans on **Bradley**.

Mrs Stokes   This twenty-three-year-old man was executed for those ideas. Hanged to death outside the entrance to what is now Cardiff market.

Beat.

But he's come back from the grave for one afternoon to help you pass your GCSEs. So class, let's welcome – (*to* **Bradley**) Dic Penderyn. Who has a question for our hot-seated martyr? Lisa?

Lisa   Um . . . well, uh. Oh, um . . . I was gonna say . . . no. I. Whatyoucall? I had it then. No! Hang on. What's your, what's your real name?

Bradley   Richard Lewis.

Gavin   How old are you?

Bradley   Twenty-three.

Mark   Are you gay?

Class *hilarity.*

Offended, **Bradley** *starts to get out of his seat and give up.* **Mrs Stokes** *indicates for him to take a breath.* **Bradley** *sits down and takes a deep calming breath.*

Bradley   No. I'm not.

Mark   Have you ever kissed a boy?

Mrs Stokes   Thank you, Mr Pritchard, I think this line of questioning has been exhausted.

Anthony   What was it like being hanged to death?

Bradley *shrugs.*

Mrs Stokes   Mr Penderyn?

Beat.

The **Class** *is silent.*

Mrs Stokes   You have the class's attention, Mr Penderyn.

Bradley   I didn't like, all the people watching and not doing anything. If I'd seen someone innocent getting punished for no reason I'd do something about it. All these people who I thought were my friends. Just let me die.

Silence.

Mrs Stokes   Just to clarify, Mr Penderyn, there was a petition with over eleven thousand signatures urging the government to release you, but yes. That must have awful for you. What were your last words?

Bradley   I don't remember. I was too busy dying.

The **Class** *laughs.* **Bradley** *enjoys the moment.*

Mrs Stokes   Your last words were '*Oh arglwydd, dyma gamwedd*'. What do they mean? Test your Welsh.

Bradley   *Arglwydd* is God, right?

Mrs Stokes   'Oh Lord, what an injustice' or 'Oh Lord, here is iniquity'. Why did you say that?

Bradley   Because I'm innocent. I didn't stab that soldier in the leg. I didn't stab anyone, they got the wrong guy.

Gavin   What's it like being a martyr?

Bradley   I'm not a martyr. / That's the frustrating thing, I'm dead but I can't control what happens to my name.

Gavin   You are butt.

Bradley   A martyr is someone who wants to die. I didn't want to die.

Mrs Stokes   That's not necessarily true.

Bradley   It is.

Mrs Stokes   A martyr is someone who died for a cause, not someone who killed themselves for a cause, there's a difference.

Bradley   Okay, well, I'm not a proper martyr.

Mark   What's someone who's not a proper martyr?

Bradley   I'm not a martyr; I just got caught, and got blamed for something I didn't do. How does that make me a martyr?

Lisa   Because you got punished.

Bradley   Those guys that flew the planes into the World Trade Center, they were martyrs. Suicide bombers in Afghanistan, they're martyrs. A martyr is someone who believes in something so much they'll kill themselves for it. Not someone like me who just got caught.

Mrs Stokes   Anyone agree with Mr Penderyn?

Pause.

Anyone want to disagree with him?

Lisa   It's not. It doesn't matter. What it is, is. Like you haven't got to. Just because you haven't done something, if the army or government or whoever make you pay, then . . . I don't know. I just. I don't know.

Mrs Stokes   Why were you protesting?

Bradley   Uh . . . poor working conditions. Debtors' court. Um.

Mrs Stokes   Anyone else?

Mark   Truck shops.

Lisa   Low wages.

Mrs Stokes   You wanted reform? Yes?

Bradley   Yes.

Mrs Stokes   Mr Penderyn. Hanging you to death was a very severe punishment for maiming a soldier. Do you think the government was threatened by your fighting skills or your ideas?

Pause.

You're not very good at fighting, are you?

Bradley   I don't know.

Mrs Stokes   As a government, you can't punish an idea, so you punish the man.

Beat.

And hope it acts as a deterrent. Is it Bradley's actions that threaten? Or the ideas he subscribes to?

Class   Ideas.

Mrs Stokes   What does that make you?

Bradley   A martyr.

Mrs Stokes   Very good, Bradley. Excellent. Round of applause for Bradley.

Class *claps.*

Scene Eleven

October 2007.

Basic training at Fort Leavenworth.

Clapping becomes the sounds of military drums.

Through movement, **Bradley** *is ripped from his digital self. He is given a haircut, inoculations, and blood samples, given a duffel bag, mouth guard, and fatigues.*

Chorus *is given the same treatment, as* **Bradley** *becomes part of a unit.*

Chorus *becomes a platoon performing fitness training – squat thrusts, burpies, calisthenics. Platoon marches to company area lead by* **Drill Sergeant***.*

They perform the 'bag drill'.

Drill Sergeant   My name is Sergeant Adams! You may call me 'Sergeant'. You may not call me 'sir'. I work for my money. Why are you blinking like that?

Recruit 1's *eye twitches.*

Recruit 1   It's a nervous / thing, Sergeant.

Drill Sergeant   Stop blinking.

Beat.

STOP BLINKING.

Beat.

STOP BLINKING.

Beat.

I am your drill sergeant for BCT. The Patriot Phase of your training. Most of you will quit. I want you to quit. I don't want weak soldiers. I don't want soldiers I cannot trust. I don't want soldiers who think for themselves. I want soldiers who think for their platoon. WHY ARE YOU STILL BLINKING? STOP IT!

Beat.

Everyone empty your bags on the ground in one pile.

Recruits *empty their bags in a pile on the floor.*

Drill Sergeant *scoops up the stuff, messes it about, walks all over it, and then gets a stopwatch out.*

Drill Sergeant   Thirty seconds to reclaim your property.

He blows a whistle.

Screen shows a thirty-second countdown clock.

Recruits *scramble for their stuff; immediately it's a nightmare of pushing, shoving, arguing, and* **Bradley** *gets consumed in the mêlée. He vanishes.*

Another **Bradley** *is thrown out of the group – he is isolated and can't get to his property.*

Thirty seconds is up: whistle blows.

None of the **Recruits** *has their stuff.*

Drill Sergeant   Fail! Empty your bags again.

Recruits *reluctantly empty their stuff in a pile again.*

Drill Sergeant *approaches* **Bradley**.

Drill Sergeant   Name!

Bradley   Bradley Manning, Sergeant!

Drill Sergeant   Are you the runt of the platoon, Bradley Manning?

Bradley   I don't think so, Sergeant!

Drill Sergeant   I think you are. Are you going to prove me wrong, Bradley Manning?

Bradley   Yes / Sergeant!

Drill Sergeant   Until then what are you?

Bradley   I don't understand, Sergeant.

Drill Sergeant   I think you're the runt until you prove me wrong. So what are you?

Beat.

WHAT ARE YOU?

Beat.

WHAT ARE YOU?

Recruit 1   Say you're the runt.

Drill Sergeant   Am I talking to you, recruit?

Recruit 1   No, Sergeant.

Drill Sergeant   On the floor. Twenty.

Recruit 1 *starts press-ups.*

Drill Sergeant   What are you, Manning?

Bradley   I'm . . . I'm the, the runt, Sergeant.

Drill Sergeant   What?

Bradley   I'm the runt, Sergeant.

Drill Sergeant   Louder.

Bradley   I am the runt, Sergeant.

Drill Sergeant   I can't hear you.

Bradley   I AM THE RUNT, SERGEANT.

Drill Sergeant *blows his whistle. Thirty-second countdown clock starts.*

Bradley *is slow off the mark, unnerved by the bullying.*

This time it's an even more ruthless scramble for property. **Bradley** *fights tooth and nail to get some stuff. Another* **Bradley** *pops out of the mêlée.*

Drill Sergeant *blows his whistle.*

There is still property on the floor.

Drill Sergeant *empties everyone's bag again, scoops up all the stuff, messes it up, walks all over it.*

Drill Sergeant   Thirty seconds! Starting from now.

He blows whistle. Thirty-second countdown clock.

Bradley *is reluctant to try.*

Drill Sergeant   Manning! Are you defying an order?

Bradley   No, Sergeant!

He tries to gather some of his things.

Whistle blows.

Another **Bradley** *pops out of the scrum.* **Drill Sergeant** *starts emptying bag, platoon is disappointed.* **Drill Sergeant** *scoops up all the stuff, walks over it, throws it on the floor.*

Drill Sergeant   Thirty seconds.

He blows whistle.

Platoon *starts to work together and sort out their property, passing it to each other.* **Bradley** *still struggles to get all of his stuff.*

Another **Bradley** *pops out of the mêlée. Everyone has a bag packed except* **Bradley** *who is on the floor scrambling for some final pieces.*

Whistle blows.

Drill Sergeant   Empty your bags!

Platoon *groans.*

Recruit 2   For fuck's sake, Manning.

Drill Sergeant *scoops up all the clothes, jumbles them up and walks over them.*

Recruit 3   Manning, get your shit together this time.

Recruit 1   Let's just help him.

Drill Sergeant   Looks like I'm not the only one who thinks you're the runt, Manning! You fail and the whole platoon gives me fifty.

Whistle blows. Countdown clock starts again.

Recruits scramble. **Bradley** *is exasperated.*

Bradley   Why me?

Scene Twelve

March 2008.

A street protest against Proposition 8.

Reporter   Because of the military reference on your sign. You're a soldier, right?

Reporter *puts a microphone in front of a surprised* **Bradley**.

Tyler *watches from a distance.*

Bradley   Who are you with?

Reporter   Syracuse.com. What's your name?

Bradley   How about I just don't tell you my name? Best way to keep a secret is to never have it.

Reporter   That's fine.

Bradley   I'm here to protest against Proposition 8. I'm currently serving in the military awaiting deployment to Iraq. I was kicked out of home and once lost my job because I'm gay. The world is not moving fast enough for us at home, work or the battlefield.

Reporter   Is 'Don't Ask Don't Tell' the worst part about being in the military?

Bradley   Totally.

Standing in drag, **Tyler** *catches* **Bradley***'s eye.*

Bradley   My job, is about life and death, you'd think the army would value personal integrity. Instead they'd rather ten per cent of their employees lie and mislead every single day about who they really are. Excuse me . . .

Bradley *leans towards* **Tyler** *and* **Chorus** *holds him back.*

Bradley   Hey?

Tyler *looks* **Bradley** *up and down.*

Tyler   Hello.

Bradley   I'm Brad.

Tyler   Tyler.

Bradley   Are you going to the rally?

Tyler   Probably, not.

Bradley   Oh.

Tyler   Speeches bore me.

Bradley   Me too, yeah.

They start to walk together.

Tyler   I'm guessing small town, something geeky, web developing, something with good health insurance.

Bradley   Soldier.

Tyler *laughs.*

Bradley   I am.

Beat.

I'm with the 10th Mountain Division. (*Off* **Tyler**'s *bemusement.*) I'm an intelligence analyst.

Tyler   Computers.

Bradley   Any kind of intelligence, cell, pamphlets.

Tyler   Computers / right?

Bradley   Basically computers, yeah.

They laugh, as they follow the march.

Tyler   You like it?

Bradley   I do a really important job. If I do my job well, brief a brigade commander right, I save lives. I feel a great responsibility.

Tyler   Well, good luck with that.

Bradley   I'm not. I don't see myself, having a military career. I figure I can do a couple of years, get some kick-ass credentials. Get into politics. Pull ideas together.

Tyler   I don't even know what shoes to wear and you've got two careers mapped out.

Bradley   If you had my upbringing you'd work on your exit strategies. How about you?

Tyler   Brandeis. Neuroscience major.

Beat.

I'm also a classical musician and drag queen.

Bradley   That's. That's . . .

Tyler   Shall we go / find a bar?

Bradley   Yes. That's. Absolutely. Yes. I. Yes.

Tyler *walks off and* **Bradley** *follows.*

Scene Thirteen

January 2011.

Quantico brig.

But the door slams in **Bradley**'s *face.*

Chorus *becomes a 'Free Bradley Manning' protest.*

Bradley *stands up. He listens hard. The chanting gets a little louder.*

He tries to press his ear as close to a wall as possible. The chanting becomes a little clearer. 'Free Bradley, Free Bradley Manning, Free Bradley Manning.'

Bradley *is stunned. He stands stock still as he tries to digest what he's hearing.*

He is sure. He's hearing 'Free Bradley Manning'.

A sob escapes him, and he tries to compose himself.

He stands listening, with a huge smile on his face.

He stretches his arms out.

He starts to feel the adrenaline and begins to fidget.

He hops up and down, then tries to stand still.

He hops again and this time runs a little in the room. Punching the air. He jumps on his bed and jumps off it. He runs around the cell.

Marine 1 (*offstage*)   No exercise.

Bradley (*delighted*)   Okay!

Bradley *stands still. He can't help himself – he lets out a howl, punches the air and runs around his cell.*

Clunking sound of a door opening.

Pumped up, four **Marines** *enter.*

Marine 1 *applies handcuffs to* **Bradley**, **Marine 2** *applies leg-restraints.*

Marine 1   Attention!

Bradley *stands at attention.*

The **Marines** *pace around.*

Marine 1   Detainee 4333453, at parade rest!

Bradley *stands with his feet shoulder-width apart.*

Marine 2 *sticks his face in* **Bradley**'s *face.*

Bradley *tries to look ahead but can't help look at* **Marine 2**.

Marine 2   Are you eyeballing me, 4335453?

Bradley   No, Sergeant!

Marine 1   Turn left!

Bradley *turns left.*

Marine 3   Don't turn left!

Bradley *corrects his direction.*

Marine 1   I said turn left!

Bradley   Yes, Corporal!

Marine 4   In the *Marines* we reply 'Aye' not 'Yes'. Do you understand, Private?

Bradley   Yes, Corporal.

Marine 3   YOU MEAN AYE!

Bradley   Aye, Corporal.

Marine 1   Turn right.

Marine 2   Don't turn right!

Bradley   Ye – Aye, Sergeant!

Marine 1   I said turn right!

Bradley   Aye, Corporal!

Marine 1   Stand still so we can remove your restraints.

Beat.

I SAID STAND STILL.

Marine 1 *eyeballs* **Bradley**, *who starts to shuffle in retreat.*

Marine 1   I told you to stand still!

Bradley   Yes, Corporal, I am standing still.

Marine 4 *approaches* **Bradley** *menacingly.*

Marine 4   I thought we covered this, you say 'Aye', not 'Yes', do you understand?

Bradley   Aye / Corporal.

Marine 1 (*screamed*)   STAND STILL!

Bradley   Yes, Corporal, I am standing still! I mean –

Marine 4   Are we going to have a problem? Do you have a problem with following orders?

Marine 2   Do you have an attitude problem, 4335453?

Marine 4   Sergeant asked you a question, 4335453.

Bradley *starts to step backwards in fear.*

The **Marines** *loom towards him.*

Marine 2   SERGEANT ASKED YOU A QUESTION.

But **Bradley** *is too scared. He staggers and sits down.*

Bradley   I . . . I . . . I'm not . . . I'm not trying to do anything. I'm just trying to follow your orders.

Marine 4   DO YOU HAVE A PROBLEM WITH ORDERS?

Bradley   I'm. Please, I'm just / trying to follow orders.

Marine 4   DO YOU HAVE A PROBLEM WITH ORDERS?

Silence.

Bradley *(quietly)*   No, Corporal.

Marine 4 *holds his face in* **Bradley***'s face for an age.*

Bradley *looks at the floor.*

The four **Marines** *stand at the corners of a square.*

Marine 1   Commence your recreation, 4335453.

Very long pause.

Marines *stand stiff and straight, contrasting with* **Bradley***'s slump.*

Slowly, **Bradley** *stands up.*

Keeping within the square the **Marines** *have formed,* **Bradley** *starts to walk.*

It becomes apparent that **Bradley** *is walking figures of eight.*

Scene Fourteen

September 2009.

Tyler's *student house.*

Bradley *walks into* **Tyler**'s *arms and they kiss in a passionate, drunken embrace.*

Tyler *pulls at* **Bradley**'s *clothes.* **Chorus** *pushes and pulls them apart.*

Tyler   Been too long.

Bradley   I know.

Tyler   Get your shirt off, get your shirt off.

He pulls off **Bradley**'s *shirt.* **Bradley** *is covered in bruises.* **Tyler** *startles.*

Tyler   What the fuck is all that?

Bradley   It's okay.

He tries to re-engage **Tyler**, *who resists.*

Bradley   Don't worry about it.

Tyler *turns* **Bradley** *around to see all his bruising.*

Silence.

Bradley   You don't need to be worried / about this, okay? It's my business.

Tyler   This is / your job. Normal people don't get beat up in an office.

Bradley   I fight back.

Beat.

Why are you looking at me like that?

Beat.

It's fine.

Tyler   Do you have people you can talk to?

Silence.

Bradley   Pete.

Tyler   What does / Pete have to say about all this?

Bradley   Yeah, he talks to me.

Beat.

If he hears me crying.

He stops putting his shirt on and stares at it.

It won't be for much longer anyway.

Tyler   How come?

Silence.

Overwhelmed, **Bradley** *puts his face in his shirt.*

Tyler   Hey.

For a few moments, **Bradley** *holds his face in his shirt.*

Tyler   Come on.

Bradley *recoils from* **Tyler.**

Silence as **Bradley** *gathers himself.*

Bradley   You go to class today?

Tyler   Uh, yeah.

Beat.

Missed the first one, I slept in.

Bradley   Right.

Silence.

Tyler   You can sue them.

Bradley   You sound like such a fucking idiot. Do you know how you sound sometimes?

Beat.

Like a fucking idiot.

Beat.

I'm outta here.

Bradley *gathers his things.*

Tyler   No.

Bradley   Out of my way.

Tyler   Please stay.

Bradley   GET OUT OF MY WAY.

Silence.

Tyler   I've seen guys like this. You don't have to stand for it.

Bradley   What the fuck do you know about anything?

Beat.

I'm going through this every day, so I can be where you are, and you can't even get out of fucking bed for class.

Beat.

I'm beat up every day, I'm called faggot, and runt and chapter fifteen, people spit on me and – I do it to get where you are and you can't get out of fucking bed?

He rips his shirt open.

You wanna stay in bed with this?

Silence.

I only signed up so they'd pay for me to go to college but I'm such a fuck-up I can't even pass basic training!

Beat.

They're kicking me out.

Beat.

So all this? It's for nothing anyway!

Tyler   Why are they kicking you out?

Bradley   Does it matter?

Scene Fifteen

January 2003.

Tasker Milward V C School.

Anthony   Not, not to me.

He sits at a computer.

I'm just saying.

Beat.

You're meant to have a hall pass to be in here.

Bradley *sits at a computer. The two work in silence.*

Bradley   What game you playing?

Anthony   I'm not playing a game.

Bradley   Jesus, Anthony.

Beat.

I'm just asking.

Silence.

Anthony   I'm writing.

Beat.

A program.

Bradley   Oh yeah?

*He leans into **Anthony**'s screen. **Anthony** quickly hides it.*

Bradley   What is it, secret?

Anthony   It's not finished.

Bradley   I'm building a website.

Silence.

I could help. I'm pretty good with code.

Anthony   Thanks.

Bradley   Do you want help or not?

Beat.

Anthony?

Beat.

*He goes over to **Anthony**'s screen. Again **Anthony** shields it from him.*

Bradley   Let me see.

Beat.

I'm not going to steal anything – I've got enough of my own ideas.

Beat.

Come on.

Anthony *shakes his head.*

Bradley   Why not?

Silence.

Anthony   It's fine. I don't mind if it's going to take ages.

Exasperated, **Bradley** *returns to his computer. They both sit in silence as they work on their projects.*

Anthony   I don't like . . . going on the yard.

Silence.

Bradley *moves over to **Anthony**'s screen.* **Anthony** *doesn't hide it.*

Bradley   What are we doing here?

Scene Sixteen

November 2008/2003.

Boston University hackerspace / Tasker Milward V C School.

Tyler   I want you to meet some of my computer geek buddies. David!

A group of BU students sit around, checking out hardware.

David   Oh hey! Tyler.

Tyler   This is Bradley. This is more his kind of thing than mine.

David   Okay! Are you familiar with the open software, open hardware movement? 'Builds' is a space where students can advocate for that movement as well as a space for student-led DIY learning to take place.

Beat.

So! Hang around, check things out, if you've got the know-how, share it. We've got the Open Organisation of Lock Pickers coming along to do a demonstration later, and Free Software Foundation dropping by to talk to us too.

David *leaves.*

Bradley   I want to go home.

Tyler   We're here for *you*, this is *your* thing. You need to meet other geeks and I don't know. / Make some new friends.

Bradley   They're *all* students.

Tyler   You're smarter than all these people put together.

Kyle   Hey?

Tyler   Hey.

Kyle   Kyle.

Tyler   Tyler, Bradley.

Kyle   What happened to your face, man?

Pause.

Tyler   He's a soldier.

Kyle   You're a *soldier*?

Bradley   Intel.

Kyle   Wow! Check out this red robot mouse I built.

He produces a remote control and drives a robot mouse into their personal space.

Bradley, **Tyler** *and* **Kyle** *look at the floor, as* **Kyle** *reverses the mouse, turns it around in circles, sends it back and forth.*

Silence.

Tyler   That's great.

Bradley   Yeah great – work.

Tyler *and* **Bradley** *drift away from* **Kyle**.

Bradley   Can we go home?

Tyler   Seriously?

Bradley   I'm about to lose my job and my one chance of going to college, and you bring me to a place full of people getting computer science majors and all they're doing is building fucking *robot mice*.

David *overhears this.*

David   So! Bradley, how about you come meet Alison?

Bradley   Um, I don't know.

Tyler *indicates for him to go.* **David** *brings* **Bradley** *over to* **Alison***'s group.*

Tyler *drifts away from* **Bradley** *and joins another group of people who are sitting around debating and drinking from red plastic cups.*

Alison   Levy outlines six hacker ethics. 'Access to a
computer and anything else that might teach you how the
world works, should be unlimited.' 'All information should be
free.' 'Mistrust authority – promote decentralisation.' Um,
how many have I said? Oh – 'Hackers should be judged on
their hacking, not on anything like education, race, sexuality.'
This is my favourite: 'You can create beauty on a computer.'

David   Six?

Alison   Fuck, man.

David   'Computers can change your life for the better.'

Kyle*'s mouse darts past the group, followed by* **Kyle** *running after it.
Everyone watches him exit, chasing the red robotic mouse.*

Silence.

Alison   I said the thing about not judging anyone, right?

David   Yeah.

Alison   Where we are now. This is the Mesopotamia of
hacking. MiT, BU sort of.

Everyone laughs.

Hacking, cyber activism / this is where it all started.

David   Is she doing her enlightenment / schtick again?

Alison   Yes, I am!

David   She always / does this.

Alison   I'm sharing information!

Everyone laughs at the in-joke.

Okay. When Gutenberg built the printing press it took thirty
years for the first porn publication and a *hundred* years for the
first scientific journal. We've had our cyber-porn goldrush.
Now it's time for our global enlightenment. The printing
presses tore down the self-interest of the church in Europe.
Web 2.0 will tear down the self-interest of the corporate state.

Beat.

I'm asking how do we do that?

Bradley   Oh, I'm sorry, I thought you knew.

Alison   No I'm, I'd like to know how we do that.

David   I think it's something to do with reverse engineering. Have you seen the lock-pickers over there?

Bradley   Yeah, what's that about?

David   It's symbolic.

Alison   Like a metaphor for hacking.

David *picks up a lock, brings it over to them and hands it to* **Bradley**. *He gives him a pin.*

David   When you pick a lock for the first time, you learn that the only barriers in the world are psychological. You hold the key to your life, not corporations, parents or university administrators.

Alison   And so, the more people who think like that . . .

David   The bigger things we can reverse engineer.

Bradley   Like what?

Alison   We can do anything I guess?

Bradley *pops his lock open – everyone is pleased.*

Tyler   You want to head off before they start chanting?

Bradley (*to* **Alison**)   How could we, reverse engineer a government?

Mrs Stokes *picks up a bin.*

Mrs Stokes   By throwing conventional wisdom into this bin.

She drops a book into a bin.

Come on, books in the bin.

Class *scrambles towards the front of the class to throw their history books into the bin.*

Mrs Stokes   Today we're looking at the Rebecca Riots of 1839. All of you find a costume.

This action takes place as **Mrs Stokes** *talks.*

Mrs Stokes *lifts another bin up, the class scramble to it and pull out traditional Welsh clothes and start to dress up as traditional Welsh women.* **Anthony** *gets there first, but gets robbed of everything he gets his hands on, so his outfit is the least complete.*

The **Class** *individually giggle and communicate to each other their delight.*

Mrs Stokes   We're going to help you remember some facts about the riots. And we're going to do it by having a riot of our own.

Confusion as she jumps up on to a table and starts stamping on the table.

Who's with me?

Silence.

I said who's with me?

Gavin   What? We're rioting?

Lisa   In class, like? In class.

Mrs Stokes   Yes!

She bangs on the desk.

I said who's with me!

Class *(ad lib)*   I am! Yeah! Fucking come on! Let's do it!

Mrs Stokes   I'm not taking / any more of this! Are you with me?

Class (*ad lib*)   Yeah! Let's go nuts! Come on! Go on, Stokesy! Let's go down town!

The **Class** *get up on the chairs and desks and push chairs around a bit.*

Mrs Stokes   Gavin! Why are you here today?

Gavin   I don't know / I'm. It's!

Mrs Stokes   Who knows why we've come here, dressed as women, in the cold?

Mark   For a meeting!

Mrs Stokes   What am I standing on?

Gavin   Desk!

Anthony   A toll gate!

Mrs Stokes   A toll gate yes! And what are we going to do?

Bradley   Tear it down!

Mrs Stokes   Why?

Bradley   Because we're sick of having to pay every time we go to market!

Class *cheers.*

Lisa   And we're sick of paying tithes to the church!

Class *cheers.*

Mark   I hate the vicar!

Class *cheers.*

Gavin   Vicar's a prick.

Class *cheers.*

Anthony   Wet harvest.

Class *cheers.*

Gavin (*under*)   You can't riot about the weather, or we'll be out every night.

Bradley   English landlords!

Gavin   Sidebars!

Lisa   Poor rates!

Anthony   Taxes!

Lisa   Why are all the landlords English?

Bradley *gets up on the desk.*

Bradley   We're the ones who know how to farm.

Cheers.

Know how to raise cattle and harvest corn! What the fuck does the council do except collect money?

Cheers.

What does the church do? Except collect money?

Cheers.

What do the landlords do except collect money?

Cheers.

And what do the fucking turnpikes do for us? Collect money!

Class   COLLECT MONEY!

The **Class** *tips over the final tables and wrecks the 'toll gates'.*

In the background **Anthony** *picks up a chair and throws it.*

Anthony   I'm not a fucking pushover!

Silence.

Everyone stares at a panting **Anthony**.

Mrs Stokes   Anthony, step out of the room.

Silence.

Step outside.

Gavin   Why are you / such a knob, Anthony?

Lisa   You spoil everything.

Mrs Stokes   Step outside, Anthony.

Anthony   But . . .

He leaves the room, **Bradley** *feels terrible for him.*

Mrs Stokes   Right . . . tell me now. Why did the riots keep happening? What did messing up the classroom feel like?

Mark   It was good. I didn't know I knew all that stuff.

Lisa   I've never . . . you know. What it is, I've never done nothing like that before in a classroom. Not with a whatyoucall there. Teacher.

Mrs Stokes   You felt free of normal school rules? Just as these people felt free of the normal rules of society?

Lisa   Yeah.

Gavin   That was awesome.

Mrs Stokes   What do you think, Bradley?

Bradley   I don't know.

Mrs Stokes   If you feel stupid just take a look round at your classmates.

Bradley *looks at his classmates dressed as women.*

The **Class** *giggles.*

Bradley   I don't know. I guess, for a moment; I didn't feel like –

Mrs Stokes   What?

Bradley   I didn't feel like the new kid.

Beat.

People were listening.

Mrs Stokes   Can you see why the riots kept happening?

Lisa   It was fun.

Gavin   Can we do it in Maths?

Mrs Stokes   I wouldn't recommend it. Anyone else got any thoughts?

Mark   Sort of. Like if. By showing no respect to the toll gate, we sort of got . . .

Bradley   Self-respect.

Mark   Yeah.

Bradley *takes his bonnet off.*

Mrs Stokes   Why is dressing up as women important?

Lisa   That's fun too.

Mrs Stokes   Absolutely. Gives a sense of occasion. There's something else.

Beat.

What did dressing up give them?

Bradley   Anonymity.

Mrs Stokes   And what does that give you?

Bradley   Freedom.

Mrs Stokes   Yes. If society casts you as powerless, why follow society's rules? Put a hoodie on and move freely. Act without compromise. Right, tidy up the class while I talk to Anthony.

Bradley   Miss, I don't think you should punish Anthony.

Mrs Stokes   Take a deep breath, Bradley.

Scene Seventeen

January 2011.

Quantico brig.

Bradley *takes a deep breath and stands to attention.*

Commander Browning *enters.*

Commander Browning   At ease.

Bradley *stands at parade rest.*

Commander Browning   What happened today at recreation call?

Bradley   I was trying to follow orders, sir, but the Marines seemed intent on causing me distress by giving conflicting orders, sir, and demanding I respond as a Marine even though I am not.

Beat.

I'd like to make a complaint sir, I'd like you to investigate / those Marines.

Commander Browning   I am the commander and no one tells me what to do.

Silence.

There a problem, detainee?

Bradley   I'm making a complaint, sir.

Commander Browning   I am the commander here. That means, for practical purposes, I am God.

Silence.

Bradley   Everyone has a boss who they have to answer to.

Commander Browning   Did I hear that right?

Bradley   You still have to follow brig procedures, sir, whatever. It's not my fault if there's a protest outside.

Commander Browning   Marines!

The **Marines** *enter the cell.*

Commander Browning   Place Detainee 4335453 under Suicide Risk Status and POI.

Bradley   What? No! Why are you doing this? I HAVE DONE NOTHING WRONG.

Commander Browning   Strip Detainee 4335453 of his clothes.

With no ceremony two **Marines** *strip* **Bradley** *of his clothes.* **Bradley** *starts crying.*

Bradley   Why are you doing this to me! What have I done? Please, no? Please! I'm begging you.

Beat.

Tell me what you want me to do and I'll do it!

Beat.

Just tell me! I don't understand! What have I done?

Commander Browning *leaves followed by the* **Marines**.

Bradley *stands naked in the cell, crying.*

Scene Eighteen

November 2003/January 2009.

The Tasker Milward computer room/US Army Discharge Unit.

Another **Bradley** *and* **Anthony** *sit in the computer room.*

Anthony   It's okay. Let me see.

He fixes something on **Bradley**'s *screen.*

Bradley   Mrs Stokes can be a dick.

Anthony   Everyone thinks she's tidy, but . . .

Beat.

Only if you do exactly what she wants.

The rest of the **Class** *enters.*

Mark   Bradders!

Lisa   Bradley!

Gavin   Here he is!

He jumps up on a desk.

We will fight them on the beaches, we will fight them in Wetherspoon's, we will fight them in Pwll! We will fight them in Llanidloes!

Mark   Come on Bradley / give us another speech.

Bradley   I'm in the middle of something, guys.

Gavin   We / will fight them in our underwear! We fight them in their underwear, we will fight them without underwear!

Class   Speee-eeech! Speee-eeech! Speeee-eeech!

The gang lift **Bradley** *up in the air.* **Bradley** *is laughing, everyone is laughing and joking and throwing him up in the air like a hero.* **Anthony** *is isolated.*

Bradley (*laughing*)   No, guys, put me down! Put me down! Come on guys, please.

Suddenly the actions turn less playful and **Bradley** *is in pain.*

He screams.

We are now in Fort Leonard Wood, Missouri – the Discharge Unit. **Bradley** *is held by a group of American* **Soldiers** *who are inflicting pain on him.*

Soldier 1   Say 'I am chapter fifteen'!

Bradley   Fuck you!

Soldier 1   Say 'I'm chapter fifteen'!

Bradley   Let me go!

Soldier 1   Say it!

Bradley   Let me go! Get the fuck off me, you fucking assholes, GETOFFME!!

Soldier 1   Say it, Manning! Fucking say it! You like to suck dick and you're a chapter fifteen!

Bradley   AAA / HHHH FUUUCCCKK YOU!

Soldier 1   SAY IT!

Bradley   GETTTT OFFFF MEEEE!

With a huge effort **Bradley** *kicks himself free. The* **Soldier** *and his gang burst out laughing;* **Bradley** *grabs a chair and holds it over his head.*

Bradley   Stay the / fuck away from me!

Soldier 1   What you gonna do / chapter fifteen? Fuck the chair? Come on, pretty boy, let's see you drop your pants and fuck the chair.

Bradley   STAY THE FUCK AWAY.

Soldier 2   Drop your pants.

Silence.

You're on your own, Manning.

Bradley   Stay the fuck away from me, I'm warning you, I'll fucking, I'll fucking kill you.

Soldier 2   What you gonna do? Cry on me?

Soldiers *laugh at* **Bradley**.

Soldier 2   My nephew's tougher than you – he's eight.

Bradley   I'll fucking kill your nephew.

Soldier 2 *starts towards* **Bradley**. **Soldier 3** *holds him back.*

Soldier 3   You know how hard it is to sleep with you crying all the time?

Beat.

Crying and fucking screaming like a bitch.

Beat.

Like some kind of freak.

Beat.

Crying like a baby.

Beat.

Soldier 1   Got anything to say, chapter fifteen?

Beat.

Soldier 1 *goes for* **Bradley**. **Bradley** *swings a chair.*

Soldier 1 *goes for him again.* **Bradley** *swings a chair.*

Bradley *wets himself.*

Soldier 2 *leans into* **Soldier 1** *and points at* **Bradley**'s *trousers.*

Soldier 2   Hell, Manning, you just pissed your pants!

Private Miles *enters.*

Everyone tries to act normally.

Private Miles   What the hell is going on here?

Beat.

Specialist Manning, put that chair down.

Pause.

Specialist Manning!

Bradley   NO / SIR!

Private Miles   Put the chair down!

Bradley   NO! I'm fucking . . .

Private Miles   Specialist Manning, this may be a discharge unit but you are not a civilian yet. Put that chair down, that's an order.

Pause.

Bradley *throws down the chair to guffaws and cat-calling from the other* **Soldiers**.

Private Miles   Pick up the chair, Manning.

Chorus   Yeah, pick up the chair, Manning.

Bradley *catches his breath.*

Private Miles   Specialist Manning, pick up the chair.

Beat.

I SAID PICK UP THE CHAIR.

Bradley   I'M NOT A FUCKING PUSHOVER!

Private Miles *grabs* **Bradley** *and drags him towards the door.*

Bradley   No! No! Get off!

Chorus *whoops with delight and laughs at* **Bradley**'s *humiliation.*

Bradley   Let go!

Beat.

Let me go! FUCK YOU! I'LL FUCKING KILL YOU!

Bradley *is dragged kicking and screaming out of the door while the* **Chorus** *cheers and laughs at him.*

Scene Nineteen

December 2003.

Tasker Milward V C School.

Mrs Stokes   Silence!

She looks at her table.

Vandalising school property is serious.

Beat.

I want a name.

Beat.

NOW!

Beat.

Who has done this?

She points to the desk.

If I don't get a name, you will all be punished. If you're happy to protect a vandal then you shall be punished like vandals. Mark? Do you know who has carved this disgusting image on my desk?

Mark   No, miss.

Mrs Stokes   Lisa?

Lisa   Didn't see anyone, miss.

Mrs Stokes   Anthony?

Anthony *shrugs.*

Mrs Stokes   Bradley?

Bradley   Didn't see anything, miss.

Mrs Stokes   Gavin?

Gavin   Didn't see nothing, miss.

Mrs Stokes   Fine. I'll see what Mr Roberts has to say about this. All of you will see me after school for detention and I will be speaking to Mr Roberts about getting *all* of your parents involved in this.

Class *groans.*

Bradley   That's not fair.

Mrs Stokes   You have something to say, Bradley?

Bradley   You haven't got to get my mom involved for something I didn't do.

Mrs Stokes   Give me a name and I won't.

Bradley   It's your fault! / You can't say riot in one lesson and then . . .

Mrs Stokes   Shut up, Bradley.

Bradley   What have I done wrong?

Scene Twenty

October 2009.

US Army Discharge Unit.

Sergeant   At ease, Specialist.

Bradley *stands at parade rest, but is ill-disciplined with his posture – he is defeated. He has a black eye. The* **Sergeant** *goes through some paperwork.*

Sergeant   Who's supporting you through your discharge process here?

Beat.

Who's your battle buddy?

Bradley   They keep changing, Sergeant.

Sergeant   Who's it today?

Bradley   Miles.

Sergeant   Miles!

In comes a much bigger, strapping soldier – **Private Miles**, *who salutes.*

Sergeant   At ease.

Private Miles *stands at parade rest.* **Bradley** *can barely stand straight.* **Sergeant** *can't look at* **Bradley**.

Sergeant   Specialist, do you know what the term 'recycled' means?

Private Miles *double-takes.* **Chorus** *gasps and is in shock.*

Bradley   No, sir.

Sergeant   It's a term we use. Private Miles will be familiar, where the army halts a discharge process. Do you follow, Specialist?

Bradley   I / guess.

Private Miles   Permission to speak, sir?

Sergeant   Granted.

Pause.

Private Miles   Sir.

Beat.

Are we?

Beat.

Are you saying, Specialist Manning is, uh, to be. Is to be recycled sir?

Sergeant   Yes, Private.

Beat.

There a problem?

Pause.

Private Miles   No, sir.

Sergeant   So, to be clear, Specialist, we have taken a look at the assessments you failed and decided to give you a second chance.

Beat.

We're at war and the army needs you.

Beat.

You will be attached to the 10th Mountain Division as Intel Specialist. You will be . . .

Chorus *plays* **Private Miles**'s *disbelief.*

Sergeant   Private Miles.

Private Miles *tries to straighten himself.*

Private Miles   Sir.

Sergeant   You will be deployed to Eastern Baghdad at Forward . . . at Forward Operating –

Beat.

Base.

He clears his throat.

Operating Base –

Staring at the sheet, **Sergeant** *tries to focus, but is distracted by* **Chorus**. **Bradley** *sways.*

Sergeant   Hammer.

He discards the paperwork and takes a moment.

How'd you feel about . . . about serving your country, Bradley?

Bradley *sways.*

Bradley   I'd be proud, sir.

Beat.

I thought I was getting kicked out.

Private Miles *looks to the heavens.*

Sergeant   Good. (*Clears throat.*) Good man.

Private Miles   Permission to speak, sir.

Sergeant   Granted.

Private Miles   Sir, should I take Specialist Manning to speak with the Judge Advocate Group, sir?

Chorus *thinks this is a great idea and is about to bundle* **Bradley** *away when . . .*

Sergeant   I have their paperwork here, they've signed off for recycling. It's all. It's signed off.

Chorus *checks the paperwork and is in shock.*

Sergeant   Your skills, are highly valuable to us Specialist. / Highly valuable.

Bradley   Yes, sir.

Sergeant   We need every, every Intel Specialist we have to be on top of their game, because your Brigade Commander will be relying on your briefings before sending his men into theatre.

Beat.

I hope you realise what an important job you have, Specialist, and what a privilege it is to serve in the US Army.

Bradley   Yes sir, / I won't let you down, sir.

Sergeant   Before . . . before deployment, you will be stationed in Fort Drum. Good luck, Manning. You're dismissed.

Bradley *straightens himself and gives a proud salute and starts to march to the door.* **Private Miles** *and the* **Sergeant** *share a look before* **Private Miles** *follows* **Bradley***.*

Private Miles   Sir.

Sergeant   Specialist Manning. Do you have . . . do you have anyone, who can support you through deployment?

Bradley   I have met someone, sir.

Sergeant   You have a *girlfriend*, Manning?

Bradley   Yes sir, I do.

Scene Twenty-One

November 2009.

Forward Operating Base Hammer, Eastern Baghdad.

Tableau sequence.

Computers, paperwork, TV screens are on every wall with live feeds from the war as the US engages the enemy.

Post-It notes are on every computer.

Another **Bradley** *stands watching the screens as his fellow* **Intel Officers** *throw stress toys around, mess about and show each other things on screen that make them laugh.*

They are oblivious to **Bradley**, *and they are oblivious to the horrors of war footage being broadcast on the screens.*

Bradley *is drawn to the screens. He can't escape the screens, as everyone else goes about their work.*

Intel Officer 1 *steals a piece of paper from* **Bradley**.

Intel Officer 1   What you got there, Manning? Oooh! Manning's got his first commendation. Specialist Manning's dedication led to the detainment of Malik Fadil al-Ugayli, a Tier-two level target.

Intel Officer 2   Make sure you tell your mom, Manning.

Intel Officer 1   While you're there, ask her why you're such a faggot, Manning.

Waves of digital information code and intelligence crash over **Bradley**.

Bradley's *head is spun as he turns from screen to screen, standing fixed in one spot; unable to tear himself away from the images he is seeing.*

All the time his colleagues do not look at the footage.

Tableau sequence over.

Intel Officer 2   Hey, anyone else read this CIED Sigact from the Diyala province?

General 'no's.

Intel Officer   Roadside IED, targeting a convoy heading south-east on Miami, carload of civilians manoeuvre off-road to allow convoy passage, activating a roadside IED. Four civilians injured and one dead at the scene, all personnel present and accounted for. HOO-HAAA!

Intel Officers   HOO-HAAA!

Intel Officers *high-five and draw* **Bradley** *into an unwanted high-five.*

Bradley   Yeah.

Intel Officer   HOO-HAA!

Scene Twenty-Two

April 2004.

Tasker Milward V C School.

Class *erupts as* **Mrs Stokes** *is absent.*

Mark *picks up* **Anthony**'s *bag.*

Anthony   Fuck off, Mark.

Mark   You fuck off.

Mark   Your bag smells of ham. Does anyone need a protractor?

Anthony   Why don't you / fucking pick on someone else Mark? Stop being such a prick to me all the time.

Mark   Is there anything anyone needs? Lisa? Protractor, roller-ruler? This pen's got a compass in it, look at that?

That's cool, I'm having that. Bradders, you haven't got a protractor have you?

Anthony   Bradley?

Bradley   Give his stuff back.

Mark   Why? It's Anthony.

Bradley   Mark, come on.

Mark   No way, he's a wanker.

He continues to look in the bag and disregard **Anthony***'s feelings.*

Unable to take it any more, **Bradley** *grabs the bag from* **Mark** *and hands it to* **Anthony***.* **Mark** *retaliates by grabbing it from* **Anthony***.* **Bradley** *grabs it from* **Mark***, there's a tussle and* **Bradley** *finally gets the bag.*

Mark *chases* **Bradley** *around the room while the* **Class** *jeers. The chase ends with* **Bradley** *standing on* **Mrs Stokes***'s desk.*

The **Class** *falls silent as* **Mrs Stokes** *enters.*

Mrs Stokes   What the hell is going on here?

Mark   He stole my bag, miss.

Mrs Stokes   Get down.

Beat.

NOW!

Bradley *gets down from the table.*

Mrs Stokes   I leave the room for two minutes.

Bradley   Miss.

Mrs Stokes   I don't want your excuses, Bradley. Who wants to go and get Mr Roberts?

Whole **Class** *put their hands up except* **Bradley***.*

Scene Twenty-Three

February 2010.

Chorus *are* **Iraqi Federal Police** *and detainees in Iraqi jail. Movement sequence as* **Iraqi Federal Police** *mistreat detainees.*

Bradley *and* **Nidal** *are in FOB Hammer looking over some Sig Acts.*

Bradley   Major Browning asked me to assess your fifteen detainees arrested November ten.

Nidal   Insurgents.

Bradley *shuffles paper.*

Bradley   They weren't armed on arrest.

Nidal   They distribute al-Qaeda literature.

Beat.

They are insurgents.

Bradley   Right.

An **Iraqi Federal Police** *beats detainees.*

Bradley   Where were they / detained?

Nidal   Out. In street.

Bradley   Okay. They were handing out / insurgency literature, in the street.

Nidal   In the street, yes.

IFP *beats another detainee.* **Bradley** *is unnerved.*

Bradley *(urgent)*   Do you have any of their papers? / Where's their papers?

Nidal   Nothing.

Another beating – increasing pressure on **Bradley**.

Bradley   I need more information, what does the literature say?

Nidal   'America Must Die'. They are / insurgents.

Iraqi Federal Police *beats another detainee.*

Bradley   Stop! Listen! We need to find out who these people are, what group they're associated with, why they're just handing stuff out in the street.

Beat.

I need to know who they are. Can we, can we work together, on this?

Beat.

Nidal.

Nidal   Yes.

Bradley   I need to know who / they're working with. I have to write this up.

Nidal   Yes.

Bradley   When you identify these people you're going to liaise with me.

Nidal   Yes.

Bradley   I have to write a report on this. The Major wants a report on this. / I have to identify them, you understand what I'm saying?

Nidal   Yes.

Bradley *is dragged into the beating. He stops it.*

Bradley   They don't look like fighters.

Beat.

Give me what they were handing out.

Nidal *hands over the literature.*

Bradley *takes it, walks to the **Major**'s desk and stands at attention.*

Major   Specialist.

Bradley   Sir. I investigated the fifteen people arrested by the IFP on November 10th. The IFP claimed they were insurgents distributing anti-American literature and were part of a wider organisation.

Major   And?

Bradley   Sir, they're not insurgents.

Beat.

They're just. They're just protestors.

Major   I don't understand.

Bradley   This is the literature the IFP retrieved, I had it translated. It's not anti-American, sir. It's not even anti-Sunni. It's. You can read it for yourself; they're accusing the Iraqi Government of corruption. They're accusing the Iraqi Government of stealing aid.

Beat.

Major   Who authorised this translation?

Bradley   We're wasting our time on them, sir. They're not insurgents.

Major (*louder*)   Who authorised the translation?

Pause.

Bradley   I did, sir.

Silence.

I was using my initiative, sir.

Silence.

I had. I thought. I had suspicions that these weren't. They didn't look like insurgents, sir. I think. By doing this. I've, I've saved us resources so we don't spend time gathering intel on these fifteen / when, when they're just, regular –

Major (*loud*) Your role is to support our brigades on the ground by identifying and tracking insurgents.

Bradley Yes, sir.

Major How the hell does this support our brigades?

He holds up Iraqi translation literature.

Silence.

Bradley I've stopped us wasting time gathering intel / on people who aren't the enemy.

Major How does *this*, help support our brigade?

Silence.

Bradley I've saved resources, sir.

Major Do you have an attitude problem, Specialist?

Bradley Sir, no, sir.

Major Do you have a problem following orders, Specialist?

Bradley Sir, no, sir.

Major If the IFP says that's an insurgent, that's an insurgent. You do not spend time proving their innocence, you spend time finding more! Do you understand, Specialist? You want to show some initiative, come in here in two days' time, and say you've doubled the IFP haul, do I make myself clear?

Beat.

I want more / insurgents, not less!

Scene Twenty-Four

April 2010.

Tyler's *student house.*

Sound of mortar fire and **Chorus** *hits the floor. It could be a post-student house party. It could be dead Iraqi civilians. Some are dead, some are nearly dead.*

Bradley　Security is a fucking joke.

He sits at a laptop. **Tyler** *stands behind him.*

Beat.

Bradley　You forget your pass, you just knock on the door and someone lets you in. Passwords to every computer are on sticky notes pressed on to monitors. Why has no one leaked anything?

Beat.

Tyler　Sounds crazy.

Bradley　Did you read the 9/11 pagers released on WikiLeaks?

Tyler　Uh, no.

Bradley　That definitely came from someone in the NSA because I've read those on the inside.

Beat.

Tyler.

Tyler　What?

Bradley　They can't crack the encryption. Somebody leaked but the FBI can't figure out who. They've got no one. If WikiLeaks don't know who uploaded it, how can the FBI?

Tyler　Bradley –

Bradley   Do you know they brought gravel and pebbles
from Turkey so that the KBR contractors don't get their feet
too dirty when it rains?

Beat.

Man, I'm so glad to be out of that room, I thought I was
going insane. Fourteen hours a day I'm looking at a screen,
or sweeping the floor in the same room. Six days a week, I'm
bombarded with all this information that no one's allowed to
see, and I can see it, as long as I act like I don't care.

Beat.

I can read about plots to assassinate heads of state, but I can't
tell anyone about *you*.

Tyler   Bradley, *listen*, the reason / why I said you needed to
come over this weekend –

Bradley   Sorry, I haven't finished. When I was a kid I used
to hack into programs, because that was the only time I felt
free. Now I don't even need to hack, this stuff is just there.
When I was kid, it was . . . exciting to find stuff. Now, I wish
I hadn't seen half of it.

He looks at the dead bodies.

Yeah.

Beat.

Now I can't get it out of my mind.

Beat.

So. I'm thinking of leaking something myself.

Silence.

I've worked out how I can do it. It's simple. I just take in a
rewritable CD with something like Lady Gaga written on.
Stick it in a machine, and then re-write with all the classified
info and lip-synch while I drag and drop the shit out of those
servers.

He laughs nervously.

Tyler   Okay, just stop / for a minute.

Bradley   There's a video. I just found it in a zip file.

Beat.

It's an Apache helicopter shooting civilians on the street with a thirty-millimetre cannon.

Beat.

And.

Beat.

I *can't* stop watching it.

Beat.

They circle them for a while.

Beat.

You'd think they'd all be looking up at the helicopter, but they can't see or hear it because the Apache's nearly a mile away. They fire and these people don't know where they're being shot at from. Some hide behind a wall, but because they can't see the helicopter they don't realise the helicopter can see them.

Beat.

One guy sort of just . . . explodes.

Beat.

And, I can't, stop, watching it. Nobody asks any questions if you're watching stuff like that because, everyone's watching videos like that.

Beat.

We're supposed to make sense of it.

Silence.

All I can think . . . every time I watch it, I think . . .

Beat.

Maybe *this* time they'll get away.

Beat.

Tyler   Don't look at me. I don't know what you expect me to do with all this.

Beat.

Bradley   I can't be myself, because, if I try to be myself, I have to do something. The longer I'm there, the more I feel like I don't have a choice.

Beat.

I'm sorry I'm just . . . I need a drink or something.

Tyler *looks around the room – can he see the bodies that haunt* **Bradley***? Does a body reach out to* **Tyler** *for help?*

Tyler   I don't want you using all your leave to come see me.

Bradley (*flirty*)   Shut up.

Tyler   I don't want you using all your leave on me.

Bradley   I *want* to come see you.

Tyler   I know.

He backs away from the bodies.

I just think you should use your . . . Maybe some other folks would like to see you; I don't want to hog / you from your family.

Bradley   Who am I going to go and see? My dad?

Tyler   You know what / I'm saying.

Bradley   Being stupid, Tyler.

Tyler   I'm thinking of you.

Bradley   And I think of you every single second I'm in that box. I count down the hours till I can see you again.

Bradley *kisses* **Tyler**. **Tyler** *is non-committal.*

Tyler   I know.

Bradley *senses* **Tyler***'s distancing.*

Bradley   What?

Tyler   It's nothing.

Bradley   You're such a headfuck.

Tyler   I'm sorry.

He backs away from the bodies.

It's just. I've got finals coming up. You're a *soldier.*

Silence.

I'm just a student.

Beat.

We're just.

Beat.

I've got, finals coming up.

Scene Twenty-Five

May 2004.

Tasker Milward V C School.

Mrs Stokes   You've *all* got finals coming up. So today we're going to concentrate on Chartism and the Newport Rising. Lisa, stop talking.

Beat.

In 1839, the last armed rebellion against the government on mainland Britain descended on Newport. Who's John Frost, Gavin?

Gavin   Chartist, miss.

Mrs Stokes   Chartist leader, Gavin. He'd made more public speeches, written more pamphlets than anyone else. But now the rising was happening, he wasn't sure it was the right thing to do and he tried to persuade the workers to go back home but they refused. Mark, stop talking.

Beat.

So did John Frost turn his back on history and go back to writing and thinking about change? Or did he take action? Lisa?

Lisa   Um . . .

Mrs Stokes   What did John Frost do?

Lisa   Um . . . he like. Was he. / No, hang on. I know.

Mrs Stokes   Bradley, stand by the board and write the names of anyone who tries to talk while I'm talking. The last person on the board at the end of the class gets detention. You keep an eye on the class, in case I miss anyone.

Bradley *gets up, picks up a piece of chalk.*

Mrs Stokes (*to* **Bradley**)   Lisa.

Bradley *writes 'Lisa' on the board.*

Mrs Stokes   He took action, and led the uprising. He was arrested and sent to Australia for his part. (*To* **Bradley**.) Gavin.

This time **Bradley** *takes his time writing 'Gavin'.*

Mrs Stokes   John Frost is one name in a long list of Welsh radicals. I want you to show wider reading in your exams, so you have a task. Go home and research on the internet the following people: Gwynfor Evans, James Keir Hardie,

Tyrone O'Sullivan, the Women for Life on Earth, Aneurin Bevan. All these people found themselves at pivotal moments in history and had no choice but to act – such was the power of their convictions. Mark, are you chewing gum?

Mark   No, miss.

Mrs Stokes   Then you're talking. Bradley.

Bradley *doesn't respond.*

Mrs Stokes   Bradley, put Mark's name down.

Bradley *doesn't. He puts the chalk down and heads to his desk.*

Mrs Stokes   What are you doing, Bradley?

Bradley   I'm not putting anyone else's name on the board.

Mrs Stokes   Why not?

Bradley   I'm just not.

Beat.

Mrs Stokes   Fine, I'll get someone / else to do it.

Bradley   I don't think anyone else should either.

Mrs Stokes   What do you mean by that?

Bradley   I don't think any of us should. We don't have to help you punish us.

He sits down.

Mrs Stokes   Lisa. Go to the front please, pick up some chalk. As I was saying, these figures in history –

Lisa *doesn't move.*

Mrs Stokes   Lisa.

Beat.

Go to the front.

Beat.

Gavin. Front of the class please. Pick up a piece of chalk.

Gavin   No, I'm alright here, miss, I want to get all this down.

Mrs Stokes   Mark? Front of the class.

Beat.

Mark   I've done it before, miss.

Mrs Stokes   I don't want to have to put you in detention. What's the matter with you?

Scene Twenty-Six

May 2010.

Forward Operating Base Hammer.

One ensemble member plays **Counsellor**. *Rest of ensemble play* **Bradley** *as he increasingly 'fractures' into two, then three, then four, then five, further and further apart. Ensemble are to elaborate on choral delivery.*

Bradley   If I knew I wouldn't be here.

Counsellor   How is work? And your relationship? What do you want to talk about, Bradley?

Bradley   You have no idea, what it's like trying to talk to you.

Deaf Counsellor   I'm a trained army therapist. I know acute stress when I see it. What's the first thing that comes to mind?

Bradley   Command, asked me to look into . . . why, these two groups were meeting in Basra.

Beat.

Recommended a sourcing mission.

Beat.

Did not recommend; engagement.

Counsellor   But they were engaged. What did the log say, was it enemy or friendly action?

Bradley   Log said enemy.

Silence.

Why would, the CCIR warn against negative publicity?

Beat.

Why say that, if they were enemy kills?

Beat.

Counsellor   You have to trust the OIC.

Bradley   I do.

Beat.

I don't know, what, they're dealing with.

Counsellor   Why is this troubling you?

Silence.

Bradley   I read, on my girlfriend's, Facebook status . . . She now considers herself . . .

Beat.

Single.

Counsellor   Your relationship is over?

Bradley   Not for, for me, seems that way for hi – her.

Counsellor   How were things when you last saw her?

Very long silence.

Bradley   She's in Brandeis so.

Beat.

Everyone.

Beat.

That's her status. Only it's patently not.

Beat.

There's someone halfway, halfway round the world, in a warzone. Crying. I'm crying every night because I, because she, she won't reply to any messages.

Beat.

What he . . . What she's put. I want. I. Her relationship status is not true. It's not true. It might be what, she wants, but it's not that's not . . . how it is.

Beat.

I've.

Beat.

She's got all the . . .

Mute Counsellor *nods in understanding.*

Bradley   I can't see how, someone . . . can try to just, wipe someone from existence. How can? How can someone just deny a year-long relationship ever existed, with a sentence?

Pause.

And . . . it's got me thinking, you know. About the logs.

He looks at the bodies.

Why would we ever record a mistake?

Silence.

Counsellor   Because we're the professionals.

Bradley   That gives us every reason not to record mistakes.

I. Some guy . . . left his house today, and four hundred klicks away I couldn't decide what his politics were from his fucking cell use, so he got shot in the head.

Beat.

You know, it's, it's just one. It's just one letter . . . on a, on a keypad. Add an E to the KIA and no one asks any questions. Enemy killed in action.

Beat.

The world can't be like this, or I can't be in it.

Scene Twenty-Seven

February 2011.

Quantico brig.

Bradley *makes sounds to reacquaint himself with his voice.*

Bradley   I'M KINDA BUSY K-K-K KINDA BUSY.

Beat.

K-K-K-K-K-K-K-KINDA BUSY.

I-I-I-I-I-I'M KINDA CHAPTER FIFTEEN.

CH-CH-CH-CHAPTER FIFTEEN.

CHA-CHA-CHA!

He makes more sounds reacquainting himself with his voice.

I-I-I-I-I-I-I-I-I-I-I-I-I –

Beat.

I missss.

Beat.

MMMMmmmiiiissssssss –

I miss.

Beat.

I missssssss –

Beat.

My mother.

He makes sounds.

Beat.

Gay.

Beat.

Chapter fifteen.

Beat.

Gay.

Beat.

G-uuhh –

Beat.

G-uuuuuuhhhh –

Beat.

G-uuuhhhaaaaayyyyy. Gay. Gay. Gay. Gay.

Maximum!

Beat.

Maximum.

Beat.

Maxi-mum.

Beat.

Maxi-mum. Maxinum. Mnaxinum. Aximum. Maxinum. Manaximum. Manningaximum. Manaxing. Man. Man. Mannnnnnning. Mannnnning. Manning.

Beat.

Manning. Mmm.

Manning. Mmm.

Beat.

MMMMmmmmmmmm.

He makes sounds as if he's warming up his voice.

A meal slides out from under the door into the middle of the room.

FOOD! F-F-F-F-FOOOOOOOD. DUH. DUH. DUH. Beans!

Thanks!

Beat.

Thank you!

Beat.

Thank you for my food! Foood!

Silence.

Confronted with the silence, **Bradley** *turns to his food. He tries to eat but can't.*

He stares at the plate.

Beat.

He screams with frustration and hurls the plate and food against a wall.

As the plate hits the wall, a female **Chorus** *hits the floor.*

Scene Twenty-Eight

May 2010.

Forward Operating Base Hammer.

Chorus *stands as one with* **Commander**.

Commander   Specialist Manning, you have been reported for striking an officer!

Holding his gun, **Bradley** *stands before a* **Commander**.
Chorus *bodies sprawl around.*

Commander   Do you have anything to say on the matter?

Bradley   No sir!

Commander   I am issuing you with Company Grade
Article Fifteen; you will be reduced in rank to Private.

Beat.

Hand me your weapon.

Bradley   My weapon, sir?

Commander *takes* **Bradley**'s *gun from him.* **Commander**
stares at **Bradley**. **Bradley** *looks straight ahead.*

Commander   Behavioural Health sent me your psych
files.

He turns pages.

Anything you want to say, Private?

Long pause.

Bradley   No, sir.

Silence.

I thought . . . my medical files were, confidential, sir.

Commander *thumbs through the files.*

Commander   Anything else you want to say, Private?

Silence.

He turns a page.

Silence.

He turns a page.

Silence.

He turns a page.

Silence.

He turns a page.

Silence.

He turns a page.

Bradley   Can I ask why you took my weapon, sir?

Commander *turns a page.*

Commander   Because I have to ensure the safety of everyone on this base. Including yourself, Manning.

Bradley   I'm not a risk to myself or anyone else, sir.

Commander   I have a female sergeant with a bust lip that might disagree with you, Manning.

Silence.

He turns another page.

Silence.

The Behavioural Unit has put your actions down to 'adjustment disorder'.

Beat.

Your time at FOB Hammer is over. In three days' time you will be back in Fort Leavenworth where the Discharge Unit will start to process you and end your military service.

Beat.

I want you to take the last few days of your security clearance to finish any unwritten reports, liaise with Specialist Marino so we have continuity with briefings, then you will be assigned to the Supply Office while you wait for redeployment to the States. Your discharge cannot jeopardise any ongoing operations. The war is over / for you, Manning.

Bradley   Sir, I lost my temper, but I still have a lot to offer the Brigade.

Commander (*reading*)   'The persona I'm forced to take on, is killing the fuck out of me.'

Bradley (*rising*)   Sir, I understood my counselling to be confidential.

Commander (*rising*)   'I don't know, I think I'm weird, I guess. I can't separate myself from others. I feel connected to everybody, like they were a distant family.'

Bradley (*rising*)   Sir, that's . . .

Commander   'Specialist Manning recalled dressing as a woman while on leave.'

Bradley (*rising*)   THAT IS NOT YOUR BUS / INESS.

Commander   IT IS MY BUSINESS BECAUSE I DON'T TRUST / YOU.

Bradley   AND I DON'T TRUST YOU! I'M NOT A FUCKING PIECE OF EQUIPMENT!

Commander   YOUR CAREER IS OVER, MANNING. AND SO IS YOUR WAR. DISMISSED.

Bradley *turns.*

Commander   Salute your superior officer.

With zero respect, **Bradley** *salutes.*

Scene Twenty-Nine

May 2010.

Bradley *and the Lady Gaga huge download.*

Intel Officer 2   Hey, Manning, I've sent you the video of the Hellfire taking a guy's head off.

Bradley *stands in the Intel room.*

Intel Officers *sit around, as usual chewing gum, watching videos, listening to music and throwing stress balls around.*

Bradley   Great.

Intel Officer 2   Boom!

Bradley *sits at a computer console.*

The rest of the department go about their business. Passing files around, logging reports. Answering phones, working on computers.

Trying to hide his fears, **Bradley** *looks around the room.*

He takes a deep, long breath.

Pause.

Professionally, **Bradley** *goes to his bag and gets a CD out. He puts headphones on.*

He puts a CD into a computer and starts to mine the data and transfer it to his CD.

Quietly, **Bradley** *starts mouthing the words to Lady Gaga's 'Born This Way'.*

Bradley *finally finds himself using his anonymity for good.*

Tableau sequence.

Spotlight on Bradley at his computer, spotlight on **Lady Gaga** *singing 'Born This Way'.*

Lady Gaga *intercepts* **Intel Officers** *as they try to engage* **Bradley** *with work; she acts as an intermediary, passing papers, cables, passes, coffee, around to protect* **Bradley**.

Secret embassy cables and war logs from the Afghan and Iraq Wars fall on the audience.

At some point in the sequence, all **Intel Officers** *hit the floor and form the dead bodies that have haunted* **Bradley**. *One by one one, they come alive to become:*

Another **Bradley** *at the Prop 8 March.*

Another **Bradley** *dressed as a soldier cries, surrounded by his property.*

Another **Bradley** *lies in cell.*

Another **Bradley** *serves coffee.*

Another **Bradley** *stands on a desk in a Welsh costume.*

Scene Thirty

March 2011.

Bradley *in Quantico brig.*

He breaks down as he is tortured with repetitive questioning.

Marine   Detainee 4335453, are you okay?

Bradley   Yes.

Marine   Detainee 4335453, are you okay?

Bradley   Yes.

Marine   Detainee 4335453, are you okay?

Bradley   Yes.

Marine   Detainee 4335453, are you okay?

Bradley   Yes. I'm fine.

Marine   Detainee 4335453, are you okay?

Bradley   Yes.

Marine   Detainee 4335453, are you okay?

Bradley   Yes.

Marine   Detainee 4335453, are you okay?

Bradley   Yes.

Marine   Detainee 4335453, are you okay?

Bradley   Yes. We don't have to do this every five minutes.

Marine   Detainee 4335453, are you okay?

Bradley   Yes.

Marine   Detainee 4335453, are you okay?

Bradley   Yes.

Marine   Detainee 4335453, are you okay?

Bradley   Yes.

Marine   Detainee 4335453, are you okay?

Bradley   Yes.

Marine   Detainee 4335453, are you okay?

Bradley   Yes.

Marine   Detainee 4335453, are you okay?

Bradley   Yes.

Marine   Detainee 4335453, are you okay?

Bradley   Yes.

Marine   Detainee 4335453, are you okay?

Bradley   Yes.

Marine   Detainee 4335453, are you okay?

Bradley   Yes.

Marine   Detainee 4335453, are you okay?

Bradley   Yes.

Marine   Detainee 4335453, are you okay?

Bradley   Yes.

Marine   Detainee 4335453, are you okay?

Bradley   Yes.

Marine   Detainee 4335453, are you okay?

Bradley   Yes.

Marine   Detainee 4335453, are you okay?

Bradley   Yes.

Marine   Detainee 4335453, are you okay?

Bradley   Yes. I'm not a risk to myself.

Marine   Detainee 4335453, are you okay?

Bradley   Yes.

Marine   Detainee 4335453, are you okay?

Bradley   Yes.

Marine   Detainee 4335453, are you okay?

Bradley   Yes.

Marine   Detainee 4335453, are you okay?

Bradley   Yes.

Marine   Detainee 4335453, are you okay?

Bradley   Yes.

Marine   Detainee 4335453, are you okay?

Bradley   Yes.

Marine   Detainee 4335453, are you okay?

Bradley   Yes.

Marine   Detainee 4335453, are you okay?

Bradley   Yes.

Marine   Detainee 4335453, are you okay?

Bradley   Yes.

Marine   Detainee 4335453, are you okay?

Bradley   Yes.

Marine   Detainee 4335453, are you okay?

Bradley   Yes.

Marine   Detainee 4335453, are you okay?

Bradley   Yes.

Marine   Detainee 4335453, are you okay?

Bradley   Yes.

Marine   Detainee 4335453, are you okay?

Bradley   Yes.

Marine   Detainee 4335453, are you okay?

Bradley   Yes.

Marine   Detainee 4335453, are you okay?

Bradley   Yes.

Marine   Detainee 4335453, are you okay?

Bradley   Yes.

Marine   Detainee 4335453, are you okay?

Bradley   Yes.

Marine   Detainee 4335453, are you okay?

Bradley   Yes.

Marine   Detainee 4335453, are you okay?

Bradley   Yes.

Marine   Detainee 4335453, are you okay?

Bradley   Yes.

Marine   Detainee 4335453, are you okay?

Bradley   Yes.

Marine   Detainee 4335453, are you okay?

Bradley *gathers himself.*

Bradley   Yes.

Marine   Detainee 4335453, are you okay?

Bradley *stands up and stands to attention.*

Bradley   Yes.

Marine   Detainee 4335453, are you okay?

Bradley   Yes.

Marine   Detainee 4335453, are you okay?

Bradley   Yes.

Black.

On screen:

February 28th 2013, the US Government finally brought Bradley to court. He had been in jail for 1,025 days.

The legal limit without trial is 120 days.

Bradley took full responsibility for the leaking of information to WikiLeaks, pleading guilty to ten of twenty-two charges.

Amnesty International has called on the US Government to drop the charge of 'aiding the enemy', which carries the death penalty.

Judge Colonel Denise Lind ruled that any sentence Bradley receives will be reduced by 112 days, due his torture at the Quantico Brig.

The twenty-five-year-old has been nominated for the Nobel Peace Prize three years running.

President Obama has imprisoned more whistleblowers than every other President in the history of the United States of America, combined.

Bradley's court martial continues.

Scene Thirty-One

May 2004.

Tasker Milward V C School.

Mrs Stokes   Detention over!

Class *bursts out of its chairs.*

Mrs Stokes   Except you, Bradley.

He sits back down. They are alone.

Do you like it here?

He shrugs.

Think you might stay here?

Bradley   I don't know.

Silence.

Mrs Stokes   I thought you were going to try and take a deep breath for me before opening your mouth and getting into trouble.

Bradley   I kept my promise.

Mrs Stokes   So why did I just have a whole class revolting against me?

Bradley   I did what you / said.

Mrs Stokes   No you didn't, you got into an argument like you always do.

Bradley   No, I did what you said.

Beat.

Mrs Stokes   And?

Bradley   It worked. I got clarity.

Silence.

Mrs Stokes   I don't know how your mam copes with you.

He shrugs.

Bradley   I'm sort of. Taking care of her.

Beat.

Me and Anthony, we've built this website, it's sort of like a news aggregator, and social network for the county. People can come and post local news and stuff. Hoping that'll take off.

Beat.

We need the money.

Mrs Stokes   Is that what you'd like to do? Run something like Apple?

Silence.

Bradley I don't know.

Beat.

I'm smart, I can do stuff. But I want to use it to help people. I see all these people walking around and. None of them know how much I can help them.

Mrs Stokes That's very noble. I don't hear many boys your age talk about a desire to serve their community.

Beat.

Bradley I guess that's why I think I'll probably join the US Army.

Mrs Stokes Why's that?

Bradley We have to protect our country. I love America.

Beat.

Mrs Stokes Don't you love Wales?

Bradley Yeah. But.

Beat.

If I want to help people, make the world a better place I can't think of anywhere better than the US Army.

Mrs Stokes I don't want you to join the army.

Beat.

Bradley I don't have a choice, miss.

Lights down.

The End.

I'm With the Band

For my band
Franklin and Chloë

'People who make music together cannot be enemies,
at least while the music lasts'

Paul Hindemith

I'm With the Band was first performed at the Traverse Theatre, Edinburgh, in a co-production with Wales Millennium Centre, on 2 August 2013. The cast was as follows:

Aaron   Declan Rodgers
Barry   Andy Clark
Damien   James Hillier
Gruff   Matthew Bulgo

Director   Hamish Pirie
Designer   Neil Warmington
Composer, Sound Designer Gordon McIntyre
Lighting Designer   Philip Gladwell
Fight Director   Raymond Short
Movement Director   Tom Pritchard
Assistant Director   Ronan Phelan

Acknowledgements

Orla O'Loughlin and all at the Traverse, Gareth Lloyd Roberts and all at Wales Millennium Centre, all at the British Council Showcase, Gordon McIntyre, Ronan Phelan, Matthew Bulgo, Andy Clark, Declan Rodgers, James Hillier, Lynda Radley, David Ireland, J. S. Duffy, Andrew Hawley, Roger Evans, Cian O'Siochain, Nicky Lund, Cathy King, Anna Brewer and all at Methuen Drama, Gary Marsh, Mark Jefferies, Menna, Philip, Matthew, Maryline, Joseph and Sophia Price.

Special thanks to: Hamish Pirie, for knowing when to be true to the sentiment rather than the word, and for teaching me that risk is the only way to play safe.

Note on the music

In the Traverse / Wales Millennium Centre production of this play in 2013 the brilliant Gordon McIntyre wrote the music and lyrics. In future productions, the music should be created anew for each distinct band. As such, the lyrics to the song in Scene Five and the instructions Damien shouts should be changed to suit any new music and lyrics. Scripted lines that are sung can be rearranged to fit music, as long as the sentiment and key information remain the same. Any references to music in the script can be changed to suit the music.

Characters

Damien Ross, *England – piano*
Barry Douglas, *Scotland – guitar*
Gruff Mwyn, *Wales – bass*
Aaron Adair, *Northern Ireland – drums*

The cast is to remain on stage at all times, creating music and sound throughout the play. A theatrical grammar should be found to signify when characters are not in the scene. The band is never quite in a song, and never quite in a play.

A large comma **,** used on a line by itself is a beat or pause. It can also indicate when music is being played.

A dash – indicates an interruption of thought or hesitation.

An oblique / indicates when the next line should be spoken.

A double oblique // indicates when the line after the next line should be spoken.

Parentheses (. . .) indicate words or phrases that can be left unspoken, at the discretion of director and cast.

Asterisks ******** indicate a sound effect that masks a word or line of dialogue.

Text in ***boldface italic*** indicates a line of dialogue that is not spoken but expressed through a musical instrument.

Quote marks ' . . . ' indicate lines that are sung.

Scene One

Damien   Track one. 'We're All in This Together'. One, two, three, four.

Band play soft indie-rock song called 'We're All in This Together'.
Damo *dominates the stage and performance and treats the band as a backing band.*

Track two. The Financial Crisis.

Aaron *counts four beats on his drum sticks.*

Damien   Nice one, guys, that's nearly there. Before you go we've got a bit of business / we need to catch up on.

Barry   When are we booked to record that?

Damien   I'm / not sure.

Aaron   You know it's ten years ago to the day we had our first number one? / I got us a cake.

Damien   Yeah / guys, I've got a bit of business.

Gruff   Am I allowed a piece?

Aaron   It's for all of us.

Gruff   Did you say you baked it?

Aaron   I baked it, aye.

,

So I baked a cake? / What's wrong with that?

Barry   You'll be menstruating / next.

Aaron   Fuck you.

Gruff *pulls* **Aaron**'*s trousers down,* **Aaron** *pulls them back up without breaking thought.*

Aaron   I baked a cake, people celebrate occasions with cake, it's better than booze.

Barry   I'm sorry, mate, I just love the idea of you in an apron.

Aaron *goes to cut the cake.*

Barry   Food fight.

Gruff *and* **Barry** *try to force* **Aaron**'s *face into the cake.*

Damien   It's quite important! Barry, it's serious. So guys, um – is that cake for me?

Aaron   It's for all of us.

Damien   Right, so guys –

Barry   I probably won't get a piece.

Aaron   Have some.

Damien   Guys. It's. Everyone – so. Um . . . I've uh. When we were – When. Martin.

,

Barry   Get on with it.

Damien   I don't know how to say it.

He noodles the piano.

'Guys. I've been meaning to . . . I've been wanting to . . . I don't want to panic you. I've got something to say to you.

,

Guys, you know, Martin our manager set up a company for us? He set up a company, for the band, to manage our finances, the cashflow, the PRS, and the bills, and collective expenses.

,

But, Martin, Martin didn't our pay any VAT. For twelve years, twelve years, twelve years, twelve years, he didn't pay VAT. No VAT. return.

,

Now the taxman, taxman, taxman, taxman he wants all his dough, dough, dough, dough, and he wants something like **** million pounds!

,

And we've got to find the dough, to make the dough to earn the dough, and pay it back or we're all, going to jail.'

Barry **** million quid?

Gruff **** million?

Aaron **** million?

Damien Something like that, yeah.

Barry Oh my God.

,

Barry 'We're fucked, we're fucked, we're fucking bankrupt. We're fucked, we're fucked, we're fucking bankrupt. We're fucked, we're fucked, we're fucking bankrupt. We're fucked, we're fucked, we're fucking bankrupt. We're fucked, we're fucked, we're fucking bankrupt. We're fucked, we're fucked, we're fucking bankrupt. We're fucked, we're fucked, we're fucking bankrupt. We're fucked, we're fucked, we're fucking bankrupt. / We're fucked, we're fucked, we're fucking bankrupt. We're fucked, we're fucked, we're fucking bankrupt. We're fucked, we're fucked, we're fucking bankrupt. We're fucked, we're fucked, we're fucking bankrupt. We're fucked, we're fucked, we're fucking bankrupt. We're fucked, we're fucked, we're fucking bankrupt. We're fucked, we're fucked, we're fucking bankrupt. We're fucked, we're fucked, we're fucking bankrupt. We're fucked, we're fucked, we're fucking bankrupt. We're fucked, we're fucked, we're fucking bankrupt. We're fucked, we're fucked, we're fucking bankrupt. We're fucked, we're fucked, we're fucking bankrupt. We're fucked, we're fucked, we're fucking bankrupt. We're fucked, we're fucked, we're fucking bankrupt. We're fucked, we're fucked, we're fucking bankrupt.'

Gruff   'Can we sue him? Can we sue him? I've got mouths to feed, can we sue him? Can we sue him? Can we sue him? I've got mouths to feed, can we sue him? Can we sue him? Can we sue him? I've got mouths to feed, can we sue him? Can we sue him? Can we sue him? I've got mouths to feed, can we sue him? / Can we sue him? Can we sue him? I've got mouths to feed, can we sue him? Can we sue him? Can we sue him? I've got mouths to feed, can we sue him? Can we sue him? Can we sue him? I've got mouths to feed, can we sue him? Can we sue him? Can we sue him? I've got mouths to feed, can we sue him? Can we sue him? Can we sue him? I've got mouths to feed, can we sue him? Can we sue him? Can we sue him? I've got mouths to feed, can we sue him? Can we sue him? Can we sue him? I've got mouths to feed, can we sue him? Can we sue him? Can we sue him? I've got mouths to feed, can we sue him?'

Aaron   'This is negligence! This is negligence! I won't lose my house because of negligence! This is negligence! This is negligence! I won't lose my house because of negligence! / This is negligence! This is negligence! I won't lose my house because of negligence! This is negligence! This is negligence! I won't lose my house because of negligence! This is negligence! This is negligence! I won't lose my house because of negligence!'

Damien   'Technically, we're still trading, trading, trading, trading, so we have to pay the debt. And it might be negligent but we can't sue no no no, it's not an option.'

Barry, **Aaron** *and* **Gruff**   'Why not? Why not? Why not?'

Damien   'Because I, sacked him. I sacked him, I sacked him, I didn't follow the right dismissal procedure when I sacked him, when I sacked, I forfeited our right to sue him when I sacked him. I was really fucking angry, when I sacked him and now we've got loads of debt.' Sort of the long and the short of it.

,

But what's important guys, we're all in this together.

Gruff   Phew, I / thought I was gonna have to pay it all back myself.

Barry   Are we fuck? I fucking knew this would happen, / I fucking knew we shouldn't hand complete control – fuck you! Fuck this. Fuck all of – I'm out of here.

Aaron   We can pay it off! / We'll // do some private shows. Some Russians. Do a tour. Fucking diversify, whatever. We'll pay it off.

Damien   Yeah. Might take a bit more than that but yeah.

Barry   Can we fuck? Have you any idea how long it'll take to pay that off? / We're absolutely fucked. I'm out of here.

Aaron   It's just a rough patch. Like when they lost my bike at the Sydney Iron Man. / I didn't quit. I just did it on a . . .

Damien   I can't handle another Iron Man story right now, Aaron.

Aaron   Where's he gone?

Gruff   Anyone want this?

Barry   Track three. The Referendum.

,

,

Three, four.

Scene Two

Damien *and* **Barry** *square up in a guitar duel.*

Barry   I don't want it.

Damien   *Everyone else took their slice home.*

Barry   I don't want anything to do with you or your cake.

Damien   *But if you don't have your slice, I'll never hear the end of it.*

Barry   I don't feel like celebrating.

Damien   *It's double chocolate gateau. Remember that one we had in Rome. After Aaron was arrested. This one's not so good. Come on, I've brought it round for you, / I want you to have it.*

Barry   I kind of feel like someone's already had my piece. I kind of feel, like you're throwing me some crumbs.

Damien   That's not fair.

Barry   *Why don't you stick your cake up your arse?*

Damien   That's just rude.

Barry   *Maybe, maybe I need to bake my own fucking cake? Maybe it's time I bake a cake exactly how I fucking like it. Madeira, sprinkes all that shit you don't like. And if it's just me at the table no one can take it away from me. I'm a good chef. No one / seems to realise that.*

Damien   Look. I hear what you're saying. Loud and clear. But we sort of need you to get over it and get back to work.

Barry   *I'm baking my own fucking sweet little Madeira with cherries and cream and all the works, just for me.*

Damien   Is this one of your tantrums or is this serious?

Barry   *What's it fucking look like to you?*

Damien   There's no point talking to you when you're like this.

Barry   *No point talking to me ever again.*

Damien   Are you being serious? We always said, we'd talk about this, if this day ever came, I deserve a – We need to talk through / together because – we need to make this decision together.

Barry   *You don't get a say if I leave the band or not.*

Damien   We always said we'd talk about this.

Barry   *We're talking now.*

Damien   I'm not saying you need my permission to leave the band (I didn't say permission, you said permission), I'm saying, we always said, if either of us ever wanted to leave we'd talk about it before doing anything. You can't – you shouldn't do anything until we've talked about it, it's not fair.

Barry   *I don't need your permission to leave the band.*

Damien   (Why are you talking as if there's a band left?) The band *is* me and you, we are the band, if you leave, there is no band it's just me and a pair of fucking clowns.

Barry   *Not my problem.*

Damien   This is the way you want to leave the band? Shouting and swearing at me? When we're good there's no one who can touch us. You think I want to sing about girls for *another* ten years?

Barry   You can sing about whatever the fuck you like. I'm not gonna stop you now, am I?

Gruff   This song's called The Red Hand of Ulster Grips. One, two, three.

Scene Three

Aaron *enters and 'warms down', co-opting* **Barry** *into various routines.*

Aaron   You're not stopping me, no, I was running this way, and, my route passes this way and I saw Karen and we were chatting and she said I should pop by, say hello.

,

Hello.

Damien   'Barry and Aaron. They're old friends. Have you ever seen old friends, who love each other? That don't really know each other. Old friends.'

Barry   I was rehearsing.

Aaron   Sounds good. I can totally see why you don't want to tour, we've got no techs, no hotels, no catering, it's like we never released a record.

,

Sinead knows something's up. She knows because my training's been all to cock since all this Martin business. I keep getting lost. I go for runs, I've got my route sorted out, and then I start thinking about, and before I know it, I'm in a car park, or a motorway.

,

I had to ring her the other day to come pick me up. Yeah – that was. And.

,

Stuck in a field!

,

One day I didn't even leave the house. Just sat there in my

,

kit. Sh / – Yeah.

Barry   I've got to crack on with this.

Aaron   Yeah sure, I've got another

,

fourteen, fifteen miles to do so, you know we can sort – you know. I can talk to Damo. He listens to me. Just don't. You know, I know the tour sounds shite but, don't lose sight of the goal. Don't lose sight of the – me.

Barry   Aaron.

Aaron   Whatever it is / we can figure it, Damo listens to me.

Barry   Aaron.

Aaron   Whatever you need.

Barry   I can't be arsed.

Aaron   I get up at five every morning to cycle twenty miles, that's not good enough.

Barry   I really can't / be arsed.

Aaron   Be arsed. Be arsed for me. Talk / to Karen.

Barry   She wants me to leave.

Aaron   Let me talk / to Karen.

Barry   I can't be arsed with it any more.

Aaron   What's the real reason? What's the real reason? / There's a real reason, what's the real reason? Is it me?

Barry   The real reason is, mate, the band, which I was getting tired of anyway, is fucked. Do you understand that? It's over. It's fucked. And I cannot be arsed trying to make something work, that I can't be arsed with any more anyway. I'm forty-two.

Aaron   That's not the real reason.

Barry   I'm forty-two.

Aaron   You don't think I can cope with a tour.

Barry   Leave it, Aaron.

Aaron   Iron Men / not good enough for you?

Barry   Fuck off, Aaron. / It's not about you.

Aaron   Give me a reason then.

Damien   'Old friends. Nothing like old friends. Nothing can hurt like an old friend. Nothing left to hurt but an old friend.'

Barry   Because the first time I picked up a guitar to just play, in years, was this week. / I'm a guitarist and I only play if someone pays me.

Aaron   Please come back. For me. Without you it's the fucking / Damo-show.

Barry   It's the fucking Damo-show anyway, it's always been the, and I'm out of it now anyway. I don't care, even if we didn't have massive – this afternoon making music my own in my pants has been the most fun I've had in, ever. / I've been thinking about leaving for ages and I just didn't have the guts. There's the real reason. I got sick of being a coward.

Aaron   You just need some stamina. You are perfectly capable of living alongside someone you detest; I know.

Barry   I'm not talking about you and Sinead.

Aaron   Me and Sinead still live under the same roof. Doesn't mean I don't wish her a long and protracted terminal illness. But I'm focused on the goal, the finish line. I will get the deeds to that house or I will die trying. Or she will. Your problem is –

Barry   What?

Aaron   No, it doesn't matter.

Barry   What?

Aaron   No.

Barry   Go on.

Aaron   I play music like this. I can see the – everything. It's all there and I feed off it. You. You're like this. No matter what's going on around you. You're like this. There could be people having sex on stage with kitchen utensils and you wouldn't know. Because it's all about your pedal board. Your monitors. Your sound. So for you it's always the grass is greener because you're always looking down. You can't even see what's in front of you because you're so fucking – you can't even see that you've hurt me.

,

That I'm sad. You've made me sad. And you're making me. / And you don't even know.

Barry   I'm just leaving the band, I haven't died.

Aaron   You're the fucking reason I joined the band!

Barry   That was like, / fifteen years ago!

Aaron   You're the reason I joined the band, / you fucking navel-gazing prick!

Barry   What a weird thing to say? / Why would you say that?

Aaron   The other two are bandmates. *We* are mates. We were mates *before* the band.

,

It doesn't matter.

Barry   It obviously does because you / wouldn't have come all the way over to my – to say . . . to make me . . . you obviously . . .

Aaron   Why didn't you even talk to me about this? Why didn't you consult me? Didn't you think I deserved a heads-up, I'm trying to train for an Iron Man, do you know how it made me feel hearing you were leaving *from Damo*? / It was like . . . I'm *no* different. Like we've got *no* history.

Barry   I only made up my mind / when I was talking to Damo.

Aaron   You could have taken me aside, / you could have said, hang on, Damo, I need to speak to Aaron about something.

Barry   This wasn't planned, I wasn't out to – I didn't think, how can I maximise / the amount of pain Aaron feels in this situation, I wasn't thinking about you!

Aaron   You said you'd been thinking about – exactly! That's exactly my point, you didn't think about me. / You gave me no thought whatsoever! Thank you. Thank you very –

Barry   The debt was the final straw.

Aaron   Why leave me out of it till the final straw? Why not tell me about all the other straws? I should be in your – I should be the *first* person you tell if you're thinking of – I should be the first – Why didn't you tell me you were planning to leave? / I tell you first whenever I'm doing a new race.

Barry   I don't know, maybe because you're always jogging / or swimming or fucking doing yoga.

Aaron   Well, maybe I'm doing that because you got me addicted to cocaine and booze and turned your back on me. Think about that? I don't *want* to run twenty miles a day. I don't want to do any of this shit. It's boring. Look at that. That's not meant to be that colour. But I'm *scared* what will happen if I don't.

Damien   'Hold him. Hold him, he wants you to hold him. Hold him. Hold him or you won't hold on to him.'

Barry   Mate.

,

Aaron   No! You brought me into this band, and you fucked me up, and now you're leaving me. But do you know what drives me insane? That I've got to fucking explain this shit to you. Do you even want a drummer?

Barry   No, / I'm doing it all myself.

Aaron   Fuck you.

Damien   Are you two ready? 'Welsh Self-Esteem' by Gruff Mwyn and Barry Douglas. Take it away, guys.

Scene Four

Gruff *hands* **Barry** *a guitar.*

Gruff   You're welcome.

Barry   Here's my new demo I've been working on.

,

,

,

Barry   But you know, there's a version that could be really like, you know, Radio Two-friendly, you know, clean and then there's the sort of Radio Six version that's dirty and massive and goes on for fourteen minutes, you know, and there's the version sort of somewhere between Radio Six and Radio Two. / It's sort of got that flexibility.

Gruff   What? Radio Four?

Barry   It could be anything right now, that's the good thing about this song, it's not really one thing or the other, it could go either way really, you know. I could do this version.

,

,

Then there's this sort of version. It's dead flexible.

,

,

Then there's this one.

,

,

,

Or a bit more –

,

,

,

Not into it? OK, maybe even there's sort of this –

,

,

,

No? How about?

,

,

,

There's this?

,

,

That's rubbish? This?

,

,

How about this?

,

,

No? Got loads.

,

,

Or maybe?

,

,

This

,

,

Or

,

Or

,

Or

,

This

,

This

,

Nah, that's shit or –

,

That's shit too, how about?

,

Fucking hell, I'm just making up on the spot. What about –
no that's shit, give me a minute, give me a minute.

Gruff   I'm not / sure what you want me to –

Barry   Give me a minute give me a minute. I can do this.

,

,

,

Fuck's sake. Give me a, give me a, just a general – and I'll
figure it out – just general, you know, and I'll fucking nail it.

Gruff   General what?

Barry   Throw me a fucking bone, Gruff? Just a general –
what kind of thing are you looking for? And I can do it. I'll do
it for you.

Gruff   I'm not looking / for anything.

Barry   You've got to give me some fucking kind of fucking
direction or I'm just flailing around here, like a fucking – and
we're never gonna get anywhere.

,

Gruff   I don't.

Barry   JUST TELL ME WHAT TO PLAY.

Gruff   Um.

Barry   And I'll fucking play it.

Gruff   I'm not that into music, Bar. I haven't even got an
iPod.

,

Barry   I don't know what I'm doing. It's all – normally I'd
come up with ideas and Damo would say that's the one and –
he'd be right, and then we'd – that's how it works. That's
how it works, I come up with ideas and then he says which
one – Did you not think any of those were any good? / There
wasn't one that stood out?

Gruff   They were all great. All of them.

Barry   I don't know how the fuck I'm gonna do this.

Gruff   You'll be / fine.

Barry   I won't if I haven't got someone else to tell me what to play.

Gruff   You should play whatever you want. Don't listen to anyone else.

Barry   If I listened to myself I wouldn't be playing guitar.

Gruff   Sound like me now.

Barry   You're a good bassist, Gruff.

Gruff   I'm not.

Barry   You're a good / musician.

Gruff   I'm not.

Barry   I fucking know / what I'm talking about.

Gruff   Thanks, Bar, but I know I'm the weak link.

Barry   I know what / I'm talking about. Listen to me. You're a good fucking musician. Don't let anyone tell you you're not.

Gruff   Leave it, Bar. I'm the weak link and I know it. I know that that's a – so just fucking leave it, OK. I don't want to talk about anything like that so – leave it.

Barry   You fucking listen to me.

Gruff   I'm not listening because I don't agree / with you, and I can't listen to this.

Barry   Get back here now. You fucking listen to me. You don't listen to anything that prick says. Look at me. Look at me. I'm not around any more, so you've got to stand up for yourself, OK? Stand up for yourself. Look at me. You're a good musician.

,

You're a good musician.

Gruff *bursts into tears.*

Some time as **Barry** *doesn't know where to look.*

Gruff *continues to cry,* **Barry** *still doesn't know where to look.*

Gruff *continues to cry.*

Barry *doesn't know what to do.*

Gruff *continues to cry.*

Barry *makes an awkward attempt to comfort* **Gruff.**

Barry   Don't be like that.

,

Stop crying.

,

Listen. Listen. If I promise to follow my gut and pack the guitar in and find something new to do, will you stop crying and stand up for yourself?

Gruff *nods.*

Barry *takes his guitar off and gives it to* **Gruff.**

Barry   Take that back to the studio so I don't get tempted.

Gruff   I don't understand.

Barry   If I play guitar, I'll always want Damo's opinion. I need to find a new way of working.

Gruff   What are you going to do?

Barry   New Country for Old Men, take one.

Scene Five

Gruff *tries to familiarise himself with* **Barry***'s guitar, an anxious* **Damien** *gets more irate.*

Damien   We'll wait for Aaron and then figure it out.

,

,

,

,

Damien   How long has it been?

Gruff   Five minutes.

Damien   Really?

,

,

,

,

,

Damien   We should wait though.

Gruff   Yeah.

Damien   He was cc'd in the email, you got it? Both of you got it. The no-pressure thing.

Gruff   Yeahno, / the no-pressure thing, yeah.

Damien   The no-pressure thing.

Gruff   Yeah, gives everyone a / a chance to, yeah.

Damien   Chance to sort / out, yeah everything.

Gruff   Sort out, yeahno, it's a good idea.

Damien   That's what I thought, clean / slate.

Gruff   Yeahno, it's.

Damien   Yeah, because you know everyone / who is here
then.

,

It's. / You know –

Gruff   Everyone's / yeahno.

Damien   Committed. / And that's.

Gruff   On it, committed.

,

,

,

Damien   How long has it been now?

Gruff   Five and a . . . half minutes.

,

,

,

,

,

Gruff   Six minutes.

,

,

Damien   What if it's just us?

,

,

What if he doesn't come, and it's just me and you?

,

,

Gruff   Won't / be so –

Damien   How long has it been now?

Gruff   Six and ten seconds.

Loud guitar crash.

Damien   Fucking hell! What if he leaves too? What's that gonna look like? How can we be the best band in the world, with everyone quitting?

Gruff   Well it's only been –

Damien   We haven't got a drummer or a guitarist. We're not a band then, are we? We can't be a band then? We can't do any of this stuff, we can't play any of the music. It's over.

,

,

This is going to look so bad.

,

,

I'm gonna have to put out a statement or something and say it was my decision. This is ridiculous.

,

,

Everyone has quit the band.

Gruff   He might be stuck in traffic.

Damien   He runs everywhere! We'll never pay this debt off.

Gruff   As long we're together we'll be alright.

Damien   How humiliating will that be? The band splits up and we're bankrupt?

,

My life will be over.

Aaron   Oi oi.

Damien   Oi oi!

Gruff   Oi oi!

Damien   Sorry I'm late, had a bit of trouble at home.

Gruff   Damien / was flapping.

Damien   So I guess / we've got a band then!

Gruff   Thought / you weren't coming.

Damien   Alright!

Aaron   Sinead's been giving it all that.

Gruff   Shit / himself.

Damien   Guys, this is gonna be so great. I've had a great fifteen years, and I'm gonna have another great fifteen years, making music, with you. Here's to The Union!

Gruff   Are we keeping the name? / Wasn't that Barry's idea?

Damien   Absolutely. The name's – no, it fucking wasn't Barry's idea! It was both of ours. He's left the band, that's all, the band hasn't broken up.

He gets some champagne out and an orange juice for **Aaron***.*

To The Union and all who sail in her!

Gruff   The Union.

Aaron   The Union. So, we're a threesome then?

Damien   Three / some!

Gruff   Yay, threesome!

Aaron   Always wanted to be in a threesome!

Gruff   Ba-dum-psh! Yeahno.

Aaron Yeah, Sinead was giving it all that about Barry. Haven't spoken for years, and suddenly she's all 'we need to talk'.

Damien Nothing's / going on, is it?

Gruff You don't want / to be going back there.

Aaron No, Jesus Christ! I am so over that. She thinks we're screwed without Barry.

Gruff She / might have a – yeah, what does she know?

Damien What / does she know?

Aaron Mind games. She doesn't. It's all about me. I'm not being – whatever, it's all about me.

Damien We might be better without him.

Gruff Ha!

Damien What?

Gruff Yeahno.

Aaron It's not about the band. It's about me. And the house, that's her goal. She thinks if we're screwed / she's got me where she wants me.

Damien I think, you need to ignore her.

Aaron I do.

Damien I think you should just put her to one side / and forget about her.

Aaron I have.

Damien Just don't even give her the time of day.

Aaron I don't.

Damien The best way to put her out of your mind, is for me to play one of my new songs. You guys pick it up.

He plays his new song 'The Parade' on the piano. The band picks it up, badly.

Damien   This is 'Parade', it's in G C E minor D, pick up as I go along.

'

> 'It started with the drums' – C next.
> 'They are rolling down the street' on to E minor.
> 'The buildings shake'
> 'And you shake next to me.' Then drop out.
>
> 'Hold on to my hand.' That's great.
> 'And release it again'
> 'In that simple moment'
> 'I knew my life had changed.'

Break it down, go into chorus. Gruff, something swooping.

> 'Let's go swimming in the river tonight
> Feel the cold on our warm skin.'

Goes to C then D resolves in G.

> 'Let's go swimming tonight.'

Guys! That was, ah . . . that was. Really good.

'

Aaron (*not convinced*)   Yeah.

Gruff (*not convinced*)   First / run out.

Aaron (*not convinced*)   For a first run out, it wasn't bad at all.

Damien   Let's carry on another verse and chorus without me shouting out.

> 'The noise from the street
> And the crowd compete
> When you speak to me
> I almost cannot hear

In a single heartbeat
The confusion clears
Then I can hear, I can hear
What you want me to hear

Let's go swimming tonight
Feel the cold on our warm skin
Let the water take the place of the air
Let's go swimming tonight.'

And then it goes to the bridge. Yeah, guys, I think you're
probably not going to get it in one rehearsal, shall I just
record it and stick it in Dropbox, and you two can learn it?

Gruff   We're picking it up.

Aaron   Yeah, we've got it.

Damien   It's alright I'll stick it in Dropbox.

Gruff   We're picking it up fine.

Damien   OK, let's go again and let's go into the bridge.

*The band strikes up again, but this time **Barry** joins in as a figment of
Gruff's musical imagination. With the guitar the song sounds great.
Throughout the song **Gruff** can't get this sound out of his head.*

Damien
'There's a hand-painted sign on the fire escape
Say it's Midsummer's Day. Let's celebrate
And the tarmac releases the heat of the day
Let's go swimming tonight.

Diving naked side by side
Singing half-known songs in the middle of the night
Dancing like children in the car's headlights
To warm our blood up again.

It started with the drums
They were rolling down the street
My body shook
And you shook next to me.'

Barry *stops playing.*

Damien
'Let's go swimming tonight
Let's go swimming tonight
It started with the drums and it ended like this
Let's go swimming tonight.'

Yeah. Needs a bit of work. I'll do a bit of rearranging.

Gruff   Yeahno. You know what? I think it's. I'm just. I haven't – I'm just.

Damien   Let me bang it over to you.

Gruff   I don't think that's going to fix it. I think. I think, it's probably. I think it's missing / something.

,

The guitar.

Aaron   Yeah, the guitar.

Gruff   *Maybe* we need some guitar.

Damien   Guys, I can rewrite this, I can write this refrain, here with C, and G in the bridge, I'm not expecting you to understand but this –

,

Does everything the guitar part did, but not the same because it's a different tone, it's the same sort of texture, so it's got to be more light and dynamic.

,

So . . . I'm using pentatonics which I can explain to you if you want but it's really boring. But to reassure you, the final sound, we won't miss the guitar. I'll arrange it so. It's what I do.

,

Shall we try it again?

Damien *starts playing again, but* **Gruff** *gets their attention.*

Gruff   Mad thought. What about getting a new guitarist in? Just / a thought.

Aaron   Aye? / Why not?

Damien   I'm not getting another / guitarist in.

Gruff   You're always off collaborating with other people. Warchild all that. / Maybe there's someone.

Damien   I'm not bringing – listen, you don't need to worry about this. This. / Guys, when have you ever had to worry about our sound? Honestly I've got it covered. Just play your parts and I'll take care of the rest.

Gruff   Or a session guitarist, we can use him just for tours. He's not a proper part of the band then. He's just a . . . you know, someone you give parts to.

Damien   Just play your parts and I'll take care of the rest.

,

I'm all for you guys being involved in the creative process as long as you get to the right decisions.

,

,

Guys, if you want to take ten, you can leave this with me. This creative stuff. It's not really your forte.

Damien *starts playing.* **Gruff** *starts exploring the guitar* **Barry** *gave him.*

Gruff *picks up the guitar and starts to play. After some time.*

Gruff   What about?

Damien *ignores him and carries on playing.*

Gruff *strikes upon something.*

,

Gruff   What about that?

Before he knows it, **Damien** *has slowed down his playing to join in with* **Gruff**. *They start to play together beautifully.*

Gruff   Is that?

Damien   Play it again.

'

That works.

Aaron *pours champagne into his empty glass and drinks.*

Damien   'Let's go swimming in the river tonight, feel the cold on our warm skin, let the water take the place of the air.' Aaron?

Aaron *puts the glass down quickly.*

Aaron   I'm fine.

Gruff   Was that?

Aaron   I've been training really hard. One little drink. I'm fine. What are we playing? What are we playing?

'

Damien   OK, let's crack on with this. Gruff, grab your bass.

Gruff   It's stupid having a bass guitar, and no lead. It sounds, well it sounds shit.

Aaron   OoooooOOOOO!

Damien   Since when do you care?

Gruff   Yeahno, I know, it's just I was just thinking it's a bit / you know, bottom-heavy.

Damien   We're just rehearsing; I haven't arranged it properly yet. Get on the bass, you're the bassist. I thought you were just having one?

Aaron   One / bottle.

Gruff   Yeahno, I know, but it sounds shit without / guitar.

Damien   We haven't got a / guitar any more.

Gruff   We're a guitar band! My musical – you know I'm right. You know I'm right. We're a guitar band, so one of us needs to play guitar. And I think I can do it.

He starts to play guitar. After some thought, **Damien** *joins him, and they start to make music together.*

Aaron   An Independent Scotland.

He shakes his rattle.

Scene Six

A file of papers is open. **Damien** *sits behind his piano, playing.* **Barry** *enters with rucksack.*

Barry   Oi oi.

Damien *stops playing.*

Aaron *makes a rattle sound as if this is a Western stand-off.*

Damien   Alright.

,

,

,

Barry   Didn't think you'd be here.

Damien   I'm always here.

,

,

,

Barry   Bank stuff here?

Damien   There.

,

,

,

Barry   I'll sign this and then I'll be off.

Damien   You're gonna need a witness.

Barry   It is just me and you?

Damien   Just me and you.

Barry   So I need you.

Damien   Yeah. You need me.

His pen doesn't work so they have to share **Barry**'s.

Barry   And here. And here. And here. Hang on, I haven't done that one.

Damien *gives* **Barry** *the pen.* **Barry** *signs and then hands it back to* **Damien**.

Barry   And there.

Damien *signs.*

Damien   Last time our names will be on anything together.

Barry   Aye. Look at the size of this?

Damien   Lawyers, mate.

Barry   Who's gonna fucking read all that?

Damien   Haven't seen any gigs advertised.

Barry   Still early days.

Damien   Us too. Let us know when you do book one.

Barry   Won't be a kind of gig vibe.

Damien   Oh?

Barry   Yeah, won't be that kind of show.

Damien   What kind of show will it be?

Barry   It's early days so.

Damien   Why you being cryptic?

Barry   I'm not, it's just all a bit new.

,

I'm fucking on the old. I bought a fucking Mac, didn't I?

Damien   You're making music on a laptop?

Barry   Trying to, aye.

Damien   Garageband?

Barry   Cuebase.

Damien   Cuebase?

Barry   That not good?

Damien   No, I'm just surprised. You still have a flip phone.

Barry   I know.

Damien   Cuebase? What kind of stuff is it?

Barry   Ah, it's early days.

Damien   I'd love to hear it.

Barry   It's not ready, I really am just trying to figure out how it works.

Damien   When it's ready I'd love to hear it.

Barry   It's just a couple of ideas at the moment.

Damien   Cuebase is great to get started on. I prefer bits of Cuebase to Pro Tools.

Barry   You use it?

Damien   Yeah. It's great for when I'm putting down ideas quickly.

Barry   Right.

Damien   Yeah, when I'm building sequences with loops I use Cuebase.

Barry   How do you do that?

Damien   Well. You sort of. You know the main edit window?

Barry   No.

Damien   In the . . . uh . . .

Barry   No, it's all fucking new to me.

Damien   Where's my laptop? It's around here somewhere.

Barry   Here, I've got mine.

He gets his laptop out and they sit together and look at the screen.

Damien   OK, so you go here. And then you open this, this is your edit window. Is this your stuff?

Barry   I don't know, it's not finished.

Damien   Let's have a listen.

He cues one of **Barry***'s songs. He then gathers a cable and plugs it into the laptop.*

Barry   What do I – this fucking / mouse, fucking thing.

Damien   Stroke it. This is great.

Barry   Yeah?

His electronica fills the room. **Barry** *is coy.* **Damien** *is respectful. Slowly* **Damien** *gets into and appreciates decisions* **Barry** *has made. Ad-lib to music.*

Damien   Nice.

Barry   Yeah.

Damien   Oooh. Nice cowbell.

He mimes a cowbell.

Barry   That's not a sample. I recorded that in my / toilet. I couldn't find a sample.

Damien   It's like late-night electronica, but clubby, bit British-Balearic.

Barry   Yeah.

Damien   I like it. It's – yeah. It's new.

Music changes. He jumps with excitement.

Ooh yes!

Barry *can't hide his delight and tries to move as enthusiastically as* **Damien**, *but he's more self-conscious.*

Damien   This needs – Tell you what. Gruff, the airborne pig, has been a fucking revelation. Did you know he can play guitar?

Barry   He's a good musician.

Damien   Well, he's not, but he can definitely play guitar. Couldn't believe it.

,

,

You know, this could do with a bit of guitar, you should get the Tele out, it wants something rolling.

Barry   No, I'm not playing guitar any more. I'm just on this now, but I can only get eight tracks working and then I get a CPU error.

Damien   What?

Barry   I'll show you, look.

Movement sequence as **Damien** *guides* **Barry** *through Cuebase.*

Damien   No no no, you just have to go into your settings.
Here. There's loads of channels on this, if you properly set it up.

,

,

Yeah, see them. They're channels. You can duplicate any of
those and that saves power. See, open up this.

Barry   What's that?

Damien   That's your library. You've got all these samples
to choose from.

Barry   Fucking hell.

Damien   Barely scratched the surface, mate.

Barry   Fucking he – Look at all this.

Damien   And there's other libraries here. Have a go. Just
drag one in.

Barry *starts to add samples.*

The music gets better and more complex.

Damien   We need some guitar.

Gruff *starts playing along.*

Damien   Oh yes!

*He gets on the piano and joins in, following **Gruff***'s lead.*

Barry *introduces another layer.*

Barry   Let's get some fucking drums!

Aaron *joins in and the song takes on more power.*

Musical sequence.

*With growing confidence, **Gruff** plays increasingly elaborate riffs.*

*With growing equality, **Damien** encourages everyone, from **Barry** to
Gruff to **Aaron**, to be the best musicians they can.*

With growing security, **Aaron** *plays more complicated rhythms.*

With growing freedom, **Barry** *plays more complex layers of electronica.*

For a short time the four musicians play harmoniously.

Barry *and* **Damien** *are back looking at the laptop.*

Barry   That was amazing. That was the best thing I've written in – that was music.

'

Just need to get the hang of this.

Damien   Yeah, it was great – I got a few ideas / then too.

Barry   With this I can do anything.

Damien   Great to bounce ideas around the room again.

Barry   Do you know what the weirdest thing was? Felt like I could see, like I could see loads of people enjoying that. I don't know, there was – I don't know. People might not buy that, but there's more value to it than the fucking price the industry puts on it and that's the first time I've worked that out. It doesn't matter if the label don't want to put it out.

Damien   They won't.

Barry   It doesn't matter, though – It's not about – it's about being an artist. Not a commodity. That might be sentimental, but I'd rather be poor / and happy than fucking rich and – why won't they want to put it out?

Damien   Exactly right. We're musicians first.

Barry   Aye, it's the music. Not the money. So even if the label doesn't want to put it out –

Damien   They won't want to put it out.

Barry   Why the fuck not? It's brilliant.

Damien   They just won't.

Barry   How can you be so certain? I don't want them to, but if I did, they'd love it.

Damien   I just know they won't want it.

Barry   I know that's good, why are you being cryptic?

Damien   I'm not.

Barry   You are, you're doing that patronising thing.

Damien   What patronising thing? What a ridiculous thing to say.

Barry   You're the most patronising person I know, everything about you is patronising.

Damien   What?

Barry   You are, the way you talk / everything –

Damien   Utter bollocks.

Barry   Your music is patronising.

Damien   *What?*

Barry   It is.

Damien   Go on.

Barry   You know it is.

Damien   You'd better fucking explain yourself. How is my music patronising?

Barry   You know it is.

Damien   Explain it.

Barry   If you don't want to admit it, then fine.

Damien   Fucking explain yourself.

Barry   I'll tell you, if you tell me why the label won't want that.

Damien   OK.

Barry   You've been churning out the same, soft-indie rock bullshit for a decade. The world's moved on but you don't care as long as you get a hit. The only person who hates playing that stuff more than me, is you. At least I know who I am.

Damien   Fuck you.

Barry   Your turn now. Oh! I should have known, once a patronising prick always a patronising prick.

Extended pause. Everyone looks to each other.

Gruff   What are we doing?

Aaron *checks a set list.*

Aaron   The Troubles with You.

Scene Seven

Gruff *is testing his pedal board.*

Aaron *is hiding his pain and drinking alcohol.*

Damien *starts opening and installing lots of new instruments around him. He tests them but doesn't play them.*

'

'

Barry   WHOA! Listen to this?

'

Blowjob city. I'm not being funny, right, whenever anyone slept with me, I always thought they'd made a mistake. Any minute they were gonna wake up, or sober up and go 'Whoa! Hang on, what the fuck? You're the bassist?' So I always, you know, I always went quick, in case they'd made a mistake. But now! I am *taking my time*. I'm gonna take *all* my clothes off, I'm gonna film them, anything. Talk to them, the works. Because I am the mother-juggling guitarist.

Aaron   You're also forty-one, married and bald.

Damien   We still sound fresh, right?

Gruff   We're still rocking and rolling. Fucking rocking and rolling.

Damien   People / like to know what they're getting, right?

Aaron   I might, I might have to disagree with you there.

Gruff   Exactly, we can still tear it up. Shagging. And. / Stuff. Pills.

Aaron   I don't know about that.

Damien   What's rock and roll about doing an Iron Man?

Aaron   I've pulled out / of the Iron Man so.

Gruff   Wahay!

Damien   Why?

Aaron   I'm injured.

Gruff   Shagging?

Aaron   Last night, after the rehearsal, I was all – pumped, you know? I was buzzing, you know for the first time, I could actually see us as a band, as a new band, and it was exciting because it wasn't just us limping along, it was a new band, with a new sound and . . .

,

So on the way home, I went to the pub to have a little celebratory.

,

I know. And I'm not really sure how it happened but I seem to have gotten quite drunk.

,

And when I got home.

,

Sinead was up, and, we got talking and I think she was a bit pissed as well and we.

,

And when she's talking, she runs her finger along the line.

Gruff   What / line?

Damien   The chalk line.

Aaron   We have a chalk line that goes through the house.

Barry *starts to play drums, with brushes – giving a beat-poetry beat.*

Aaron   She runs her finger along the line.

,

She's pissed. But it's like she's running it along me.

,

It would be more, *this*, it's more sexy, than if she actually touched me. Because that's our *line*. That's the line. You don't mess with the line. But, she's not only crossing the line, but, the line that's kept the peace for so long she's *toying* with it.

,

She's toying with me. We haven't spoken for years, Barry leaves the band and we talk *every* day! Granted sometimes it's a lot of abuse, but still.

,

Even if it's abuse it feels like flirting.

,

So I'm in the kitchen and it's . . . with the line, fingering.

,

It's nice and.

,

After a while. I can't really remember because I was pissed.
But for some reason I took my shirt off and we kissed.

,

We kissed.

,

I'm not meant to be near her, and she's stuck her tongue
down my throat!

,

We haven't kissed for eight years and it's amaz – I can't
describe it.

,

And it's hot.

,

So hot. It's so hot.

,

I wanna . . .

,

Pull her hair, when we kiss.

,

So I pull her hair. And she doesn't complain. In fact, she likes it.

,

And you know why she likes it?

,

It's because of, because of the *build-up*.

Gruff *and* **Damien** *join in.*

Aaron   Ten, years. Ten long years. Ten years, in the cold,
ten years on one side of the bed, ten years eating meals for
one, ten years driving with just the satnav for company.

,

Ten years, and now we're man and woman.

,

Ten years . . . and now I'm kissing her and pulling her hair,
and pushing her against a wall and you know what? She
likes it.

,

She's up against a wall and she likes it.

,

I'm up against a wall and you know what? I like it!

,

She's up against a wall, and I can see the chalk line and I'm
like 'Fuck you, chalk line! Fuck you, I've crossed the line, I've
crossed the line so far I've got my hand in her pants! That's
what I think of you, chalk line!' I see the chalk line, I cross the
chalk line and I finger your momma, that's what I think of
you, chalk line! And the chalk's all smudged like a tiny
miserable bitch, and I'm like 'I SMUDGED YOU, CHALK
LINE! I SMUDGED YOU!'

,

And then I realise, that's not in my head. That I'm saying it,
I'm shouting it, I'm shouting aloud 'I SMUDGED YOU! I

SMUDGED YOU, CHALK LINE' and I look at Sinead and I'm worried I've blown it.

,

But you know what?

,

She likes it.

,

She really likes it.

,

She likes it so much she starts shouting it herself, she's got her own beef with the chalk line, she's calling him a 'SON OF A BITCH', she hates the chalk line as well, she treats the chalk line like a *racist*, she's like, 'Fuck you, chalk line! You can't repress me! I'm my own woman, I'm like *Beyonceaaay*! I will kiss, and bite, and fuck who I like, you're not the boss of me!' And she bites me.

,

Bitch bites me on the lip.

,

Got blood on my mouth, and it's dripping on my bare chest, because I took my shirt off earlier.

,

Got blood on my chest and I'm like this bitch just bit me on the lip and I look at her, and she's got blood on her teeth, and something tells me, I think it was my penis.

,

Tells me.

,

Tells me, I like it.

,

So I'm covered in blood and my mouth hurts badly but she's down to her underwear. 'Who's the boss of you?' I ask, and I've got my hands around her throat and she's like –

,

'Yoooouuuu.'

,

So, we're fucking now.

,

And by now, I'm pretty sure she likes everything.

,

So we push each other.

,

Sexually.

,

She knocks me about like a punchbag, and I throw her around like a rag doll.

,

Know what? We like it.

,

We like it, we like it 'cause together we've lived so long with so many rules and limits and regulations and now there's no rules, there's no lines, there's nothing to stop me sticking a spatula in her arse and being creative.

,

I stick a spatula in her ass and she sticks a, a spike, like roasting, what's the / thing you –

Damien Skewer.

Aaron   She sticks a skewer through my ball sack and out the other side.

,

I'm not sure if either of us likes it, but it was too late to ask, so we carry on until some point *someone* introduces knives.

,

Knives are going here, they're going there, pressed against this, pushed against that, neither of us flinching. Lightly, stabbing, cutting, sawing and fucking, and no one likes it but we're not gonna say because who wants to be *that* guy! So we carry on and I don't like it, the pain's unbearable and we can't tell whose blood is whose, and there's so much blood spilt on the floor that we can't remember how it started or what we were meant to be doing so we stop.

Music stops.

Then we got cleaned up and had a Nespresso.

,

Gruff   Where did she stab you?

Aaron   In the kit / chen.

Damien   On your body. Where on your body, were you stabbed?

,

Oh God!

Gruff   Have you had that looked at?

Aaron   So, things are a bit weird at home. I was wondering if I could skip rehearsals and see if I can talk to Sinead, see where we're at.

Damien   Tell me you don't want to get back with her.

Aaron   Jesus Christ! She put a skewer through my ball sack. How can I run twenty miles with a hole in my balls? But I would, just like to see, where her head's – bit confused. Mind if I head home?

Gruff   Yeahno, I don't have a problem with that at all.

Damien   Fine.

Aaron   Thank you.

He leaves.

Damien *starts to explore making music with his new instruments.*

Gruff   If rock and rolling means perforating your testes, then I'll stick to just playing guitar thank you very much.

He goes back to his pedal board.

Damien   You know, you've got the guitar. Aaron's got Sinead. Barry's got his new career. What have I got? What's my thing?

Gruff   Your thing's the band, you don't need anything else.

Damien   I think we need to do something new with the band. New direction.

Feedback!

Gruff   Woah! What happened?

Damien   Track eight, Scottish Diplomacy. One and two and three and four.

Scene Eight

Barry *has a plaster on his nose.*

Aaron *is drinking.*

Movement sequence as **Damien** *and* **Gruff** *wrap* **Barry** *and*

Aaron *together with cables, as they introduce more equipment and instruments to the studio.*

Barry   Karen broke my fucking nose. Stop knocking her fucking sister about, I'm warning you.

Aaron   I haven't laid / a finger on her.

Barry   She's at my house, / covered in cuts and I'm getting the fucking blame.

Aaron   I've been trying to get hold of her – what's it to do with you anyway?

Barry   They're fucking sisters, for fuck's sake. We're fucking friends. You see a fucking problem there?

Aaron   No, I don't / see a fucking problem there.

Barry   She never comes round to ours. I'm trying to fucking make a record, Karen's all upset, I say one fucking tiny thing in your defence, and she fucking twats me on the nose. She's never hit me in her fucking life! / Bled all over my laptop.

Aaron   Don't go blaming your and Karen's problems / on me. That's your shit.

Barry   We were arguing about you, you stupid cunt.

Aaron   She's probably angry about something else. / The fucking debt you're in that you've got no hope of paying off on your own.

Barry   We were fucking arguing about her sister / getting assaulted, by my fucking pal.

Aaron   That you said going solo would make things right / and it's just as shit as it always was.

Barry   FUCK YOU! Aaaoooowwww.

Aaron   You OK?

Barry   I can't –

'

fucking shout because it fucking / kills my nose. I can feel it clicking.

Aaron   Don't touch it, stop touching it, you prick.

Barry   It's fucking clicking.

Aaron   Let me have a look.

'

Aye, it's fucking broken that.

Barry   Does it look fucked?

Aaron   Aye, but you're an ugly fuck anyway, / can't get much fucking worse.

Barry   Fuck's sake.

'

'

'

'

Barry   I fucking liked my nose, you know?

'

One of the few bits of my face I like and she fucking – is it straight or – ?

Aaron   Aye, it's just got a fat fucking bump by the bridge, it's fine.

'

'

Barry   Probably fucking snore now.

Aaron   You fucking snore anywhere, it might fucking cure it.

Barry   Stop fucking trying to put a good spin on this, OK?
Let me just –

,

,

Don't fucking – Since I left the band, things haven't been
great between me and Karen for lots of fucking reasons,
which are none of your fucking business. But the one fucking
thing I can fix, is this fucking bullshit, OK? I fucking know yous
and I fucking know her, and I've never fucking got involved
before because we were in the band, and it was fucking easier
if Damo fucking sorted it out, but now I'm fucking solo,
Karen's fucking worried no one's fucking trying to sort it out,
and if it doesn't get fucking sorted out, Karen's gonna fucking
flip. So I thought I might as well, you know, use my fucking
unique insight on the fucking situation, being as I was the
cunt who fucking introduced yous two to each other, I might
be able to exercise a bit of fucking, you know, insight and sort
this fucking shite once and for all.

Aaron   OK. What do you think I should do?

Barry   I think you should stop fucking hitting her / you
stupid cunt. Simple as that.

Aaron   She fucking started it! / She stuck her tongue down
my throat after years, years of nothing! We were fine till she
started all the fucking nonsense again, you know what a
psycho fucking bitch she is.

Barry   Hang on hang on. Stop stop stop, that's no use. I'm
not interested in who did what when. / Boring, man. It's
fucking boring.

Aaron   You want to talk to her. She's the one who needs
getting / her head sorted out. She fucking –

Barry   Listen fucking. Shut up. Shut the fuck up.

,

You and her.

,

Right, you're a pair of fucking cunts, right. You think she's a cunt. She thinks you're a cunt. Truth is, you're both a pair of fucking cunts, right. Now I know, you're a cunt right, and I know she's a cunt and all. I fucking know yous both. I'm no fucking – I fucking *know* you're a pair of cunts, right? But what I'm saying is, right, if yous pair of cunts stopped being a pair of fucking cunts right, treated each other with a bit of fucking – you wouldn't treat each other like a pair of cunts, you know what I'm saying?

Aaron   I think so.

Barry   You know what I'm saying, yeah?

Aaron   Yeah.

Barry   Stop, being, a cunt. All this fucking shit'll be sorted. I'm not on anyone's side, I think you're both a pair of cunts.

Aaron   Was this your idea? Coming round.

Barry   Aye.

,

Actually it was Karen's but. You know.

Aaron   Karen's saying the same thing to Sinead.

Barry   Aye, not in so many words, aye.

Aaron   You know why Karen sent you round?

Barry   Because you fucking hit her sister, you cunt.

Aaron   No, because she's getting fucking nowhere with fucking Sinead. So she's sent you here. You're here *because* Sinead wants me.

Barry   Sinead isn't in fucking love with you, you stupid cunt, / she can't just leave you alone.

Aaron   The only two people who have any fucking idea what this is like is me and Sinead. / You haven't got any fucking special insight.

Barry   I fucking put yous two pair of cunts together.

Aaron   That was like fifteen years ago.

Barry   You wouldn't be in this fucking situation if it wasn't for me. I've fucking known you, and her, longer than you've fucking known each other.

Aaron   That doesn't stand for shit.

Barry   I fucking put yous together, I can fucking pull yous two apart.

Aaron   Me and Sinead had the best sex of our lives the other day. Look at that?

He lifts his shirt.

No one's getting in the way of that happening again.

Barry   Listen, you stupid cunt. I've fucking told Karen you'll fucking listen to me. Leave. Sinead. Alone.

Aaron   No.

'

'

Barry   If I go home and tell her I fucked this up she'll fucking leave me.

Aaron   I don't care.

Barry   I'm begging you.

Aaron   I stopped caring a long time ago. Do you have a problem with that?

He drinks.

Gruff   Um . . . uh . . . Scottish Diplomacy.

Barry   We've just played that one, you twat.

Gruff *fumbles a set list.*

Gruff   Um . . . uh . . . How to Lose Friends and Alienate
People.

Barry   Fucking hell.

Scene Nine

Playing guitar, **Gruff** *is struggling to make sense of his pedal board.
Still tied to* **Aaron,** **Barry** *turns to* **Gruff.** *As he speaks he struggles
to untangle himself from* **Aaron.**

Gruff   No, it's the pedal board I'm struggling with. How
did you remember what does what? I can barely remember
which pick-up is which.

Barry   It's not a good time Gruff (bit tied up).

Gruff   Once I've learned all these I'm sure I'm gonna be
fine. Yeahno, I'm sure, it'll all slot in. It's just I don't know
where to start. I'm feeling a bit of an idiot and Damo wants
all these particular sounds and I don't know where to start. So
I was wondering if you could give us a crash course on the
pedal board? Once I've got it logged I'll be fine. This is
what's holding me back. I'm not sure how you're supposed to
sequence them. / Because, when I arrange them, some of
them cut each other out. And then there's the feedbacking.

Barry   Gruff, mate. Gruff, Gruff. I haven't got time for this.
Karen's left me, which I knew was gonna happen anyway.
And Damo set up some program on Cuebase that I can't
fucking work out. And I've sent my stuff to the label and
they're not fucking returning any of my calls. It's a pedal
board, it's not fucking rocket science. What are you doing?

Gruff   Sorry, I can't figure it out. Is that one? If I press that
one . . . does that?

,

Yeahno, Damo's been saying stuff like 'more ethereal'. Who are they? Or tickly and fuzzy and round. How can a sound be round? And then he's always talking about bands I've never heard of. Then he gave me an iPod with loads of music, but I can't figure out how you turn it on.

Barry   Gruff, man!

Gruff   Sorry, it's just we wrote a song together the other day.

,

I've never written a song with him before.

,

I really want to do it again but he hasn't done it since.

Barry   You can't remember which one your fucking delay pedal is. You are never going to write a song.

Gruff   Well. I did. With Damo.

Barry   If Damo's not writing with you any more it's not because you can't figure out your fucking pedal board.

Gruff   Eh?

Barry   He's not fucking writing with you any more because he doesn't think you're fucking good enough. You can fucking blame your pedals all you like.

Gruff   Yeahno, sorry, I just wanted a hand with the pedals, I don't need any – me and Damo are fine.

Barry   You're fine, are you?

Gruff   Yeah. He's got a new sound we're working on for the band.

Barry   New sound, right. And you're fucking involved in that are you?

Gruff   Yeah. Sort of.

Barry   He's asking for lots of fucking sounds is he?

He takes the guitar off **Gruff***, steps on the pedal board creating different effects.*

Barry   Wants something exotic?

,

Or something crunchy?

,

Something space-age.

,

Something cold.

,

Hot. Spiky, smooth, coarse, rusty, sad, broken, noisy, flat. Name it. Name a sound. Go on, name a fucking sound he wants.

Gruff   I don't know / what he wants.

Barry   Name a sound!

Gruff   I don't / know.

Barry   Name a fucking sound!

Gruff   I don't / know.

Barry   Name a fucking sound name he wants!

Gruff   I don't know!

Barry   No. You don't, do you? 'Cause you're a *bassist*. And that's all you'll ever be.

Gruff *packs up his guitar and pedal board.*

Barry   When you see Damo, tell that cunt to give me a fucking call about this label bullshit, he thinks he fucking knows what's going on.

Gruff   They won't sign you.

Barry   Why the fuck not?

Gruff   Because we're on the label.

Barry   That should make them fucking want me.

Gruff   Yeahno, there's twenty-eight other bands on the label. If they give you a deal, then every guitarist who wants to go solo will leave the bands. And all the bands will break up. And then the label won't have anyone making albums. And the label is all about keeping the peace. Yeahno. The only guitarist they ever signed, they made them record at the band's studio and the singer produced the record. Sounded *exactly* like the band. Can you do that sound?

Barry   Hell is an English Garden.

Damien *loops that line over and over.*

Scene Ten

Movement sequence as **Damien** *tries to save the band by creating a successful new sound. He rushes around the studio with a loop pedal playing every instrument like the Sorcerer's Apprentice.* **Damien** *sings into a mic, loops it, and distorts it.*

Gruff *and* **Aaron** *try to join in, but* **Damien** *needs total control to create the right sound.* **Gruff** *and* **Aaron** *want to help but find them-selves redundant. As the power of* **Damien**'s *music grows, so does the redundancy of* **Gruff** *and* **Aaron** *as musicians.*

A dawning realisation for **Gruff** *and* **Aaron** *that the band now works better without them.*

A swell in the music results in **Gruff** *and* **Aaron** *startling; the music begins to hurt.*

They shield their ears in pain. Oblivious to their suffering, **Damien** *strives for the sound, believing that this is the sound that will secure the band's future, but as he does so he causes suffering to* **Gruff** *and* **Aaron**.

Gruff *and* **Aaron** *try to get relief from the sound, away from the amplifiers, but there's no escape from it.*

Desperate, they try to get **Damien***'s attention, but he's too engrossed in the music he's making to save the band.* **Damien** *makes a breakthrough and the sound grows, but so does* **Gruff** *and* **Aaron***'s pain to the point where they are filled with agony.*

The louder/more complex the sound, the more pain **Gruff** *and* **Aaron** *feel and the closer to the goal* **Damien** *believes he gets. The music torments* **Gruff** *and* **Aaron** *but liberates* **Damien.**

The music explodes and **Aaron** *and* **Gruff** *tear at their clothes in agony and* **Damien** *tears at his clothes in abandon.* **Gruff** *and* **Aaron** *flagellate themselves with cables for relief.*

Damien *frees himself of the shackles of collective music, so the studio shackles* **Gruff** *and* **Aaron.**

For **Gruff** *and* **Aaron** *the pain is unbearable and they writhe around naked in a sea of cables, while* **Damien** *stands atop the drum kit, master of the band's destiny.*

Barry *enters and sees the hell* **Gruff** *and* **Aaron** *are in.*

He tries to help them, but they are too far gone.

He appeals to **Damien***, but he is too far gone.*

He tries again to pull **Aaron** *and* **Gruff** *from the cables but the music starts to hurt him too.*

His ears hurt as he tries to help them.

He can't take it any more, he appeals to **Damien** *again.*

Barry *finds a power cable and pulls it.*

The music stops.

Gruff *and* **Aaron** *wail in pain on the floor.*

Barry   What the fuck are you doing to them? / Look at them. Look at them!

This is the first time **Damien** *has been confronted with the consequences of his actions and is appalled.* **Barry** *and* **Damien** *rush to disentangle* **Gruff** *and* **Aaron.**

Damien   I was trying / to save the band.

Barry   You're killing them.

Damien   I was trying to save the band / with the new sound.

Barry   The band is them, without them there is no band.

Aaron *and* **Gruff** *attack* **Damien***'s amps with instruments.*

Aaron   I'm not / fucking // taking it any more!

Gruff   Fuck you! Fuck all of this shit!

Barry   Guys! / Guys! Stop that.

Aaron   Fuck you! / Make some sound now! Come on! Try and hurt me now! You can't hurt me more than I can hurt myself.

Gruff   Leave me alone. / I can't take fucking do this! I can't!

Aaron *and* **Gruff** *trash equipment.*

Aaron   I know you think I deserve this because I'm weak. We all did the same drugs. You think I fucking deserve it / because I'm weak.

Barry   What / are you on about?

Aaron *smashes some equipment.*

Gruff   You're not the only one who's fucking – You haven't got a fucking monopoly on being fucked about. I'M NOT A GUITARIST. / I AM AN AVERAGE BASSIST!

Aaron   I'm fucking weak and worthless.

Gruff   I know you only asked me to join because I had a van.

Damien   That's / not // true.

Aaron   I know all of you have wished at some point that I was dead.

Gruff   It's true, I've heard you say it. On the phone. To Martin. You've said it to my face when you're shitfaced it's – do you know he hasn't even sacked Martin? He fucking lied to us. I know! / You're so used to ignoring me you think I can't listen. He lied to us. Martin is still managing us. He's still fucking in charge. Isn't he?

Aaron   Who gives a shit?

Damien   Martin's a mate. You don't sack your mates. / He made one mistake.

Gruff   AND I CAN'T FUCKING DO ANYTHING ABOUT IT.

He drives a guitar into an amp.

I'll do whatever you want. You want to start another band? Let's start another band. I'll play bass, I'll drive the van, I'll wear a fucking grass skirt and coconuts / on my nipples, but I cannot survive without you. You have to look after me.

Aaron   You pathetic fuck. The fuck is wrong with you? *Please* look after me? *Please,* Damo! Fucking pathetic. I can't fucking believe I chose *this* over her! I fucked up my relationship for *this*!

He wraps a cable around his neck.

I fucking said to her, I said, if you want me, you can have me. You know what she said? She said, she's not over me, but she's over 'us'. What the fuck does that mean? Fuck this band.

He is about to strangle himself. **Damien** *and* **Barry** *rush to stop him.*

Barry   No! Put / it down.

Damien   Put / it down.

Gruff   Aa / ron.

Damien   Ple / ase.

Barry   Put it down, put it down, put it down. Put it down. Put it down. Put it down. FUCK SAKE, AARON. YOU THINK ANY OF US ARE HAPPY? I fucking left and I'm still dragged down by you cunts. Do you want me to say I think you're weak? Do you want me to say it? I fucking will. You're weak. But so am I, you stupid cunt, we all are. I fucking got out. And look at me. Still. Fucking. Here. Karen's left me. / I can't work my fucking laptop / but I've got a solo deal, right! Yeah, great news, yeah? Is it fuck? They want *him* to fucking produce it. *Here.* Look at the fucking state of this place.

Aaron   I don't give a shit. I fucking hate this band.

He tries to strangle himself. They all try to stop him.

The struggle breaks out into a fight. **Aaron** *slaps* **Barry**, *a guitar is smashed across* **Damien**'s *head. A mêlée ensues, breaking up only when* **Gruff** *strikes everyone with a keyboard.*

Ad-lib fighting talk.

Gruff   WHAT THE FUCK IS GOING ON? We're not / even pissed!

Damien   People would die to be in this band. People would take anything to be – they would take anything! Whatever – The shittest job in the world. Spoons! They would die to play the spoons in our band. People, would die, to have an afternoon playing, playing, fucking kazoo, session kazoo in our band. They would die. Kill themselves, for a chance to be part of our band. And we're fighting over what?

Gruff   You started it.

Damien   How?

Aaron   The new fucking sound.

Damien   You want to start a new band! You want a new career! You want to run off with your ex or / whatever.

Aaron   Because no one cares about the band any more.

Damien   Why? Because it's what? Not cool any more? Being in a band our age isn't cool? So we throw it away, because – for what? For it's uncomfortable? I don't – we feel a bit compromised? Playing with each other is a compromise now? Bit childish. We should thank our lucky fucking stars.

Barry   None of us want to be in a band any more, not even you.

,

,

Band retreats.

Barry *rights an amp and checks to see if it still works.*

He picks up some detritus. The others watch.

Damien *joins him.*

Then **Gruff.**

Then **Aaron.**

Slowly they repair the studio.

,

,

,

,

Gruff   Mad thought. Maybe there's a band we can all be in where Aaron can be with Sinead, Barry can do his own stuff and me and Damo can write together now and again? Yeahno, ignore me.

,

,

They carry on repairing the studio.

They test if instruments work. A brief moment, as the testing becomes something else.

Barry   One, two, three, four?

Blackout.

Protest Song

In memory of Antonia Bird

Can anyone make a difference any more?
Can anyone write a protest song?

Manic Street Preachers, 'Let Robeson Sing'

Protest Song was first performed in The Shed at the National Theatre, London, on 16 December 2013.

Danny   Rhys Ifans

Director   Polly Findlay
Designer   Merle Hensel
Lighting Designer   Lee Curran
Movement Director   Jack Murphy
Sound Designer   Carolyn Downing
Voice and Dialect Coach   Richard Ryder
Staff Director   Sean Linnen

Characters

Danny, *forty-something, homeless alcoholic from the South Wales valleys*

Notes

The performer and director should feel free to create bespoke interaction with the audience and space.

Jenny's second phone call is not intended to be heard by the audience.

A dash (–) indicates an interruption of word or thought.

Words or phrases in brackets (. . .) are unfinished thoughts or sentences and where possible should remain unspoken. This is to be discovered in rehearsal at the director's and performer's discretion.

A forward slash (/) indicates when the following line should overlap.

One

In the space, **Danny** *sits in audience members' seats until he is moved along. This continues until there is nowhere left for him to sit.*

Improvise his transgressions with audience members.

He makes it down to the stage.

Danny (*to patron*)   Ow, have you got a pound for a hostel?

He looms.

Patron gets purse out and gives him a pound.

Danny   Thank you, thank you.

He realises he can make more.

It's three-twenty actually for a hostel. Have you got three-twenty?

Patron gets purse out.

Danny   Come on, you're minted.

Patron gives him the money.

Danny   Happy Christmas.

Beat.

A mobile phone starts ringing from **Danny**'s *bag. A moment before he realises it's his phone.*

He scrambles to open his rucksack. He pulls out a plastic bag tied with rubber bands. Desperately he pulls the rubber bands off and pulls off the bag, to reveal another. This goes on for some time as he unties layer after layer of plastic bags, the phone ringing all the while. Finally he gets to the phone.

Danny   Yes!

But his celebrations are cut short when the phone stops ringing.

Fuck.

The phone beeps with a text message.

Voicemail (*on answer phone*)   You have one new message. To listen to your messages, press one.

Danny *presses the button.*

Jenny (*voice only*)   Danny it's Jenny, I'm at Waterloo Bridge, got the paperwork, bit of a scramble but I've got it. Just need you to sign now. So. Hurry up! I'm a bit pushed for time. Give me a call yeah, let me know you're on your way.

As **Danny** *listens he winces, realising he'd forgotten. He scrambles and starts packing all his property back into his bag.*

Danny   Housing charity give me this, just got to look after this, keep it charged, and I'll get indoors by Christmas, my own bed, central heating, the fucking works. I done all the pathway shit, counselling, life-skills, detox.

He packs some cans of lager.

I know what I'm doing – when I was indoors, I was the one who sorted everything out, knew where everything was.

In his haste, he forgets to pack the phone.

I fucking like order, not in an OCD way but y'know . . . 'Where's my kit, Dad?' 'Where's my bag?' And they wanna test my fucking reliability. Fucking mugs.

He swaggers off.

Then realises he hasn't got the phone and runs back.

Fucking hell!

Holds phone.

Nearly failed the fucking test, fucking first day. Oh you fucking cock-head.

Beat.

Last time I did the pathway I didn't even get to the phone test and Occupy came along and fucked it up. The Square Mile's perfect for rough sleepers 'cause it's dead at night. Non-residential, seven years I've been there, it's quiet.

Beat.

Quiet until three thousand people turn up on your doorstep with tents and bongos.

Two

'OI! FUCK OFF! THIS IS A FUCKING CATHEDRAL.'

I'm a free spirit, don't get me wrong. I think people should do
what they want.

'FUCK OFF! TAKE YOUR DRUMS, AND STICK
THEM UP YOUR ARSE OR I'M GOING TO FUCKING
STAB YOU. FUCK (OFF). THIS IS MY HOME.'

Do what you want, just don't fuck with my routine. It's all
I've got.

'Desperate? I'm fucking desperate for you lot to fuck off. How
can I sleep? Go on, fuck off.'

Fucking five hundred tents on my doorstep. It was the noise
that got to me you know. I think anyone would have done
what I did. Any right-thinking member of society.

Beat.

So, I piss on a few tents. Early hours, take a stroll. Piss on a
few. Pull a few poles out. Slash a couple, 'cause it *will* happen
if you – (rough sleep in a tent). If sleeping in a tent was safe,
we'd all be doing it? No. You're a target, you mugs. Piss,
fire – (the works). So I'm doing them a favour. Better to have
my piss than a junky's.

Beat.

But what do the cunts do?

Beat.

Build a fucking wigwam. 'Fucking take it down. Fucking take
it down now. You are not. This is – (my home). Look at the
police here. Look at them. You're fucking trespassing.' Fruit.
They used to hand out. *Avocados*, which are actually quite
nice. 'Stick this fucking pear up your arse until it comes out of

your big toe.' Cunts bring me a poem instead. 'I've got a
poem,' I say, and I recite *The Snail and the Whale*. All by heart.

He drinks.

My boy's favourite, that.

He drinks.

(*To patron.*) What's your number, love? What's your number?

Beat.

WHAT'S YOUR FUCKING NUMBER? Sorry. Sorry.

Patron replies with number. **Danny** *announces it as he types it into his
phone.*

Danny   It's just I need to look like I'm using it. If I feel
ownership over it then I won't forget it, in *her* book, *this* –

Phone.

– is civilisation. So let's show her how fucking civilised I am.
What's your fucking name love?

Patron replies. **Danny** *puts it in.*

Danny (*to another patron*)   Oi. What's your fucking number?

Patron 2 replies.

Danny   Pass it round. Put all your numbers in, I'm not
having anything fuck this up, this time.

Beat.

It wasn't *just* Occupy's fault. St Paul's played a fucking part
an' all. They were like, 'Occupy, come and stay!' And then
they fucking closed the doors, not just to them but to
everyone. Fucking Jesus didn't close his doors to any cunt.
Seven years I *slept* outside that door. Wash in there every
morning. If I don't wash on the street, I get ill, I get fucking
infections, end up in hospital, they know, I told them that.

'I'm nothing to do with those cunts, you know that, Lesley. OPEN THE FUCKING DOOR.' I reckon it was fucking Boris, he made them close. He fucking put us in detention centres for the Olympics; didn't fucking know that, did you? He's a fucking shit-eating Nazi paedophile. He's the one who's behind the benches with dividers, sloping bus seats, one bag at a time in libraries. Bleach! He makes them pour fucking bleach on doorways.

Beat.

Meant to be a fucking refuge and a couple of tents – (close it down). The Blitz couldn't close that church. I was in the middle, Occupy don't want to listen, St Paul's don't want to listen. 'OPEN THIS FUCKING DOOR NOW.' I can't remember how it happened, but Allie the fruit girl turns up, and hears what's going on. 'MIC CHECK! MIC CHECK!' she shouts.

Beat.

And I shit you not; the whole fucking camp shouts it back. The human microphone they call it.

Beat.

'THE CHURCH HAS CLOSED ITS DOORS. THEY WON'T LET DANNY IN. THEY RECKON IT'S CLOSED UNTIL THE CAMP IS EVICTED', or something like that, and they all fucking shout it back. Together. And suddenly. The *whole* fucking camp is listening, every *single* one of them.

Beat.

How fucking handy would that be when you're getting stabbed or pissed on, or you can't find your . . .

He panics, can't find his phone.

Where's my phone? Who's got my phone?

He retrieves it.

He chooses a patron, hands them the phone.

You. Keep an eye.

Beat.

After that, I'm like a fucking celebrity, 'Do you want a cup of tea?' 'Do you want a tent?' 'Do you want to join the church liaison working group?' 'Come and join this group, come and meet this little bloke, sign that.' I fucking preferred it when they were ignoring me.

Beat.

They were like ants. Two days they had a fucking kitchen. With a chef. He had a hat!

Beat.

Allie took me in, food spread out. Just help yourself. Different kinds of bread, tea, coffee, soup, cheese. One meat dish, one veg dish. Queues of people, in the middle of fucking St Paul's. They'd only been there two days. Worse than the fucking gypos. There's no ticketing, just in and out. I'm in there with my can, no cunt says anything. Allie's like, 'Have whatever you want.' FUCK OFF. I don't want anything do with this shit. 'It's free.'

He double-takes.

Free food. On my doorstep.

He considers this.

Well.

Beat.

Be rude not to, wouldn't it?

Beat.

Odd bowl of soup.

Beat.

Breakfast, maybe dinner, see what's on for tea. No one says anything.

Beat.

Not long before I'm fucking rinsing them.

Beat.

Eat like a fucking oligarch. Every day. No one says anything.

Beat.

I put my bowl in the bucket. They have this big square bucket. And I remember, when I was indoors a bit of hoovering never bothered me; ironing, did it all, long as you got a bit of music it's fine, but I fucking *hated* washing up. I'd cook just to avoid it. I'd do anything to avoid it, harder when you're not working. The wife would say, 'You don't wash up 'cause you're a bum.'

He looks at the imaginary bowl.

And there's this bucket.

Beat.

And I've got the bowl, and I don't know why but I put my hands in under the water.

(*To himself.*) Drown the cow out.

Beat.

Fucking squirt some washing-up liquid, rub it, swill it round, rinse it off –

He startles.

'Fuck me.'

He holds an imaginary bowl for inspection.

'I just cleaned a bowl.'

Beat.

Wooky, this guy with dreadlocks, takes it off me, dries it and stacks it on the shelves. 'Shall we crack on?' He wants me to carry on washing up. Thinks I'm a fucking volunteer, thinks I'm gonna wash up after all these cunts, no chance.

He is confused.

But I fill up the bucket and I fucking do it.

Beat.

I was down Covent Garden, making a bit of money.

Beat.

Get my spot under a cashpoint. Put my hat out.

Beat.

And start my routine. In the mornings, I have to look exhausted and stay quiet, because that's how *you* feel in the mornings. So I get my face on.

He makes a sad, tired face.

And I make a bit of money.

He pulls the face again.

But for some reason I sort of feel, stupid. I try and ignore it and concentrate, take it serious.

He pulls his sad, tired face.

I don't know what the fuck is the matter with me. It never bothers me normally. I know the fucking game. Mornings I have to look sad and tired and not speak to you. Afternoons I have to do something productive like sell the *Big Issue* or do a drawing on the pavement, and evenings I have to act like I'm desperate to get home to a hostel. Because that's what *you* feel like in the day. Knackered, productive and homesick and it's a way of *acting* like we're connected or something. Like we're the same, I've got it fucking *nailed*.

Beat.

Rinsed it for years.

Beat.

But now, I feel stupid. With my hat on the floor.

Beat.

I sort of get to know them while I'm doing the washing up.
Wooky's got an Anonymous mask and I ask him what it's all
about.

'It's Guy Fawkes. It's from a comic book', and he goes on
about Anonymous, so I try and steer him away from politics,
I am not interested in that shit. 'Guy Fawkes, makes me think
of my boy. Every bonfire night we'd go out, and he'd always
check the bonfires for hedgehogs. Whenever I see a firework
and it looks like a hedgehog, I sort of hope he can see it as
well', that sort of thing, just making conversation.

Beat.

Wooky's like an angry uncle, gets stressed about the smallest
things, like people not bringing cutlery back, Allie is like the
mum, like a diplomat making sure everyone's being kind to
each other. She sort of makes the kitchen really welcoming
'cause she treats everyone like a long-lost friend. Hal is the
Buddhist who normally lives in communes so he's really
quiet; he's like Grandad in the corner, wise and bald. And
then Dad is Dev, he's the chef, he runs everything but he's
the most awkward man on the planet, you'd never go to him
with anything.

Beat.

Wooky's doing impressions of everyone – he does a brilliant
Hal, he's got his fucking, the way he talks just right and then
Dev he's got his walk down to a 't', it's sort of like –

He does an impression but gives up halfway through.

He must just watch everyone all day, he does Allie's greeting and everyone pisses themselves laughing it's spot-on, even Allie's fucking laughing, she can see what she's like.

He is itching to join in.

'I've got one!' I say.

He shifts his weight uncomfortably.

Pause.

Only. I haven't.

Beat.

And they're all looking at me.

Beat.

And I don't know why, but I just. Carry on washing up.

He is embarrassed.

Beat.

Sometimes an old woman in a poncho comes in to wash up, and when she does I go and stand by the shelves.

He is embarrassed.

Pass them stuff. I sort of invent a new role. Like a, like a shelf-sweeper. My first Saturday on the shelves was a bit stressful, lunchtime; there was a queue all the way past the tech tent. Wooky and Allie serving, Dev and Hal cooking and Poncho, or Carol as she likes to be called, is on the sink and me on the shelves. 'Danny, get us the lentils', 'Danny, cutlery', 'Danny, where's the fucking bread?' 'FUCKING SLOW IT UP.'

He is sheepish.

So when it calms down, I think perhaps I'd better head off, they probably don't want me around, but before I go I give the shelves a bit of a tidy. Bring a bit of *order*.

There's no system, they've got no system, it's just shoved there, so I separate them all out, get all the perishables together, all the crockery, and all the tins. Dried goods. Get a bit of fucking order in there. It only takes me half an hour and it's all sorted, easy to navigate, for the next fucking mug who's roped in.

Beat.

Couple of days later I'm in the queue and Poncho's on the shelves.

He can barely hide his irritation.

'Can I have the soup please, Carol?'

His irritation rises.

'Soup please, Carol?'

He can barely stand still.

'Carol?'

'IT'S FUCKING THERE, CAROL. TOP RIGHT. WITH ALL THE OTHER FUCKING TINS. IN THE TIN SECTION.'

He straightens himself.

I don't know why it pisses me off so much. It's just a shelving system. But it's so simple, why is she making a fucking meal of it, the fat little Mexican? I spent hours on that. The longer I watch, the more I want to fucking smash her face in.

'Kidney beans, Carol?'

He is aggravated.

'Carol?'

'Out the way, Poncho, I can't take any more of this. Right, who needs what?' And I get in front of the shelves, and I don't even think, I just fucking rinse it. Chickpeas are flying here, sweet potatoes flying there. All afternoon, everyone gets what they want. And I fucking prove that my system, my system of dividing it all up, means you know where everything is without thinking, it's just there. And I don't shout or swear or frighten anyone. Job done. Proved my point.

'Nice to see your face again, Danny,' says Dev. 'Nice to have you back.'

He is confused.

Between the washing up, and the shelves and the prep, there's always something to do, something needs doing. So when the journalist comes in I just carry on chopping carrots. She asks them all why we're here.

Hal goes first, he says something like: 'Spiritual bankruptcy.'

Wooky says, 'I want a revolution.' Allie goes on about loads of stuff I don't understand and Dev says, 'I'm not sure why I'm here, I just read about it, thought it was important.'

'And you? Why are you here?'

'I'm doing the carrots.'

'Why are you protesting?'

'Oh, I'm not part of the protest, I'm just helping out.'

Beat.

'Why are you helping out?'

'I don't know.'

'Why are you helping in the *kitchen*?'

'I don't know. It just sort of happened.'

'You must have a reason.'

'I'm lonely,' I say.

He is ashamed.

He smiles.

I like the routine. Half-six the cleaners wake me up on the steps. I know Dev's opening up on his own, so I head down there, get the water. Start poaching eggs for him. Bit of banter.

Beat.

When it's not busy, and we've done our prep, if it's just me and Dev, he teaches me how to cook. I learn how to cook – okra, mung beans, pak choy, all sorts of mad shit I'd never buy. It was brilliant, two blokes in a massive kitchen. Just sautéing all kinds of mad shit for each other. And the routine helps. If I've got a routine I don't get into trouble up here.

He taps his head.

It's great because he doesn't want to get involved or stick his nose in, not like Allie or Jenny, he doesn't want to know any of that shit. He's so awkward. He's perfect company if you want to keep things to yourself. But sometimes, you can't help it.

Beat.

We were in the kitchen, just the two of us, doing an audit for the day, and Dev reads out a, a sell-by date and I realise it's Kylie's birthday. I get a bit upset. I'm crying, and Dev goes:

'Do you wanna mint?'

He laughs.

It's just like being back in prison, there's all sorts there. Mentally ill, professors, drug dealers, soldiers, bankers, musicians. And every one of them is fucking Allie's mate. She introduces me to everyone as 'Danny from-the-kitchen', and it sort of becomes my new name. 'Danny from-the-kitchen'. Even now, sometimes when I meet someone I'm like 'I'm Danny f – '

Beat.

There's this knackered piano outside the kitchen tent, out of tune, keys missing. Every cunt plays it all the time. Fucking 'Chopsticks' or 'The Entertainer', it is torture.

Beat.

But this bloke comes along, and he spends hours pressing all the keys, over and over again. Like he was testing it, or getting to know it.

Beat.

And after a while, he starts to figure it out. He doesn't fix all the broken bits, he just learns where they are and plays around it.

Beat.

We've been fantasising about all the different ways we could destroy this fucking piano for weeks, and then this bloke comes along and it's fucking beautiful. He just knew what it needed to make music again.

Beat.

Allie is so excited, she wants to dance, but Dev is too uptight, Wooky says it's too bourgeois and Hal's a Buddhist. I don't know why they don't dance but they don't, and she looks at me, and I think I'm not getting involved in any of this.

'I'll dance with you,' I say and she nearly vaults the table.

He looks down at himself and is repulsed.

He holds his hands out at a distance.

He realises his hands are dirty and he furiously rubs his hands clean.

He holds his hands out at a distance.

He dances as if holding Allie.

'Hold me properly,' she says, and she pulls me close. People don't touch me. I'm not . . . I'm not used to it. I never bump into anyone or brush past anyone. 'Cause people go:

He recoils.

She's holding me and I'm confused, people don't touch rough-sleepers do they?

He addresses a patron.

Danny   Would you touch a rough-sleeper?

He addresses patrons until someone says 'yes'.

When someone says yes, **Danny***'s heart melts.*

Danny   You would.

Summoning courage, he offers his hand to the patron.

Danny   Would you?

Beat.

Please?

He persists until patron joins **Danny** *on stage.*

As he takes her in his arms we hear piano music. They dance, and slowly, **Danny** *turns patron so he is facing the audience and she is facing the back of the set.*

We see **Danny** *is overcome with happiness.*

Danny   We dance.

Beat.

We dance around the kitchen, and she puts her head on my chest.

Danny *and patron dance.*

Danny   We dance, and it's just me and her and I don't feel disgusting or repulsive any more.

He is in agony.

And I hold on to him and I promise I'll never let go.

He holds the patron as if it is the last time he held his son.

And then slowly he comes to.

Improvise. Perhaps he is embarrassed and apologises as he lets go of her.

Thank you.

Patron returns to her seat.

Danny *gathers himself and drinks heavily from his can.*

Beat.

Danny   I tell her my ex-wife said I'll die alone, because I'm the most selfish man she's ever met. We sit on Banksy's Monopoly board together, and she tells me Allie isn't her real name. Her real name's Lucy. 'Allie's my activist name. She's who I want to be: changing the world. Lucy's a victim.' And we get pissed and watch bankers kick tents, and tourists take pictures, London go by, and for some reason it all feels new.

Beat.

The more people I meet, the more I start to understand what's going on, like, I met a blind diabetic woman in a wheelchair, with kidney and heart problems and the Government declared her fit to work. She was fucking double incontinent.

Beat.

Met a shop owner. He'd borrow money off the bank every month to buy stock, sell the clothes and then pay off the loan. The bank just fucking stopped lending to him. Just like that. He went bust overnight with a wife and kids.

Beat.

Every day there was someone. I was in the Info tent and this bloke comes in, he's in a super expensive suit, but looks like shit. Looks like he could do with a good meal, or a good sleep, I don't know what, but he needs something. He wants to make a donation. He gets his wallet out and gives us everything he's got and he starts to cry.

He's a millionaire, he's got wife, kids, mistresses, but he's the most unhappy bloke I've ever met and *I* end up comforting *him*. That's the kind of mad shit that would happen in Occupy.

Beat.

Three

Danny But I was still avoiding the politics. All this shit.

Up-twinkles. Down-twinkles. **Danny** *gives them the 'V'.*

I didn't get involved in all that.

Allie comes in, 'Come on, you're coming to the GA tonight.'

'Thank you, no, I've got plans tonight.' I haven't got plans, but with Allie you've got to be on your toes, or you'll be roped into some nonsense.

'Please. It's a big one.'

'No, I've got plans, and besides I'm not a protestor.'

And she looks me dead in the eyes.

'It would make me happy.'

He doesn't know what to do with the attention.

It goes on for ages.

He clears his throat.

Beat.

Wooky, Hal and Dev are there already, so all the kitchen crew sit together. It goes on for an hour or so, and there's proposals about sanitation, and the church, and what we should do about the banks.

'Join in,' says Allie, 'cause she can see that I haven't voted once.

'Do you agree with anything that's been said?'

'I don't know.'

'You must have an opinion.'

Beat.

'It doesn't matter what I think.'

And as I say that, Dev goes, 'Shh shh.' It's the city liaison group, and the whole GA goes quiet for the first time, like everyone's been waiting for this proposal. This little mousey girl gets up to the mic with a piece of paper.

'The City of London has agreed not to pursue any legal actions, or attempts to evict us, on condition we agree to leave peacefully and clean up after ourselves on December 31st. How do we respond?'

(*Impersonation.*) 'I think we should accept the offer; we've made our point.' (*Impersonation.*) 'If we accept this we can leave in a non-violent manner.' (*Impersonation.*) 'Our priority is a non-violent eviction.' (*Impersonation.*) 'If we accept we can ask for a permanent, symbolic tent on site.'

'NO! NO! NO! NO! NO! NO! NO. WHAT THE FUCK IS WRONG WITH YOU? LET'S NOT ACCEPT THE OFFER. LET'S NOT ASK FOR A FUCKING SYMBOLIC TENT. YOU THINK THIS IS SYMBOLIC? WHAT THE FUCK DO I SYMBOLISE? WHAT ABOUT ALL THE ROUGH-SLEEPERS? WHERE ARE WE GONNA GO? THIS IS A PROTEST. NOT A CAMP SITE.'

He catches his breath.

He looks around.

And, everywhere, I look, I see –

Up-twinkles.

So I do it back. 'You don't do it back, it's just our way of agreeing with you,' says Allie.

Beat.

It's just our way of agreeing. With my point. Which I made. In public. I made a point. In public. In front of. Hundreds, of people. In public.

He giggles at the insanity.

And the facilitator goes, 'I think we have consensus', and they fucking jump on me! Hal, Wooky, Allie, none of them have got consensus before. And we roll around on the steps and Dev takes pictures on his phone because he doesn't like being touched and Wooky gets up and does an impression of me. And they all do it and they all take the piss out of me.

He loves it.

For me now the camp and the politics were interconnected. The camp couldn't exist without the politics, and the politics couldn't exist without the camp. You can't have one without the other. I hadn't realised, I was too caught up in my own shit.

He points to his head.

But that GA changed everything, 'cause, when you see five hundred people going –

Up-twinkles.

There was no going back.

The big picture that they don't want you to see is that everything is connected.

Because I used to think I'm just an alki. But I'm not. I'm loads of things.

He puts a can down. Points to it.

That's not gonna fix everything. What about the fact I'm a dad? And a metal-presser. A man. A fucking full-back. A divorcee. A rough-sleeper. A chef. A *ninety-nine percenter*? What about all that? I'm not just an alki, and it's not just a banking crisis.

Beat.

Those poor cunts under the bridge who you walked past. They're connected to you.

Beat.

I'd go in the tea tent and I'd sit with a paranoid schizophrenic, a banker, a runaway, a professor and a tranny, and we'd all have something in common. Getting fucked by the one per cent. I wouldn't have done that before Occupy. But now the picture was bigger. I was finally in it. Connected, affecting others.

Beat.

I don't just want to see my son again, I want to abolish tuition fees, I want civil rights in Egypt, I want to stop drilling in the Arctic, I want all of that stuff! I start going on marches. I go on every march I can. On the electricians' union one I get fucking kettled. Kettling to me was having boiling water with sugar thrown over your face, but on the streets it's about stopping you moving. Me kettled! Anyone see the fucking irony in that? Seven years those mugs have been moving me on. Now I've got to stay put! So they can set their dogs on sparks who just want to protect their jobs.

'BALFOUR BEATTY SHAME ON YOU!'

'BALFOUR BEATTY SHAME ON YOU!'

Eight hours on Blackfriars Bridge and it's fucking brilliant because we're all together fucking changing the world.

'BALFOUR BEATTY SHAME ON YOU!'

He looks at the crowd. A surge of passion.

MIC CHECK.

Audience responds.

(*Louder.*) MIC CHECK!

Audience responds.

(*Louder.*) MIC CHECK!

Audience responds.

BORIS JOHNSON –

Audience responds.

IS A MASSIVE CUNT.

Audience responds.

THE *EVENING STANDARD* –

Audience responds.

ARE A BUNCH OF CUNTS.

Audience responds.

THE METROPOLITAN POLICE –

Audience responds.

ARE A PACK OF CUNTS.

Audience responds.

Let's sing a fucking carol!

He might write the words up on the tiles, improvising as he moves amongst the audience, instructing certain sections to sing certain lines.

'On the first day of Christmas the system gave to me.
A vote in a democracy.' Got that *right*?

On the second day it's 'Two racist cops'.

On the third day it's 'Three student loans'.

Fourth day – 'Four bailed-out banks'.

Fifth day – 'Boris is a cunt'.

Sixth day – 'Six hacks a-hacking'.

Seventh day – 'Seven drones a-bombing'.

Eighth day – 'Eight sweatshops sweating'.

Ninth day – 'Nine spies surveilling'.

Tenth day – 'Ten MPs claiming'.

Eleventh day – 'Eleven bubbles bursting'.

Twelfth day – 'Twelve councils cutting'.

Once the twelfth day has been sung –

Mobile phone rings. The person holding **Danny***'s phone runs to him. When he sees who's ringing his face falls. He indicates for the audience to stop singing.*

Danny (*improvise*)   Fuck! Shh shh! Everyone! Shh! Oh shit . . . shh, fuck. Shit. Fuck. Bollocks. Everyone . . . shh . . .

He takes the phone. **Jenny***'s lines are unheard.*

Danny   Hello?

Jenny   Danny, it's Jenny.

Danny   Yes. Hi.

Jenny   Where the hell are you?

Danny   I'm, with some, with some friends.

Jenny   Drinking?

Danny   No. Carol singing.

Jenny   Carol *singing*.

Danny   I am.

Jenny   What about the HCTB1 form? I've got it here for you to sign?

Danny   Oh! Was that tonight? Shit.

Jenny   Yes, it was tonight! We arranged this morning when I gave you the phone.

Danny   Where are you now?

Jenny   I'm on a train to Kent.

Danny   I don't understand. Will I be in for Christmas?

Jenny   No. It's too late.

Danny *is gutted.*

Jenny   I had people in the office waiting for it. I've got people in Croydon waiting to process it because I rang them up and told them your story and they're using their own time, to get you in for Christmas and you can't be bothered to turn up.

Danny   Don't cry, Jenny.

Beat.

Come on. Look. Come on.

Jenny   I thought we were getting somewhere.

Danny   We are.

Jenny   I'm doing everything I can to help you.

Danny   I know you are.

Jenny   I'm doing everything.

Danny   I know you are.

Jenny   I thought we were getting somewhere.

Danny   I know, I'm sorry.

Jenny   I've had to ring everyone and *apologise*.

Danny   I'm sorry I just got, distracted. Stop crying, go home, see your family. Don't worry about me. I'll be fine. I'll be fine.

Jenny   I'm just so disappointed.

Danny   I know. Sorry Jenny. Sorry. Sorry. I'm sorry. I'm sorry. I'm sorry. Merry Christmas.

He hangs up.

Four

Danny *looks at his phone.*

The weight of the phone call hits him.

Defeated, he sits down and lights a cigarette.

Danny   Anyone done a Crisis at Christmas? (*Dry.*) They're great.

Beat.

No, you know. Good people, volunteering on Christmas Day, fair play.

Beat.

Can't drink though, so everyone wolfs their food down.

Beat.

You're not really celebrating Christmas though. Sitting around with a load of rough-sleepers and people with nowhere else to go. You're sort of getting together to mourn Christmas. To mourn Christmas, and all the Christmases you've fucked up for other people.

He toasts the sentiment.

To Christmas.

A nihilistic smile breaks across his face before he takes a hefty, medicating swig of lager.

Christmas at Occupy was good, that was the best one since – It was great, everyone who'd moved off came back for a day. Say goodbye.

Beat.

And then one night, I was doing a shift in the kitchen, and loads of my old rough-sleeping mates come in because Occupy had closed down the tea tent. The tea tent was the only twenty-four-hour tent, the only place you could stay

warm if you didn't have a tent. It was like the Occupy pub for
rough-sleepers. But the GA had enough of the noise and shut
it down. So the brew-crew all start coming in the kitchen.
Billy, Mikey with the cat on a string, Julia and Vaclav the
Pole. It was fine, they had nowhere to go. But this one night,
Mikey's cat, sort of, did a, a, a sort of a shit, on a chopping
board. And Hal and Allie get a bit upset and there were
words and then Allie storms out and Hal follows and I go after
them. I overhear them talking and Hal says, 'Why don't we
ask Danny to talk to them?' And Allie says, 'Why would they
listen to Danny more than us?'

He drinks.

'He's a rough-sleeper,' Hal says.

He smiles through the hurt.

It was fine. I knew what he meant. You know, they were all
my mates, I've known them for years, and if they were going
to listen to anyone it would be me. You know. Fair enough.
I'd get through not because I'm a rough-sleeper, but because
I'm fucking, I fucking know how to talk to them, and I know
how to talk to the GA. I'm fucking – I can do it all. So I go
back in and I round everyone up. 'Come on you lot, fuck off,
this isn't a fucking zoo, piss off, we've got work to do.' And
they all sort of fuck off one by one. And Hal comes up to me
and says, 'Nice one, Danny, that was getting out of hand.'

He hides how pissed off he was.

(*Forced.*) And I'm glad.

Beat.

I am. 'Cause now I can see how stressed everyone was, and
everyone starts talking to each other again, and it's like it's all
back to normal with Wooky doing impressions and Allie
slapping people with leeks and it's fun. Back to normal.

Beat.

Back to normal.

Beat.

Allie and Dev cooking, Hal and Wooky serving, me on washing up, everything back to normal. So I have no fucking idea why, when no one's looking, I go to the donation tin and nick twenty quid.

Beat.

Never stolen anything in my life. After losing my job, losing the dole, and the fights over money, had more fights over money than fucking – (anything), I never stole, ever. She fucking knows. Fucking standards. All you've got when you've got nothing. Fucking brought up right. Fucking bringing up a – (boy, right). You don't fucking steal. Whatever I got wrong, I taught him that. Fucking proud people. Just because I'm a rough-sleeper don't mean I haven't got any fucking pride.

He is confused.

I wanted to do some good with it. Yeah, I broke the Occupy rules, but I was doing something good with it. I bought some vodka, and found Mikey and Vaclav and shared it with them. Doesn't matter if it's a bowl of soup or a bottle of vodka, or some warmth from a fire, it's all fucking sharing. It's all about connecting people. I'd kicked them out of the kitchen, I don't want them thinking I'm taking sides. I'm not having any of that shit, I'm here to make sure no one slips out of the big picture. So we have a bit of a party, few drinks, smoke, fire going, couple of jellies. Someone gets some music going, vodka goes round. We don't need the fucking tea tent, we can have a party on the camp.

'Why don't you lot fuck off somewhere else? It's four a.m.' And there's this bloke, in his sleeping bag, trying to put out the bonfire, shouting and swearing, and literally hopping mad, fucking jumping around on the fire. And then I see. 'Fuck me.'

Pause.

'It's Hal the Buddhist.'

Pause.

It's Hal the Buddhist. In his pyjamas, hopping up and down in a sleeping bag, trying to put our fire out.

'Don't do that, Hal. Don't do that we're freezing.'

But he carries on.

'Hal, please.'

'I don't give a shit, there's fucking tents everywhere, you could kill someone, you stupid fucking pisshead.'

And I grab him.

He catches his breath.

I just grabbed him. But next time I go to the kitchen it's pissing it down, and Carol's waiting for me.

Beat.

It's weird because she's standing inside, and then when she sees me she steps outside. So we both stand there, in the rain.

'They told me to tell you, you can't come in. You're not welcome.'

'Why?'

'Because . . . '

He is ashamed.

'Because you knocked one of Hal's teeth out.'

It pains him to remember this.

I try to get past her, but each time she steps in my fucking way, like it's a fucking dance, and I fucking . . . 'OUT OF THE WAY, PONCHO', and Allie hears and steps out into the rain. And it's just me and her. And when I see her, getting soaked, to be with me, I want to say, I want to say I'm sorry. I want to say thank you. I want to say, even though I've got a hole in my life, somehow, you make it OK. I want to say, some days just standing next to you is enough.

Beat.

I've got all this stuff I want to say, and I know if I can just tell her, all this will be sorted out. But I don't say any of that. I say:

'He fucking deserved it.'

He is devastated.

Beat.

I didn't want to fight with her. I didn't want to fight with any of them. I don't know why everything I did upset everyone. I didn't want to take sides, but everyone else was. Everyone was fighting. You couldn't go two yards without getting into a fucking argument. They couldn't fucking see that I can't lose any more people in my life. Everything they were fighting about was bollocks. In the big picture it was bollocks. They got their own police force. Tranquillity. That pissed everyone off, but I didn't mind, I just wanted everyone to stay together. Everyone gets upset that they close the tea tent, but Tranquillity get a new tent with sofas and burners and DVD players. I don't give a shit, it's not important, give them a fucking swimming pool if it stops the arguing.

Beat.

I make myself eat in the kitchen. I keep my head down, don't cause any trouble. They might not want me, they might ignore me, but I'm still eating with them. I don't care, I'm not embarrassed. I'm not going back to the soup kitchens. I'll eat there even if no one talks to me, because I'm not giving up. For the first time in the whole fucking Occupation, I'm glad Carol's there because she's the only one who speaks to me. She's actually quite a nice old lady. Poncho. She's a grandmother. She chats to me and everyone else carries on. I'm in there, and Carol serves me, and we have our chat that we always have about how cold it is, and then she says:

'Danny, love, you can't bring that in here.'

Beat.

I don't know what she's talking about for ages but then I realise she's pointing at my can.

'The camp's a drug- and alcohol-free zone.'

Pause.

'Since when?'

'Since the GA decided.'

Beat.

Which is fine.

Beat.

But then I see the rest of them, all of them, Dev, Allie, Hal, Wooky, and they've all gone quiet. No one's talking. Because they all want to see what I'll do. See what the alki'll do.

Beat.

So I pour it away.

He pours it over his head.

And they ban me from the kitchen.

He is reborn as his former self.

They want an alki, I'll be a fucking alki – seven years I've been drinking on those steps and they want to try and fucking tell me what to do? Fuck off.

'WHAT THE FUCK HAS HAPPENED TO YOU? MAKING PEOPLE HOMELESS, BANNING DRINKING. GOT YOUR OWN POLICE. YOU'RE NO BETTER THAN THE CITY. The only thing we've got is this kitchen and you're not taking that away from me.'

Beat.

'WHO ARE YOU? NONE OF YOU USE YOUR REAL
NAMES.'

Beat.

'YOU CAN'T FUCKING COME HERE AND GIVE ME
ALL THIS AND THEN TAKE IT AWAY.'

I AM NOT GOING BACK. I AM NOT GOING BACK
TO THE STREETS. I CAN'T GO BACK. I CAN'T BE
ON MY OWN. I can't. I can't. I can't. I can't. I can't.'

He drops to his knees and tries to pack his bag.

I can't, I can't I can't I can't I can't I can't.

He starts to look for his phone.

I can't I can't I can't I can't I can't, where's my phone?

*Crying, he goes through his bag, he finds his phone, but he also finds an
Anonymous mask.*

*He pulls it out and holds it at arm's length. He considers it, for what
feels like an age, as he remembers his son, and Occupy.*

Pause.

You know. I could bear it. I could bear it all. I could. I had it
all figured out. How to bear living with myself. With what
I've done. I could bear it. And then you lot come along. And
now look at me.

He grabs the phone and throws it against the set.

He smashes the set up.

Five

LOOK AT ME.

At patrons.

DON'T FUCKING LOOK AWAY. LOOK AT ME.

At patrons.

WHAT DO YOU SEE?

At patrons.

WHAT AM I MISSING?

At patrons.

A FLAT?

Beat.

A BEDSIT IN FULHAM?

Beat.

THAT GONNA MAKE EVERYTHING OK, IS IT?

Beat.

DOES IT MAKE YOU HAPPY?

Beat.

WITH YOUR PHONES.

Beat.

AND YOUR MORTGAGES. ARE YOU HAPPY?

Beat.

ARE YOU SAFE?

Beat.

YOU WISH THAT FOR ME?

Beat.

A BEDSIT?

Beat.

I DON'T WANT IT. I don't need reminding my life is
ruined. You think I don't know that? You think I don't know
everything worth living for is gone. For ever.

Beat.

I don't need reminding of that. I need, I need reminding I
have something to offer.

Beat.

I have something I can do. I can make something better. I
can make someone's life better. Even if it's just a bowl of
soup.

Beat.

I can do that.

Beat.

I know I can. I might be able to help you with something.

Beat.

Just need the chance.

Pause.

I don't want a bedsit, I want someone to talk to. If I wake up
frightened I want someone there. If I'm sad I want someone
to cheer me up. If I feel useless I want a job. If I feel stupid
I want to learn. And I'll only ever get that from you.

Silence.

Occupy screwed my life up.

Beat.

Because it gave me hope.

He discards the mask.

The mobile starts to ring, but he doesn't answer.

He turns his back to the audience and starts to walk out.

We are left with three points of focus. The mobile phone, the rough-sleeping gear, the Anonymous mask.

Danny *walks offstage.*

Lights down.

Under the Sofa

Under the Sofa was originally performed as a script-in-hand reading as part of Paines Plough's *Later* season at Trafalgar Studios, London.

Julie   Raquel Cassidy

Director   Duncan Macmillan

Julie   I went to Tesco's before coming here.

Beat.

I've changed my big shop to Thursdays. Makes Sunday less of a hell.

Beat.

Day-to-day is good. It's the day-to-day stuff that is the best really. Packing, doing a lot of packing. Upstairs and the kitchen are nearly done.

Beat.

I'm trying all the all the dried fruits. It's sad I know but they last so much longer, it's better than a load of fresh fruit going off by Sunday.

Beat.

I saw a woman pushing her trolley around with her bag in the, in the front bit? I wish I had the confidence to put my bag in the front bit like she does. I did try it once, but I went round so fast I missed the tinned fish.

Beat.

No tuna for a week.

Beat.

So I picked up some flowers. Then I got into a bit of a state, I couldn't remember if it's bad luck to buy yourself flowers. Is it flowers or rings? Why is it that they terrify you about such nice things? I picked up some flowers. They were lovely fresias, I'd forgotten how fresh flowers smelled I'm so used to air fresheners, they were so strong. As I walked round Tesco's I was breathing them in, it was lovely.

Beat.

I got to the checkout and felt wrong so I took them back.

Beat.

Sunday night I let a bad cat in. He's well known around by us.
But I let him in anyway. Just to see what would happen. He
was very curious. He didn't seem that interested in me. I tried
giving him some milk, I didn't try to pick him up I knew that
would offend him. I talked to him. It was nice. Better than
the telly.

Beat.

He was so *superior*! So it was nice looking down on him. And
him being in my own house, made all his posing look
ridiculous. I was telling him 'There's no point looking like
that, I know you like the nice house and I know you love me.'

Beat.

He went under the sofa for a while, and I got self-conscious
waiting for him to come out so I got on with some packing.
But it was nice, it was nice thinking of him behind me. All
brooding and wide-eyed.

Beat.

I drove to Croydon on Tuesday night to buy Stephen some
pornography. I've got in the habit now of judging corner
shops on their pornography. For years I never noticed it. But
now it's the first thing I look for when I walk into a new one.

Beat.

There are still plenty, I'm pleased to say, that don't stock any
kind of pornography. They're usually the same ones who'll
stock soy milk and headache tablets. But then there are
others, where there'll be a shelf the length of the shop, with
magazines catering for all sorts of tastes.

Beat.

I found a shop in Croydon and went in, and it had a top
shelf, but they were covered in little white plastic sleeves
which is good.

Beat.

I always have this crisis about what to buy *with* the pornography.
Sometimes I actually need things, especially at the end of a
shopping week. But being a thirty-eight-year-old woman with
a copy of *Asian Babes* and a box of vegetable stock is no way to
escape scrutiny. But also, in my mind is the fact I don't want
to walk in there and buy *just* the magazine. It's very stressful
and there isn't any advice about it anywhere.

Beat.

So, I've got in the habit of buying chewing gums as a companion
purchase. Family packs, so it looks like a purchase not an
afterthought.

Beat.

I can't face asking him what he likes so he gets the first thing
I get my hands on.

Beat.

Sometimes I look at them. Not very often because it makes
me feel so cold. Part of me wants to see the women he looks
at. I want to see if any of them look nice or kind or reliable.
But these women are cartoons, there's nothing pretty about
them.

Beat.

I'm fine with it.

Beat.

It's something he has to do. Nothing to be ashamed of.

Beat.

I was driving home from Croydon. I stopped at some lights.
I had the chewing gums and the magazine on the passenger
seat and I had to pull over because I couldn't see very well
because I was crying again.

Beat.

I pulled over and wiped my tears with a wet-wipe which made my eyes sting. I knew I couldn't drive for a while so I decided to kill a bit of time and ring Dad. I tried telling him I loved him but he didn't want to know. I was shouting at him trying to tell him all sorts of things, about moving out, about Stephen, about my job, the letter. But he was speaking over me not saying anything in particular just building up to hanging up.

Beat.

I got home and went looking for the cat. I walked around the streets, I put milk by the doorstep, I even stood by the door and called out his name 'Blacky' but I don't think that's his name. I call him that because he's got a black head and white nose like he's wearing a hood. He never responds to it anyway.

Beat.

Day-to-day it's been fine. I had a nice chat in work on Tuesday morning it was really natural. We were both waiting to speak to HR and it was taking ages. Claire, she works in a pod behind me, so we don't have much cause to chat really. But she's pregnant so we talked about pregnancies and shared lots of stuff it was lovely.

Beat.

She was waiting for some tests after an amniocentesis. She's been through it before but I could see it was worrying her. When we started talking about it she would wipe away a tear now and again. Like you do when you're pregnant, you don't cry but things well up and spill out. That feeling never really goes away I suppose but when you're carrying the baby it's all too much for you.

Beat.

I remember when I fell pregnant with Stephen. It wasn't planned, but it wasn't not planned either. I couldn't wait, because I wanted to show everyone that I was good at something. That I wasn't a trophy any more. I wasn't an ornament, I was going to do something, raise a child and I was going to do it well. I never let myself dream about Stephen becoming a barrister, or doctor or politician. I just dreamt that he'd rely on me.

Beat.

I'd dream about meeting him for lunch and he'd tell me about problems with his girlfriend.

(*Aside.*) She was moving things too fast.

Beat.

He'd tell me he was getting bullied at work, and we'd come up with a strategy together to get over it. We'd go to Habitat and choose cushions for his new place.

Beat.

But it's not my place to think about what I've missed out on. I don't have the right to list the things I missed out on. My father reminds me of that every time I see him.

Beat.

The only girl Stephen ever brought home was a young girl called, Stephanie. I made a joke about them both having the same name Steph and Steve. It wasn't really a joke, I just noted it. She was really nice and smiled, but Stephen was so angry. 'Why are you talking to us like that, Mum?' 'Like what? I'm not doing anything wrong,' I said. 'You're talking to us like a teacher,' he said. 'How do you want me to speak to you, Stephen?' and he said, 'Just don't,' and walked upstairs. I couldn't say I'm speaking like this because I'm nervous. I'm speaking like this because I'm excited, because I want your friend to like me and I want her to feel like she can come round and relax. I couldn't say that, I just had to stand there and take it.

Beat.

This had been on my mind when I went to see him Wednesday night. We were talking about the food he'd eaten in there and I told him about the dried fruit and how it lasts longer and before I knew it I was telling him he was rude. He couldn't remember. 'You know, when, when you brought Stephanie around, you were rude to me,' I said. He didn't remember, and refused to apologise for something he couldn't remember. He looked so bored. Which made me even more mad.

I slapped him.

Beat.

I slapped him in the face. For a moment I thought I was going to hit him some more but I sat down. A guard came over and asked if everything was alright and I didn't know what to say so I just looked at the floor. Stephen said something to him about everything being fine. I couldn't look at him.

Beat.

All I wanted was to grab him and hold him tight. I looked up and he was clicking his jaw, brooding. He ate some of the dried fruit and said if I was just going to have a go at him and hit him he'd rather be in the gym, or the library.

Beat.

He saw it. I tried to hide it. I tried to mask it but he saw a flicker of approval in my face, and that set him off. Swearing and shouting about me being nosey. Then we just got into the same argument we've been having for years. He was saying, even in prison he can't get any privacy from me, I was upset that showing an interest in him was wrong.

Beat.

I got home and the cat was waiting outside the door. I opened the door but he wouldn't come in. He just stood there, stubborn. I asked him what he wanted. 'Why are you here? Why don't you just do what you want?' I closed the door and ignored him. I watched him from the top window, he stayed for quite a while and then walked into next door's garden and I lost him. I taped up my final kitchenware box and put it with all the others. My kitchen used to be where everything happened.

Beat.

I bagged up some old clothes and took them to the dumper by the park and noticed that the gates to the park were bent out of shape so you could crawl through them. I scagged a tight on the gravel but it was lovely being in the park in the dark.

Beat.

I sat on a bench where I taught Stephen about heartbeats and we timed our pulses. My mind drifted to Stephen pushing a knife through someone's neck so I grabbed my mobile and flipped it open, it's one of those flip ones. And I got the light on and reread the letter, the only thing that has comforted me the only person I can rely on whose words never fail never let me down. Whose words I recite to myself, in supermarkets, corner stores, at work and in bed. Pressing the button on my phone every now and again, I read, 'I pray for you and your son every day, in the hope that you will be judged fairly for the pain you have caused me. In the moments I stop being angry, I tell myself there are no winners or losers in this, only you and I in the middle.'

Beat.

For the first time in so long I knew where I was going and it was my father's kitchen.

Beat.

He stood in front of me holding five playing cards close to his chest. It was poker night and he'd put the round table in the lounge. I imagined his friends sat looking at an empty seat and listening to me in the other room. He told me I should have rung ahead and closed the door. I didn't care about that

I told him I wasn't selling the house. I wasn't moving out and I wasn't running away any more. He asked, 'What about the fresh start?' 'What about all the stories?' 'What about the gossip?' and lots of other questions all of which led to, 'Why now, did I want to stay after what had happened?' And all I could think of saying was 'The cat.'

Beat.

I told him I'd hit Stephen because I was upset. Thinking about it now, I hit Stephen because I didn't want to leave my home. I blamed him.

Beat.

I don't know what he said but for some reason, for the first time in our lives he seemed to understand me. He put his cards down on the worktop and we agreed to talk the next day but I knew he'd surrendered.

As I left he asked if I'd leave the cake (I'd taken a cake . . . don't ask).

I felt a change in me. So I didn't hand it to him I just slid it on to the worktop, which gave me the biggest tingle I've felt for years, I can still feel it now just thinking about it.

Beat.

I got home and as I got through the door, the phone was ringing, I got to the phone, but didn't have time to close the door. It was Stephen. He never uses his phone card for me.

Beat.

He asked how I was, and even though I had so much to say, I didn't say anything, I just said I'm fine. But I had the biggest smile on my face, I know because I caught myself in the mirror looking like a bashful schoolgirl. He'd forgotten to tell me something. He wanted to tell me about the music he'd been listening to in prison. I stood in the hall looking at the black night where the door should be and fiddled with my hair for the first time in a year.

Beat.

Apparently all the prisoners listen to either, happy hardcore. Or Tracy Chapman. He said I should go and buy some Tracy Chapman. He said if he was outside he would have burnt it for me on to a CD so I could listen to it in the car when I drive to visit him.

Beat.

When he was talking to me I looked at the packed boxes in the lounge, and the table I was going to keep.

Beat.

I said I'd go and buy it in the morning. He said he was sorry he couldn't burn it for me. We hung up and I had one last look for the bad cat before closing the door on the night. I walked up the stairs, I emptied my mind of all the day-to-day stuff and just listened to Stephen saying to me 'Night night, Mum. Night night.'

The End.

For a complete listing of Bloomsbury
Methuen Drama titles, visit:

www.bloomsbury.com/drama

Follow us on Twitter and keep up to date
with our news and publications

@MethuenDrama

www.ingramcontent.com/pod-product-compliance
Ingram Content Group UK Ltd.
Pitfield, Milton Keynes, MK11 3LW, UK
UKHW020719280225
455688UK00012B/420